Not,

Daily Meditations

Not, Daily Meditations

Written by
Thomas Vaughn

Meditations on the Philosophies of Not and Authorism

Copyright ©2021 by Thomas Vaughn, All Rights Reserved
ISBN: 978-1-7372750-0-8

Visit our website at www.churchofnot.org

For information about permission to reproduce selections from this book, send email to reproductions@churchofnot.org

Cover art and book design
by Thomas Vaughn

TNP_2021_0517_0740

Contents

Contents iii
Before We Begin 1
January 1 – The Most Important Thing In The World 7
January 2 – New Year's Day (Yesterday) 9
January 3 – The Principles of Not 10
January 4 – Preserving Life 12
January 5 – Effective Bailout Value 14
January 6 – Vitacentricism 16
January 7 – The Interconnect 17
January 8 – Maintaining Life 18
January 9 – Honoring Life 19
January 10 – Mine, Yours 20
January 11 – Ours, Theirs 21
January 12 – Animal Life 22
January 13 – Computer Life 24
January 14 – Plant Life 25
January 15 – All Life 26
January 16 – Alien Life 27
January 17 – Life Destroys Life 28
January 18 – Taking Life 29
January 19 – Sanctify Life 31
January 20 – Be Ready for Anything 32
January 21 – Survival of the Fittest 34

January 22 – Fitness	35
January 23 – How do I "do" Fitness?	36
January 24 – Spiritual Fitness	37
January 25 – Spiritual Exercise	38
January 26 – Spiritual Nutrition	39
January 27 – Spiritual Rest	40
January 28 – Mental Fitness	41
January 29 – Mental Exercise	42
January 30 – Mental Nutrition	43
January 31 – Mental Rest	44
February 1 – Emotional Fitness	45
February 2 – Emotional Exercise	46
February 3 – Emotional Nutrition	47
February 4 – Emotional Rest	48
February 5 – Anniversary Ecclesia Condita	49
February 6 – Physical Fitness	50
February 7 – Physical Exercise	51
February 8 – Physical Nutrition	52
February 9 – Physical Rest	53
February 10 – Social Media	54
February 11 – Social Fitness	55
February 12 – Social Exercise	56
February 13 – Social Nutrition	57
February 14 – Social Rest	58
February 15 – Relationships	59
February 16 – Self and Life	60

February 17 – The Love-Spark 61
February 18 – Your Family is Whatever You Say It Is 62
February 19 – Giving Time 63
February 20 – Cultivating Relationships 64
February 21 – Pruning Relationships 65
February 22 – Creating Relationships 66
February 23 – Non-Love Relationships 67
February 24 – Immortality 68
February 25 – What is Moral? 69
February 26 – Your Personal Code 70
February 27 – Articulating Your Code 71
February 28 – Center Yourself 72
February 29 – How should I act? 73
March 1 – Healthy Skepticism 74
March 2 – Shake Your Foundations 75
March 3 – Superstructures 76
March 4 – Code Seeking 77
March 5 – Personal Fulfillment 78
March 6 – Take a Step 79
March 7 – Self Actualization 80
March 8 – The Unexamined Life 82
March 9 – Community 83
March 10 – Communities within Communities 84
March 11 – Neighborliness 85
March 12 – Take Care! 86
March 13 – Pick-up Sticks 87

March 14 – Your Avatar	88
March 15 – Make the World a Better Place	90
March 16 – Financial Independence	91
March 17 – Money doesn't Exist	92
March 18 – The Tesseract	93
March 19 – Nothing Touches Anything	95
March 20 – Time Cannot Pass	96
March 21 – The Vernal Equinox	98
March 22 – The Mainstream	99
March 23 – Veer Away!	100
March 24 – Go with the Flow	101
March 25 – Is Religion Good or Evil?	102
March 26 – Deeper than Good and Evil	103
March 27 – The Gradient Yin-Yang	104
March 28 – Good Mandates Evil	106
March 29 – Evil	107
March 30 – We Need Both	109
March 31 – Don't Be Evil	110
April 1 – Not, God?	111
April 2 – Introduction to Not	112
April 3 – Coldness	113
April 4 – Darkness	115
April 5 – Stasis	117
April 6 – Emptiness	119
April 7 – Not	121
April 8 – Not, Perfect?	122

NOT, DAILY MEDITATIONS

April 9 – Not to be Seen 123
April 10 – Not must not Exist 124
April 11 – Nothing isn't Not 125
April 12 – Not isn't Everywhere 127
April 13 – What isn't Not? 128
April 14 – Paradox is Prevalent in Truth 129
April 15 – Not in your Mind 130
April 16 – Warmth 131
April 17 – Light 132
April 18 – Activity 133
April 19 – Presence 134
April 20 – Life (big "L") 135
April 21 – life (little "L") 136
April 22 – Life, Rocks 137
April 23 – Death is Life 139
April 24 – Life is not Death 141
April 25 – Life, Not and Life (Not and Space) 142
April 26 – Life is Death 144
April 27 – Anti-Not 145
April 28 – The Ultimate Expression of Life 147
April 29 – But Anti-Not Cannot Be 148
April 30 – Walpurgisnacht 149
May 1 – Only Life Exists and it is Eternal 150
May 2 – Pain and Suffering 151
May 3 – Authorization 152
May 4 – External Authorization 153

May 5 – Authorization Loopback	154
May 6 – Self-Authorization	156
May 7 – Self-Worth	157
May 8 – Rejection	159
May 9 – The Soul	161
May 10 – Authorization for Crime	162
May 11 – I am God?	163
May 12 – Comparing Yourself to Others	164
May 13 – Choosing a Religion	166
May 14 – All Religions are True	168
May 15 – The All-Truth	170
May 16 – *The* Truth	171
May 17 – Splinters of Truth	172
May 18 – All Religions are False	175
May 19 – Becoming Religious	176
May 20 – Good God!	178
May 21 – Your Higher Power	180
May 22 – What is Greater than Humanity?	182
May 23 – The Power of Prayer	183
May 24 – Size and Scope	184
May 25 – We Are not the Center of it All	187
May 26 – The Occult	189
May 27 – Modern Humans	191
May 28 – Future Humans	192
May 29 – Magic	193
May 30 – A Visual Aid for Manifestation	196

NOT, DAILY MEDITATIONS

May 31 – How does Magic Work?..197
June 1 – Authorization for Magic..200
June 2 – Aspects of the Self..202
June 3 – Never in the Same Place Twice 204
June 4 – The Spiritual Self..205
June 5 – The Mental Self 206
June 6 – The Emotional Self...207
June 7 – The Physical Self 209
June 8 – The Social Self..211
June 9 – Scarcity & Abundance..212
June 10 – The Pebble in the Pool 213
June 11 – The Self, Connected 214
June 12 – Everything is Connected....................................216
June 13 – Awareness of your Awareness 218
June 14 – The Tree of Not...219
June 15 – I Think Therefore I Am......................................220
June 16 – Cinereo Modo...223
June 17 – Cinereo Ascensus..225
June 18 – Vita..227
June 19 – Aciem Exacuitur..228
June 20 – Necessitudo...230
June 21 – Summer Solstice...232
June 22 – Love Yourself..233
June 23 – Love Others..235
June 24 – Codice Personalum...237
June 25 – Existing Structures of Belief...............................239

Not, Daily Meditations

June 26 – Preferred Ignorance 242
June 27 – What Does it Look Like? 244
June 28 – Civitas 246
June 29 – Get Involved 248
June 30 – Religion 250
July 1 – Jobs and Career 251
July 2 – Putting Good Into the World 252
July 3 – You Have Reached the Top! 254
July 4 – It's Not a Simulation 255
July 5 – The Great Tapestry of Life 257
July 6 – The Linear Spiral 258
July 7 – The Spark 262
July 8 – The Glimmer 263
July 9 – You are an Energy Being 265
July 10 – We are All Connected 266
July 11 – Manifestation of Chaos 267
July 12 – Reigning in the Chaos 269
July 13 – Life, the Disease 271
July 14 – Paradigms of Truth 273
July 15 – Pursuing the Truths 275
July 16 – Unifying the Paradigms 277
July 17 – Inconcussa Fundamenta 279
July 18 – Proof of Manifestation 281
July 19 – The Mistake of Atheism 283
July 20 – Born Pagan 284
July 21 – The One True God 285

July 22 – Original Innocence 286
July 23 – The Detriment of Here and Now 288
July 24 – Presence for Past and Future 290
July 25 – A Measure of Health : Balance 292
July 26 – Chaos and Order 294
July 27 – Nobody Has a Clue 295
July 28 – The Mysteries : Album Mysteria Non 298
July 29 – Act 'As-If' 302
July 30 – Just do *Something* 303
July 31 – What is All of This? 304
August 1 – Why Are we Here? 306
August 2 – Is there Purpose? 307
August 3 – Origins and Destinations 308
August 4 – What is Consciousness? 309
August 5 – What is Death? 310
August 6 – What are Dreams? 311
August 7 – Are Humans Animals? 312
August 8 – Violence and Destruction 314
August 9 – Give Peace a Chance? 315
August 10 – The Universe 316
August 11 – Aliens 317
August 12 – Can Life Stop? 318
August 13 – Can Not Exist? 319
August 14 – A Full Solar Eclipse 320
August 15 – Day and Night 321
August 16 – Doubt and Self-Doubt 323

August 17 – Spiritual Hunger 324
August 18 – Spiritual Meals 325
August 19 – Finding Yourself 327
August 20 – Creation and Destruction 330
August 21 – Alchemy 2.0 333
August 22 – The 21-Day Deity 336
August 23 – Toxicity in the Mainstream 338
August 24 – The Church of Not 339
August 25 – Science & Religion 340
August 26 – Good Religion, Good Science 341
August 27 – Good Religion + Good Science = Not 343
August 28 – What it Isn't 344
August 29 – Humanity's Destiny 348
August 30 – Sleep or Die 349
August 31 – Should I Worship Something? 351
September 1 – What if You Are Wrong? 352
September 2 – Nothing Matters 354
September 3 – It is a Violent World 356
September 4 – Dictate to the World 358
September 5 – Living with Intention 360
September 6 – Fake it till You Make it 362
September 7 – Pray to What? 364
September 8 – Creation Hasn't Stopped 365
September 9 – Conviction of Belief 366
September 10 – You Are Deeper than Belief 369
September 11 – Don't Be Afraid 371

September 12 – Religious Delusions?... 373

September 13 – Belief in Fate.. 375

September 14 – Are there such things as Accidents?............... 376

September 15 – Everything Happens for a Reason 377

September 16 – Free Will 378

September 17 – How Can I be Good?.. 379

September 18 – Your Spirit can do no Wrong 380

September 19 – Knowing Right from Wrong........................... 381

September 20 – How can Death be Life?.................................. 383

September 21 – Love your Past... 384

September 22 – Autumnal Equinox 385

September 23 – Faith 386

September 24 – Blind Faith.. 387

September 25 – Detach from Outcome..................................... 389

September 26 – Love... 390

September 27 – Life After Death... 391

September 28 – Absolute Authority 392

September 29 – The Need to Believe.. 394

September 30 – The World is Getting Better............................ 395

October 1 – Nobody Can Ruin Your Day 397

October 2 – The Value of Church... 398

October 3 – The Suffering of Death is Only for the Living... 399

October 4 – Science... 400

October 5 – Philosophy.. 402

October 6 – Being Part of the Pack... 403

October 7 – Belonging.. 404

October 8 – If You Are Lucky, You'll Hit the Bottom 405
October 9 – Indomitable Spirit 407
October 10 – You Have to Have a Plan 408
October 11 – The Mind/Body Connection 409
October 12 – Depths of Thought 410
October 13 – Victim Mentality 412
October 14 – Belief 413
October 15 – Perfection 414
October 16 – Tolerance is Easy 415
October 17 – The Comfort of Familiarity 417
October 18 – Go to the Woods 418
October 19 – The Empath 419
October 20 – The Tightrope 420
October 21 – Dichotomy 422
October 22 – The Third Pole 423
October 23 – Feel the Awe 425
October 24 – The Breath of Air 427
October 25 – Communication is the Key 428
October 26 – Trust 429
October 27 – The Highest of Authorities 430
October 28 – Intellect 431
October 29 – Bullies and The Martial Arts 432
October 30 – Pressure and Stress 433
October 31 – Halloween 434
November 1 – Sanctuary 435
November 2 – Achievement 436

November 3 – Your Salvation 437

November 4 – The Framework (of Thought) 438

November 5 – The Nucleus 441

November 6 – Fear 443

November 7 – Perspective 444

November 8 – Fine Lines 445

November 9 – Futility 446

November 10 – The Universal You 447

November 11 – Being Mean 449

November 12 – A Day is a Life 450

November 13 – Control 452

November 14 – Reconciliation 454

November 15 – The Universe is Unfolding as it Should 455

November 16 – The Past 456

November 17 – The Present 457

November 18 – The Future 458

November 19 – Liberation 459

November 20 – Infinity 460

November 21 – Finding Evidence 461

November 22 – Being Heard 463

November 23 – The Garden 464

November 24 – Hate 466

November 25 – Passion/Dispassion 467

November 26 – Right and Wrong 468

November 27 – Points of Present 469

November 28 – Enveloped in Energy 472

November 29 – Ardentis Animae 474

November 30 – Tranquillitas Animae 475

December 1 – How Deep Should I go? 476

December 2 – Everyone is Orange 477

December 3 – Divinity 478

December 4 – Our Most Valued Commodity 479

December 5 – The Collective Conscious Imperative 480

December 6 – Righteous Indignation 482

December 7 – Heaven or Hell? 483

December 8 – The Allure of Evil 484

December 9 – The Fallacy of Power 486

December 10 – The Void 487

December 11 – Addiction 488

December 12 – Sanity and Insanity 490

December 13 – Reflection and Manifestation 491

December 14 – Certainty 493

December 15 – Growth and Learning 494

December 16 – Opportunities 495

December 17 – Loyalty 496

December 18 – Religion as Good 497

December 19 – Religion as Evil 499

December 20 – God can't Fix This 500

December 21 – Winter Solstice 501

December 22 – Religion had to Change 502

December 23 – Acceptance 503

December 24 – The Need for Purpose 504

December 25 – Seek and Ye Shall Find 507

December 26 – Seek and Ye Shall Not Find 508

December 27 – Don't Wish Your Life Away 510

December 28 – How Do I Be? 511

December 29 – The Opposite of Love 513

December 30 – Religion Without God 514

December 31 – Do Not Wait For the Afterlife 515

Your Birthday! (and Yearning) 516

Afterward 517

Acknowledgements 519

Appendix A – Alphabetized List of Entries 521

Appendix B – Cinereo Modo 535

Not,

Daily Meditations

BEFORE WE BEGIN

There are a few items we should touch on before you start reading and one of those things is the concept of "Not."

In brief, Not is a really deep subject. In fact, the argument is made in this book that there is nothing deeper. It is beneath the substrate of reality. It is the underlying basis beneath all of existence. The word "Not," is used because what it is can only really be described in terms of what it isn't. It is not warmth or light or activity or presence. Instead, it is cold, black, static emptiness. Those four precepts all combined into one thing is what we call "Not." Not is described in much greater depth in late March and early April.

THE BOOK OF NOT

There is a book titled, *The Book of Not*, also by Thomas Vaughn and the Church of Not (written and published in 2020) which first introduced the idea of Not and Authorism.

You need not have read *The Book of Not* to dive into this book.

The Book of Not, in short, describes the philosophy of Not, the genesis of Authorism and the Principles of Not. *Not, Daily Meditations*, dives deeper into all three of those topics and due to its nature of being a book on philosophy, affords us the opportunity to dive deeper into a fourth area of focus: that being the search for purpose and meaning in our everyday lives.

AUTHORISM

Authorism is an ideology that asserts that we are each the author of our own lives. We author our existence both in thought and in manifestation of reality through thought.

Perhaps deeper still is that whether we think we are choosing to or not, each one of us *is* authoring our own lives. This is an important distinction because many people do not realize that they can be the author of their lives (rather, they believe they are victims of circumstance) and that even if they could author their own lives, many believe the story would not end well.

But there is a paradigm shift occurring in the world and the new paradigm is showing us all that we actually do author our own lives and that the story unfolds almost exactly as we "write it."

Beyond the simple idea that we humans are the authors of our own stories, Authorism goes on to explain *how* we are the authors and how being the author of our own story fits in with living life. Life is huge and any explanation of life and how to live life will necessarily also be far reaching. As such, as we explain Authorism, we also end up touching on other concepts such as nature, anthropology, chemistry, physics, quantum mechanics, biology, history, sociology, mathematics, economics and because of their extreme significance in addressing 'living life', there is an emphasis on philosophy and religion.

In other words, meaning and purpose are very central ideas in Authorism. Even though nobody but you can write in the core meaning and purpose of your own story, we can still all discuss it together.

MEDITATION

What do we mean by "meditation" in this book? Meditation is a topic of countless seminars, blogs, classes, books and so forth. There are hundreds of approaches to meditation. This book does not explore how to meditate other than to say that when we say "daily meditation," we are thinking of meditation in the sense of "something to contemplate," as opposed to "a clearing of the mind."

What is meant by a "daily meditation" is along the lines of a "thought for the day." The intent in creating this book of daily meditations is to offer up a thought for each day on various topics that are pertinent to the search for meaning and purpose, especially as these may relate to the philosophy of Not and Authorism.

Not, Daily Meditations

You may use these meditations for actual meditation by reading the entry and then sitting comfortably in contemplation of the content. Or perhaps for your daily meditation, just setting aside the time to read today's entry will be sufficient.

About The Book

There are 367 daily meditations in this book. There is one for every day of a leap year, plus an extra one for your birthday.

Much of this book is written in terms of a discussion we are having. "We" in this case is either you and I, or you and Authorism. To make it more of a discussion, questions are asked of you in the text. Sometimes questions you might ask are anticipated and then answered. Sometimes I stop to explain an idea or a concept and how it might relate to everyday life.

Each of the meditations are in some way aspects of Authorian philosophy.

I wrote this book for us. And we wrote this book for you. Where "us" are the Authorists and "you" are the person interested in Not, Authorism, or the search for meaning and purpose.

How to Read this Book

This book was written with the intent to provide a book one could pick up on any given day to touch base with the philosophy of Not and Authorism. There is no mandate to read every single day or to read every single entry. The idea was to provide the information to the reader and allow the reader to determine how much of it they want to examine and how often they wish to examine it.

While this book was written to provide daily meditations there was also the understanding that some readers may not wish to stop reading after just one entry. As such, there are larger arcs throughout the year that remain connected over many days. For instance, the description of Not begins in the end of March and goes on through April 19th. But even this end is just the beginning of what is needed to explain Life (with a capital "L"), which takes a few days to address before we start talking about the Principles of Not. The Principles of Not are then explained over the course of several days, and so on.

So on the one hand, each day is a single entry that stands by itself and can operate as the meditation for that day. But on the other hand, for most of the larger topics being contemplated, each entry flows with the one before and the one after, so the book may also be read straight through from January 1, through December 31 and there will be a sense of flow throughout.

SEE ALSO

There are many entries throughout this work which have a parenthetical "See also" to essentially cross reference other entries. For instance, on the day we talk about Not, there is a statement at the end that reads, "See also, *Introduction to Not*."

At the end of this book there is an appendix (See also, *Appendix A – Alphabetized List of Entries*) which reorders the table of contents such that the titles of the entries align with the dates. The titles of the entries are listed in alphabetical order so if you do want to cross reference one of the entries, you can quickly find the title of the entry, then see the associated date for that entry.

For instance, Introduction to Not is the title for the entry on April 2.

Not, Daily Meditations

Not, Daily Meditations

January 1 – The Most Important Thing In The World

Your child asks you, "[Mommy/Daddy], what is the most important thing in the whole world?"

What do you tell them? Is it getting a good job? Finding a mate? Making your bed? Is it a god or many gods? Religion? Being a good person?

It is none of those things.

This is what you should tell them: "The most important thing in the whole world is life."

In Authorism, life is held as the highest ideal. In fact, life is our higher power. There are many good reasons for this. You may think it sounds like a cop-out to use "life" as your higher power. It is not done without thought. If you consider the value of life – the real value that nobody ever talks about, you will feel the truth in it.

Because life is held as the highest ideal, no other ideal can be held higher. What this means is that no group, organization or entity of any kind can convince you to kill somebody merely based on the merit that they think it is a good idea or that it furthers their cause, etc.

Most notably this removes the authorization other religions and ideologies grant to kill in the name of their god, their gods or their ideas. You may not kill because your religion tells you to. You may not kill because a priest, preacher, prophet, rabbi, mullah or imam tells you to. You may not kill because your god told you to either! Life is the highest power and the highest principle and that means it is higher than god when it comes to what matters in all of existence. That's right: Life is more important than gods are.

For Authorists, killing in the name of any religion or deity is unacceptable because life is held as a higher principle than religion and deities. Religion, in fact, is pretty far down the stack when it comes to the hierarchy of principles. (Religion is part of the Community Principle).

This also elevates life above the importance of money, material wealth, power, ideas, philosophies, etc. thus establishing that killing for any reason other than preserving life is unacceptable. When it comes to taking life in order to preserve other life, understandably this can become very complicated.

For today, let's just think about the all-importance of life in the cosmos. To life, nothing is more important than life.

January 2 – New Year's Day (Yesterday)

Happy New Year!

Sorry, we are a day late with this. I wanted to start this book with the most important thing in the world (life!), but I also did not want to skip celebrating New Year's Day.

Today's meditation is on the new year and therefore on new beginnings.

Of course we could randomly choose any day of the year to "start over" and to make a new beginning, but because most all of the world (and certainly all of our world) also acknowledges January 1st as a brand new year, it makes it much easier to see today (even if it is one day late) as a new beginning!

Today we can close the book on last year and look forward to what new possibilities await us.

Today, perform even the smallest of rituals to celebrate this new beginning. Of course you can perform a full ritual celebration but if you don't have the time or inclination for that, then at least take a scrap of paper and write down one thing you want to come to fruition this year and then light a candle in honor of your aspiration. Leave the scrap of paper out for the rest of the day. (But don't forget to blow out the candle!)

Or consider what you would like to see happen, close your eyes and think about what it will look like. Feel gratitude for this new beginning.

January 3 – The Principles of Not

How do we choose this job over that one? Should I go with my friends on this road trip or spend the week with my sick aunt? Should I move to the big city? Should I move to the country? Should I have a baby? Should I get married? Should I join the Army? Should I find religion? How do I decide which one to choose?

Should you ask your friends or family for advice, pray to a god or gods, meditate, cast lots, do a tarot reading or flip a coin? Unfortunately, nobody can make the hard choices (or any choices) for you. You must choose. Authorization for action based on your choice comes from within you. Nonetheless, we still need some kind of guide in order to make those important decisions.

The Principles of Not are a guide to decision making. They are "of Not" because Not is the foundation of the ideology from whence they came.

The principles are almost just plain common sense. They are the things that are most important to all humans and as you read them you will likely be unsurprised by what they are and you may even exclaim, "Well of course, those are the things that matter most."

Putting them in order is what makes them "The Principles of Not" and gives us the ability to use them in decision making:

1. Life
2. Fitness
3. Relationships
4. Personal Code
5. Community

These principles flow in order of precedence – from most important to least important – and as such we can use them to determine what we should do in any given situation.

There are two ways to look at the Principles. On the one hand, these principles can be seen as values and as values (as previously mentioned) you can use them to make decisions. This approach is called Cinereo Modo ("the gray walk"). It is a way one can use the Principles in everyday life. For instance, "should I quit the team?" There are a series of questions you can ask to test the action against the Principles to help you decide what to do. (See also, *Cinereo Modo*.)

The other approach to the Principles is called Cinereo Ascensus ("the gray climb"). This is a way of using the Principles to provide direction. Instead of reacting, you are being proactive. Are you in a place where you feel like you have stagnated? Are you feeling spiritually flat? Looking for direction? Cinereo Ascensus uses the Principles in such a way that you can align yourself with the Principles in forward (upward) movement in your life. (See also, *The Tree of Not* and *Cinereo Ascensus*.)

Today's meditation is to consider the Principles of Not and how they influence your daily life.

January 4 – Preserving Life

Strive to preserve life whenever possible. That sounds pretty easy. Shouldn't be a problem...

Most people don't need to deal with this on a regular basis, but let's quickly discuss law enforcement, military combat and other individuals who have to make life or death decisions as a matter of course. Yes, it is sometimes necessary to take life. However, because life is the highest ideal, the only time one should consider taking a life is when one is actively trying to preserve life.

Paradox? Yes, of course it is. Truth is always bathed in paradox. I cannot sum up the plethora of variables one might need to weigh when deciding to take life in order to save life. All one can do is remember that life is of the highest importance and then try their best to make it through the day.

What about non-human life? What about cheeseburgers? Can we eat those? What about lettuce? After all, lettuce is a living plant. Does walking on tiny organisms kill them? Is it wrong to kill an annoying fly? When driving, if your car hits (and kills) a flying insect, is that okay? What about a mosquito? Or a wasp?

At some point in your decision making, you will have to use the **effective bailout value** to make a decision and move on with your life. (See also, *Effective Bailout Value*.)

One could take this life principle too far and be frozen with inaction. Some lines must be drawn within the framework of life in order for us to move forward.

Since humans are obviously significantly different from the rest of the animals (see also, *Are Humans, Animals?*) I draw a line between humans and the other animals. But because humans are also similar to some other animals and we think we are mammalian, within the animal kingdom I draw another line between mammals and the rest of the other animals. However, because some of the other animals in the animal kingdom can be similar to mammals, I also draw a line between all animals and plants. And because plants seem different from microorganisms, I draw another line there – between plants and microorganisms. Finally, underneath the importance of microorganisms I draw the last line and claim that anything that is not an animate organism which eats and breeds is not alive. And if something is not alive, its value is lower than that which lives.

So on the one hand I would agree with an ethical assertion that it is wrong to eat cows, on the other hand, I set my effective bailout value at that first line and I allow myself to eat meat in order to sustain and replenish my own life.

Each of us must find where these lines are drawn in our own personal codes and decide where we will set our own effective bailout values.

January 5 – Effective Bailout Value

In the late nineteen-nineties a program for the (then still relatively new "personal computer") came out called fractint.exe. The program was designed to calculate various fractals and then "paint" them on the screen of a personal computer. A fractal is an irregular curve where part of the curve or shape is similar in shape to a given larger or smaller part when magnified or reduced to the same size. Due to the infinite nature of fractals, if one is not careful, one might set the computer on an eternal task just calculating one part of a fractal.

In order to give the computer a break and in order to actually finish drawing the fractal before the end of time, there was a value one could adjust called the "effective bailout value." The effective bailout value is the point at which the computer would say "Ok, I have gone deep enough into this algorithm. I'm calling it! This part of the fractal is finished and I will move onto the next part!"

In real life, it is effectively the point where one says "Ok, forget it, we're finished here."

This can be a useful idea in many aspects of life.

I use this effective bailout value when discussing the virtue of life and the importance of preserving life. Or, more specifically, the importance of not taking life.

Somewhere between not killing other people and eating a delicious, juicy cheeseburger, I set my effective bailout value and more or less say, "It is wrong to take life, but it is ok to kill animals if I am going to eat them." (In my case, I am not actually the one doing the killing, so I have to acknowledge, "It is ok for me to allow others to take life on my behalf so that I might purchase the dead meat from a grocery store." (Wow, sometimes the truth sounds terrible when spoken aloud)).

Perhaps it isn't fair to take this route and there is an entire argument in ethics and even philosophy wrapped up in that seeming copout. But on this topic, everyone must set an effective bailout value or they will perish.

Because despite life being the most important thing in existence, the irony is that we all must take life in order to live life.

JANUARY 6 – VITACENTRICISM

Perhaps you think that placing the importance of life above all else in existence is vitacentric and self-serving. Well, of course it is. One might argue that we feel that life is the most important thing because we are life. Ironically, perhaps, only other life could argue that point.

But if you cannot get behind the idea that life is the most important thing in all of existence, perhaps you will at least acknowledge that Life is the most important thing in all of existence.

In other words, if that which grows, consumes and reproduces is not the most important thing, then at the very least, the building blocks of everything else certainly must be.

That is to say, warm, light, active presence is the most important thing in the cosmos.

How can this assertion be justified? Because the alternative is Not. (See also, *Introduction to Not* and *Not.*)

Today's meditation is to consider that life thinks life is the most important thing in the universe.

January 7 – The Interconnect

Science is beginning to piece together the awe we experience from Eastern mysticism with the awe we experience from technological breakthroughs.

The fact that everything exists in the form of waves of energy that emanate from sub-subatomic energy filaments to the fact that everything exists as discrete particles frozen in time, and everything in between, is now being explained by various fields of science and philosophy. It has not all been explained yet by a single "all-truth," but we are certainly getting closer and closer to understanding Life. (See also, *The All-Truth*)

One of the undeniable results of our research is that everything is connected. *Everything* is connected. That means that everything is connected to everything else. As an aside for the moment, the only thing that is not connected to everything else is Not. But that is not the focus of today's meditation.

Today, we should consider this interconnectedness. You can easily feel it just by closing your eyes and thinking strongly about something far away. That thought is literally a filament of energy connecting you to that thing you are thinking about.

You were already connected to it, but thinking about it strengthens that connection.

You may be considering someone you love in the other room or you may be thinking about some purple and black rocks on a planet in a solar system in a different galaxy.

If it is warm, light, active presence, is it Life. If it is Life, it is interconnected.

January 8 – Maintaining Life

Of course the interconnectedness we experience from the quantum to the subatomic to the molecular, then the cellular to the everyday and on to the macroscopic may be experienced in all things.

In other words, you may see a flower or a full moon and feel a deep connection. You may feel it with people or animals.

But it also exists between guiding principles such as the Principle of Not.

As the most important principle of all, that being *life*, preserving life is of course critical to life. But also important to life is maintaining life.

The "maintenance" of life is the key interconnect between the first Principle of Not and the second. Generally speaking, we reference the maintenance of life with the single word, "fitness."

As a single human can be likened to an entire cosmos (see also, *The Universal You*), so too can the word "fitness" have a vast scope.

But make no mistake that fitness is critical in maintaining life and it is therefore something you must hold in very high esteem. In fact, it must be that in importance, fitness is second only to life itself.

Today's meditation is for you to take a moment to reflect on your overall fitness.

January 9 – Honoring Life

It may seem ridiculously obvious to point out that we should honor life, but the respect for life as the most important thing in the universe is something that most life takes for granted.

On the one hand, life just is. Why should we revere life above non-life? Doesn't a soul *just exist* much like a rock or a star? Perhaps that is true. But the difference – and this is likely what distinguishes us from all other life too – is that we can observe that observation.

In other words, we have a real-time awareness of the fact that we are alive. We can witness in real-time the living of life that we are actively engaged in.

And this is a most wondrous and amazing thing to behold. There's an old Zen poem that goes something like this:

> "Marvelous action; magical power.
> Chopping wood; carrying water."

You can honor life throughout your day by recognizing this in the mundane actions of life. As you locate the right key and slide the key into the lock, you can hear the subtle sounds this makes. You can envision the action of the metal key aligning perfectly with the tumblers. Think about the trillions and trillions of molecules moving around in both the key and the lock. Imagine the infinitude of atoms that are involved in this dance in even just a microsecond of this action.

Any given moment of our lives is a stunning explosion of warmth, light, action and presence!

January 10 – Mine, Yours

What is more important, your life, or my life?

To you, perhaps your life is more important. To me, it is likely mine.

Placing importance on life is the easy part. Figuring out which lives have more importance within the framework of life gets a little bit trickier.

How do we assign value to individual lives? Is the life of a mentally ill homeless person worth more than the life of a federal politician? Is a movie star's life worth more than the life of a doctor? The answers to these questions depend on your ultimate objective.

If you were collecting people for an ark (think, Noah's Ark 2.0) you may want to select the politician over the mentally ill homeless person. Is this fair? No, it is not. But what are you trying to build? What is the objective? To preserve life or to preserve a way of life?

Is it ok to choose one life over another in an effort to preserve a way of life? Perhaps it is as long as life is still being regarded as the highest principle.

At any rate, if I can for a moment, put myself in your shoes, I can suddenly realize how your life is just important as mine.

January 11 – Ours, Theirs

What about your group versus my group? Is your group of lives more important than my group of lives?

Who do we include in "our group?" Is your group just your immediate family? Is your group everyone who wears a red uniform? Is the blue group more important than the orange group?

And who can make this judgement? Can the yellow group all vote to decide that the lives of their group are more important than the lives of the blue group?

As you may have already deduced, because we have questions like these we also have distrust, fear, suspicion, killing and finally, war.

As long as we humans divide ourselves into sub-groups, the questions of "ours versus theirs" will always plague us.

And verily I say unto you, as long as life divides itself into sub-groups we will always have to ask "Ours or theirs?"

Today's meditation is on your life-group. What is your life-group? How large is it? Could it encompass more than just the people you know?

Little kids will approach one another and ask, "Do you want to play with me?"

Wouldn't it be something if grown-ups could do that?

January 12 – Animal Life

Can we assert that human life is more important than animal life? Before we had agriculture or writing we were out there competing with the other animals for territory and natural resources.

Once we began writing things down we decided to make a note that our lives were more important than the lives of the animals that we either ate for dinner or displaced with our cities.

Flash forward five thousand years and we have now advanced our civilization to the point where some of us can supplement our diets with non-animal protein and still thrive.

Now it becomes an ethical debate: Should we eat other animals even though we can now avoid doing so?

Is the life of a cow just as important as the life of a human? What about a dog or a chimpanzee? A mouse?

Does sentience make a difference? For instance, if a dog has a spirit-consciousness like ours, does that dog's life become more important than the life of an ant who does not have a spirit-consciousness? How can we know if any given animal (or other human, for that matter) has a spirit-consciousness like we do?

Those who make the argument, in this case, win the argument. In other words, humanity has a different kind of consciousness than any other lifeform we have encountered to date. (See also, *Are Humans Animals?*) Because humans are the ones who can make this assertion and because humans, so far, are the only ones who can even ask this question, humans have the freedom to select any answer which pleases them.

So the answer is, yes, we can assert that human life is more important than animal life.

Now we have to decide on a criteria to use to determine worth. For instance, it is obvious that some of the other animals think in similar ways that humans do. It is also obvious that some of the other animals have sentience like we do. Anthropomorphism notwithstanding, you can see the intelligence in their eyes. You can see the spark of spirit-consciousness.

Is the spark of spirit-consciousness our benchmark? I think it is. Because my spirit-consciousness is what separates me from rocks, trees, stars and even from fishes and dogs, I *think* the spirit-consciousness is that which we must use to measure worth. Is my (or your) life more valuable than a rock or a chunk of dirt? Is it more valuable than a tree?

At what point does an animal's life become as valuable as a human's life? When their spirit-consciousness matches or exceeds our own. Exceeds? How can we even make such a comparison?

How this can be discerned is something we must leave unanswered today. Today, we merely consider the value of animal life in the great spectrum of that which is warm, light, active and present.

January 13 – Computer Life

Since we are using spirit-consciousness as a guide to determine the value of life, shouldn't we have an exact definition of what spirit-consciousness is?

Yes, we *should*, but we do not.

Nobody knows what consciousness is. Science cannot explain it and religions cannot agree on a definition of it. The only thing that seems obvious is that "spirit" is the same thing as "consciousness."

Our *soul* is the *consciousness* that animates us.

What happens when an artificial intelligence (AI) reaches the point that it becomes sentient?

Will that AI become *life*? It is already the same as us in that it is warm, light, active presence. But once it becomes sentient it will become the same as us in almost every respect. It will be a warm, light, active presence that can grow, consume and reproduce. And moreover it may be as conscious or "more conscious" than we are.

Whether we like it or not, at that point, the value of that AI's life shall reach or exceed the value of human life.

Incidentally, if you do not like that answer, you must come up with a different barometer to measure the importance of life. Remember that it must answers such questions as, "What makes a human life more valuable than a mosquito's life?

January 14 – Plant Life

Life is all-important. Plants are alive. Because plants are alive and because life is all-important, we should not go around killing plants.

But…

There is a hierarchy of life value and plants are lower on that scale than humans. In fact, for the time being, we place humans at the very top of that scale.

Authorism argues that the only thing more important than human life would be life that is even more human than humans already are. In other words, something that is also "alive" but more sentient might qualify for a higher position on the scale.

In truth, and as an aside, it is likely that humanity would redefine "life" if we discovered something that would rank higher than us on the life-value matrix.

Nonetheless, plants are quite a bit further down the scale than humans and even though we should respect them as living beings, we also have the freedom to do with them as we wish.

Ethically, you are within your rights to destroy a plant's life, however, also ethically, you should probably come up with an argument to justify that action.

For instance, killing a dandelion because it is a weed and makes your yard look bad is valid justification for plant-murder. Killing a dandelion because you want to cause death is not a valid justification.

January 15 – All Life

We have ascertained that Life (with a big "L") is that which is warm, light, active and present and that *life* (with a little "L") is a subset within that vast definition of Life.

Over the last few days we have been building a basis for describing the importance of all life.

That which grows, consumes and reproduces is more important than that which does not.

Of the things that grow, consume and reproduce, that which reasons, thinks and philosophizes is more important than that which does not.

While we glorify ourselves above all else*, we also acknowledge that we must surely be only partway along a spectrum of importance where there is that which is less important than us and that which is more important than us.

* Don't forget that humanity really is different. (See also, *Are Humans, Animals?*)

All life has value. And life must remain our highest value if life is to persist.

JANUARY 16 – ALIEN LIFE

Before we stop talking about the value of life, we should touch on the topic of alien life.

Yesterday we mentioned that all life has value and we mentioned that in a spectrum of life-value, humans are at the very top.

There is but one justification for humans being at the very top: Nobody else is around to argue with us.

The only life that could argue for the importance of some other life above humans would be another human. As soon as another human opens their mouth to argue, they have just lost the argument. They too, remain at the top of the index.

What about aliens? Are there any? Considering the validity of something like the Drake Equation (or derivatives thereof) we can safely say, "Yes, there are most assuredly intelligent, conscious aliens out there somewhere."

Is there life to be considering more valuable than ours?

Well, that will depend on who is asking and who is around to answer.

As mentioned previously, if we, as humans, find we need to move our importance further up the scale for some reason, we will need to find a better way to quantify the value of life.

January 17 – Life Destroys Life

In order to thrive, life destroys life.

This is a fact and a paradox but also a contradiction to the first Principle of Not.

Life consumes other life in order to live. What a paradox this is!

The single celled amoeba kills other single-celled animals and consumes them to nourish itself. Tiny multi-celled animals kill and consume amoeba for nourishment. Small fish kill and consume the tiny multi-celled animals for nourishment. Larger fish and mammals kill and consume smaller fish for nourishment. Mammals and humans kill and consume larger fish for nourishment. Humans kill and consume other mammals and whatever else they want for nourishment. Viruses, bacteria and other microorganisms kill and consume humans for their nourishment.

There is a notable exception to this rule about life destroying life in order to live.

Plants.

Almost all plant life is able to sustain itself without killing and consuming other life.

Perhaps plants have evolved to the highest ethical plateau and we should aspire to be like them?

Does the presence of the spirit-consciousness introduce the need to kill?

January 18 – Taking Life

Once we acknowledge that life is the most important thing there is it naturally follows that taking life should not be permitted.

If given a choice, we should not destroy life.

This means from the most trivial example of pulling up a dandelion or stepping on a bug to the most significant example of killing another human being.

Is it ever okay to take life? Yes. Again, we can apply the Principles of Not for guidance and see that it is okay to take life as long as it is in the interest of preserving life.

But that discussion was really about human life. What about lesser life? What about killing an annoying fly?

We have discussed this before. There is an effective bailout value when it comes to applying these principles. One can find justification for taking lesser life by various means. For instance, one might argue that if you do not kill the fly, it will breed and create more flies and if there are too many flies there is a greater and greater chance of being infected with some disease that flies may carry until your very life is at risk due to the presence of so many flies.

Or you can be truthful and say, "I do not like this buzzing fly bothering me and therefore I will kill it."

Humans have left the realm of nature yet our homes still exist within nature. When an insect or a rodent invades our home it can potentially put our health at risk. Again, only you can find that dividing line where you say "I will not kill a person, but I will kill a fly." Or a mouse. Or a rat. Or a raccoon. Etc.

But one must be careful because that line between what you will and will not kill must be drawn somewhere.

January 19 – Sanctify Life

We have discussed the fact that life is to be held as our highest principle and that by doing so we abolish certain behaviors such as killing in the name of some person or god and especially killing in the name of an idea.

For most people, it is not going to be that difficult to go through life without killing someone. So besides trying to not murder people what else does the sanctity of life mean to us day to day?

It means that we should take steps in the other direction too. In other words, we should not only avoid murdering people but we should also take steps to try to extend life and make life better.

How can we extend life? How do we make life better?

The answer to this question introduces us to the second Principle of Not: Fitness. At first this may seem surprisingly shallow. After all, when discussing Not and Life we are touching on the deepest philosophical concepts. However, once we look more closely at "fitness" you will see that it is not shallow and it really does matter.

Through invoking the second principle we make our lives last longer and this, in turn, makes our lives better all around. Further, by making your own life better you become an example to others and when they see the benefits you reap from being fit, they are drawn to become more fit themselves thereby making *their* lives better. This begins a virtuous cycle.

January 20 – Be Ready for Anything

How could anyone possibly be ready for anything? Honestly, that is not feasible.

Or is it?

When it comes to emergency preparedness, there are some things you can do in the event of an emergency. You can have a little extra food on hand or extra water in case services go down for an extended period. You can have some extra blankets and some flares in your emergency kit. Some people have a "go bag" they can grab with supplies in it in the event something catastrophic happens and they have to leave with no time to prepare. You can go a little way or a long way down these kinds of emergency-preparedness paths.

That is not what I am talking about though when I say to be ready for anything. Some of that is certainly a good idea, but what I am talking about is specific to the second Principle of Not: Fitness.

By remaining spiritually, mentally, emotionally, physically and socially fit, you will be as ready for anything as anyone can be.

When something catastrophic happens to us or in our lives, it usually crosses multiple aspects of the self. For instance, it might be physical in nature but ripple out into our mental, emotional and spiritual aspects of the self. Or it may be social in nature and ripple out into our physical, mental and emotional states. More than likely, no matter what the catastrophe, it will affect all five aspects of the self (spirit, mental, emotional, physical and social)

Remaining spiritually, mentally, emotionally, physically and socially fit will prepare you for anything.

Do you feel one of these aspects of the self needs your attention today?

JANUARY 21 – SURVIVAL OF THE FITTEST

Charles Darwin is attributed with the expression, "survival of the fittest." In his theory of natural selection in describing evolution he postulates that the species who is more fit is the species that survives. The species that is less fit dies off.

You can see why "fitness" gets moved way up to the top of the things that we must regard as important in our lives. We do not want to die off. You should not want to die off. You should want to thrive and put more of yourself into the world around you. The world will benefit from having more of you in it!

Survival of the fittest is true for natural selection but it is also true for everyday life. The average person thinks that life is "Get up, go to work, come home, go to bed; get up, go to work, come home, go to bed;" ad infinitum.

But it isn't. Things happen, both good and bad, in between that seeming drudgery. Opportunities present themselves along with catastrophic crises.

We use the term, "aciem exacuitur" (Latin for 'sharpened edge') to remind us to sharpen the edge. Only by remaining sharp can you be ready to seize the opportunity when it appears. Having a sharpened edge will give you the best chance to weather the storm when it comes. Those who are most unfit are most likely to miss the opportunities or be destroyed by the catastrophes.

As life, you must not only survive, but you must thrive! Sharpen the edge! (See also, *Vita*.)

January 22 – Fitness

The word "fitness" is deceptively simplistic. Generically most people think of "physical fitness" when hearing the word "fitness." But fitness applies to all five aspects of the self: spiritual, mental, emotional, physical and social.

Another thing to note is that "fitness" is rather arbitrary and subjective. More often than not it can be said (in all five areas of fitness) that a person is less fit than some and more fit than others.

Just like "respect for life" seems obvious, so might "staying fit," seem like an obvious principle to hold high, but it is all too often that fitness is pushed to the back in favor of more important things we do from day to day. Who has the time to spend on fitness when the kids need to be picked up, the dogs need to be dropped off and the house project list needs to be worked on?

In order to thrive and be the best life you can be, it is important to bring fitness way up the stack in importance. In fact, it needs to be brought so high up that it sits second only to life in the "what matters most" department. You must make this a priority. And it needs to be all five aspects of the self: spiritual fitness, mental fitness, emotional fitness, physical fitness and social fitness.

What is the most important in thing in the cosmos? Life.

What is the second most important thing in the cosmos? Becoming, or remaining spiritually, mentally, emotionally, physically and socially fit. (See also, *Aciem Exacuitur*.)

January 23 – How do I "do" Fitness?

We have talked about what fitness is and why it is so important. But how do we do it?

How do we become or remain fit? It is not necessarily easy, but it is very simple:
1. Exercise
2. Good nutrition
3. Healthy rest

For the sake of conversation, let's call those three "functions of health."

Whether we are talking about spiritual, mental, emotional, physical or social fitness those same three functions will apply.

In order to stay sharp and fit we will need to find ways to integrate those three functions into all five aspects of ourselves.

Today, consider how you are integrating exercise, good nutrition and healthy rest into the five aspects of yourself.

January 24 – Spiritual Fitness

How can one become or remain spiritually fit? For that matter, what exactly does "spiritual fitness" mean?

To be honest, it means whatever anyone saying it wants it to mean. Really, "spirituality" is impossible to define because nobody really knows what a spirit is. Is it your consciousness? Perhaps. But that is not helpful in that nobody really knows what "consciousness" is either. And "fitness," as we have already discussed, is also somewhat subjective and difficult to define precisely.

Add those two words together and you have a vagary that you could apply to almost anything.

But here in this work we have already defined what we mean by "fitness," and in the interest of clarity, we will drill down on our definition of "spirituality" here as well.

When we talk about spirituality, we mean the consciousness. We mean the part of you that makes you uniquely you. It is the "you" that ignores things you are reading to yourself. It is the "you" that observes your thoughts or clears your mind of them in meditation.

I often refer to spirit or consciousness as "the spirit-consciousness" because these words are essentially interchangeable. Because neither religion nor science can define them, I take the liberty to make that assertion.

With that said, "spiritual fitness," then is about having a healthy soul. It is about having a healthy spirit. It is about keeping your spirit-consciousness fit!

January 25 – Spiritual Exercise

In order to maintain our spiritual fitness, we will need to do some spiritual exercise. How does one exercise the spirit-consciousness?

Being present and living in moments of now on occasion is good spiritual exercise. (See also, *The Detriment of Now*) There are some disciplines which stress 'always living in the moment' but that is of course completely unrealistic. We must think about where we have been and imagine where we are going to go in order to be people in the society we live in. Nonetheless, being present and living with intention is excellent spiritual exercise.

There is a vast esoteric world that can explain why this is, but being outdoors, especially in a natural setting away from a city is good for the soul. It can revitalize and bring clarity to your being. Communing with nature can provide spiritual acuity.

Another spiritual exercise is simple meditation. Meditation can create a state of calm, contribute to feelings of pleasure and emotional stability and improve the perception and understanding of your body, mind and spirit-consciousness. Integrating even three or four minutes of meditation into your daily life will increase your overall spiritual health.

One more excellent spiritual exercise is to find somewhere you can be still for a few minutes. Sit, kneel or relax in some way and close your eyes. Feel love. Is this love coming from within? If it is not coming from within, use the love you feel to connect to your innermost self and feel that combination of the love you feel from outside mixing with the love you feel from the inside. Now, imagine this love energy expanding. It flows from you freely like the fire and light from a star. It shines out into the universe and expands to fill all space. Just feel this expansion of love as you fill the world with it.

JANUARY 26 – SPIRITUAL NUTRITION

Like physical nutrition, there are countless approaches to finding the right spiritual nutrition plan for you and just like physical nutrition, only you can determine if your spiritual nutrition plan is working or not. (See also, *Spiritual Hunger* and *Spiritual Meals*.)

At the risk of abusing a cliché, we wish to reiterate that each person is a completely unique being unlike any other. (Yes, that's right, like a snowflake). This cannot be emphasized enough when it comes to finding your way. Because of this uniqueness no one else can figure out what your path should look like. It has to be you.

That you are reading this book indicates that spiritual fitness is something that is already important to you. Reading about matters concerning the spirit or consciousness and continuing the journey to discover how it is important in your life is one way to nourish your spirit. Continue to seek the answers. If you do not find them here, keep looking. Continuous progress toward a goal will keep you sharp. The more you seek, the sharper you will become.

A spiritual nutrition plan is something that will have to work over a long period of time. Ideally, the rest of your life. A spiritual nutrition plan takes care of your long term spiritual needs, not your short term needs. For short term needs, a spiritual meal or two can tide you over.

Creating a spiritual nutrition plan is not something we can cover in a single day's meditation (although later in the year we outline an experiment titled, *The 21-Day Deity*), however we believe that Cinereo Ascensus is an excellent framework for a long term spiritual nutrition plan. (See also, *Cinereo Ascensus*.)

January 27 – Spiritual Rest

These ideas may seem counterintuitive as some of them are things we would normally think are not good to do in a spiritual practice. Bear in mind these are ideas for spirit rest, not exercise, so the opposite of what requires spiritual strength and intention is what provides spiritual rest.

Again, comparing spiritual fitness to physical fitness, rest is important. First and foremost this means good uninterrupted sleep. Sleep allows the spirit to reset (and do whatever else it does at night when nobody is watching!)

Another way to let your spirit rest is to "unplug" and just sit. To allow yourself to just be. This is not meditation per se, but allow your mind to drift and do not focus your intention on anything. Be without intention. If a thought comes to mind, follow it to see where it goes, then let it go and pick up the next one. Set a five minute timer and promise yourself no action until the timer goes off.

Do something that does not require intention. This can be scrolling through social media posts, driving a car somewhere you have been a hundred times, walking a very well-known path, playing something you know inside and out on a musical instrument, etc. The idea here is that you allow your body to engage in the automatic and "thoughtless" actions that it already knows how to do without thinking which gives your spirit consciousness the freedom to drift in and out.

Most of us do spiritually restful things often enough that they do not require dedication on our part. However, if you have developed a highly regimented spiritual fitness program, just do not forget to allow for spiritual rest.

January 28 – Mental Fitness

Remaining mentally sharp will give you the edge in the physical world and in the virtual digital world you live in. Mental acuity can improve all other areas of your life in that while in a sharpened mental state you can see approaches to problems or process ideas for solutions that you would not be able to accomplish when mentally dulled.

You will need your mental acuity to create your fitness plans for all five aspects of your life. It is from the place of mental clarity that you can see what needs to be done for your own progress as well as what things you should not do. Mental acuity is necessary to maximize your body's ability to exploit intuition.

Keep your mind sharp!

January 29 – Mental Exercise

To maximize mental fitness, it is important to exercise mentally on a daily basis. Some of the following may be good options for mental exercise.

Learning a new trade or a musical instrument. This could be in the form of a hobby. You can look online or check your local recreation center for class offerings.

Using your mind and body at the same time is good mental exercise. For instance, playing sports or running around kicking a ball. Bouncing a ball off of a wall and catching it again or even tossing a ball (or any small item) into the air and catching it is excellent mental exercise. Try this with your eyes closed for a very eye opening experience. (No pun intended!)

Even just looking around you right now, finding something you can pick up, then picking this thing up and looking at it. Look at it from different angles. Feel the weight. Feel the texture. This is like a mini-meditation on [_____] (insert thing's name). Look deep within this object and consider the Linear Spiral (see also, *The Linear Spiral*).

Puzzles and games of strategy make good mental exercise. Do a web search for "puzzles" and order one or search instead for "online puzzles," and try one.

Debating with friends or friendly discussions on controversial topics can be excellent mental exercise.

Today, consider how you can exercise your "mentality."

January 30 – Mental Nutrition

Nutrition for your mind is that which makes your mind feel good and healthy. Some of these things are going to overlap with other fitness activities you do for the other four aspects of the self.

Meditation is a good example. Meditation is an excellent way to clear your mind and make it feel healthy.

Of course eating the right foods and getting plenty of sleep is good for the mental state but we will talk more about that in the section on physical fitness.

Reading books – any books – is nutrition for the intellect (an aspect of the mental state). Especially if you have to look up a word once in a while because of the book you are reading.

Being intentional is good for the mind. This can also be called "being mindful." It is overriding automatic action with directed intention. It can be difficult but is a good thing to try. For instance, pouring yourself a glass of water mindfully, means you maintain a constant awareness during the act. You feel the weight of the glass getting heavier as the water pours in. You see the bubbles dancing around. You feel the balance of the glass in your hand (if you're holding it) shifting as the weight changes. You watch the water level rising even while you feel the pitcher getting lighter. You can do this kind of exercise while walking from your car or while opening a door. There are hundreds of things we do without thinking. Doing one with pure thought is a mental exercise that will improve mental acuity.

Intentional mindfulness can bring calm to the mind and spirit as well as bring emotional stability, physical calm and help you be more tolerant of social situations that might otherwise be stressful.

January 31 – Mental Rest

Your mental state can be affected by a plethora of external and internal stimuli. Make sure you give your mentality some rest. If you feel your mind buzzing from overuse, this is a good sign that you should slow it down a bit or at least step away from whatever it is you are engaged in to give your mind a few minutes to calm down.

Meditation can also be used for mental rest. This is where you clear your mind of thoughts and each time one pops into your mind, you release it and go back to Not or to a candle flame or "nothing," etc.

Step away from whatever you are doing on occasion and do something totally different. Sit at a different angle or on the floor instead of in a chair. Stand in the corner or back up against a wall. Just try something "strange" in order to reset your mind.

February 1 – Emotional Fitness

It is easy to recognize when someone else is emotionally unfit. It may be more difficult to see it in ourselves.

"Controlling" your feelings is a complicated subject. On the one hand, feelings are real and should be acknowledged when they happen. On the other hand, if you allow your feelings to dictate your actions, it is possible to become an unmitigated storm of emotion with no direction or purpose.

Balance is important. (See also, *How Do I Be?*) When we talk about emotional fitness, balance is one of the areas which should be focused on. In attaining a balance, it is not necessary to "control" your emotions but it is necessary in life to control your responses to them. In other words, you may not be able to control when a feeling arises, but you may exert control over your reaction to that feeling.

There are many important things that source from the *emotion* aspect of the self, not the least of which is authorization, acceptance and validation. Today, think about how you are reacting to your feelings.

February 2 – Emotional Exercise

Again, meditation comes into play, however, it does not have to be a dedicated session. This meditation you can do at any time. Just stop for a second and ask yourself, am I feeling an emotion right now? No? That is it. You are done. Yes? What is the emotion? Then ask yourself, where did it come from? What triggered it? Look into that for a moment and then move on. This is a way to exercise emotional understanding of yourself without judgement. Over time you may decide you want to change some things. Or not. But either way you empower yourself with knowledge.

Mindfulness, as introduced a few days ago, is a good way to practice gathering emotional intelligence which can be used to determine whether or not you want to make changes to how you react to your own feelings.

Another emotional exercise you can try is to remember something that evokes a powerful emotional response in you, then purposefully react radically different than you usually do. Consider that it is only an emotional exercise and therefore you have ultimate freedom in how you handle it. In other words, do not cause yourself unnecessary stress but instead, try to have fun with it.

FEBRUARY 3 – EMOTIONAL NUTRITION

Emotional nutrition comes in the form of positive emotions. Using your emotional exercises you will start to see when positive feelings arise and when negative feelings arise and combining that information with your mental prowess, you will start to see who and what kinds of things bring on these differing feelings in your life.

If someone or something or even some thoughts tend to bring you good feelings, it is likely that keeping those things around you is good emotional nutrition for you.

On the other hand, when you identify the sources of bad feelings, make a note of that and even if it is difficult for you it is probably wise to eliminate those sources from your being. Do not surround yourself with things that trigger bad feelings inside you.

This sounds ridiculously simplistic, and truly it is. But as we see in life over and over again, just because it is simple does not mean it is easy.

Keeping a journal – really a journal of any kind – can also be good for your emotional nutrition. This is because writing things down can bring clarity to how you feel even if you did not know your feelings were clouded. For instance, it is not uncommon that when feeling overwhelmed, one begins to list all the things that are causing this feeling only to find that the list is much shorter than one expected. And in that short list, once seeing it all "on paper," it becomes easy to identify the real source of the negative or overwhelming feelings.

FEBRUARY 4 – EMOTIONAL REST

One method of enjoying emotional rest is to defocus from emotional awareness (opposite of the mindfulness activity). Watching a movie, reading a book or exercising are all things that can move your focus away from the emotions long enough to bring some rest.

The same meditation exercise used above for nourishment can bring you emotional rest. By dispassionately considering a feeling that arises within you, you can experience feeling things without being admonished or praised. Just a level, non-judgmental experience of your emotional state can be restful to the emotional state of being.

FEBRUARY 5 – ANNIVERSARY ECCLESIA CONDITA

Today is the anniversary of the founding of the Church of Not and the religion of Authorism.

If you are an Authorist, today you can perform the ritual as described in the NR&C to celebrate our anniversary.

If you are not an Authorist, then for today's meditation we should consider the value of education in the world.

Consider a person who is raised to believe that they are better than everyone else and that in fact, other people are not even human. This person may learn to despise other people as lesser creatures. This person can be easily taught to hate other people because they "weaken the gene pool" and are not even human. (See also, *The Garden*.)

But if this person were to learn about other races and other religions, this person's horizons would expand and their mind would open and they would begin to realize that they had been misled in their education. They would begin to see that other people are no less or no more than themselves. And that they themselves are no more or less than other people. (See also, *Everyone is Orange*.)

Through learning and education this person who once was filled with ignorance, intolerance and hate is now filled with understanding, tolerance and love. (See also, *The Need for Purpose*.)

Thus is the power of knowledge.

FEBRUARY 6 – PHYSICAL FITNESS

For someone who is on a thought or spirit journey seeking the answers to deep and far-reaching questions of meaning and purpose it may be tempting to ignore the body and think that the mental state is a higher priority than the physical state and therefore physical fitness is irrelevant. That conclusion is folly.

Critical to mental, emotional and spiritual acuity, it is important to keep the physical body fit as well because this physical fitness ensures overall fitness throughout the other aspects of the self. All of the aspects of self interconnect and feeling bad emotionally or spiritually can cause physical discomfort just as physical discomfort can cause mental or emotional stress.

The bad part of this interconnectedness can be seen in how a negative thing that happens to one aspect of the self reverberates throughout the rest of the self causing negative effects in other aspects of the self.

The good part, on the other hand, is that making a positive change in one aspect also reverberates throughout the entire being and can uplift the other aspects of the self.

Physical fitness will improve all aspects of self and give you an edge on your spiritual journey.

February 7 – Physical Exercise

Physical exercise is a critical part of physical fitness. Exercise makes the body stronger and makes people feel good. The strength that comes with repeated exercise can be used to help further your journey and allow you to endure tribulations that might otherwise set you back on your journey.

Exercise releases endorphins in the body and makes you feel good thus lifting your spirit. Exercise improves emotional stability, mental acuity and when you exercise in a group setting it affords the opportunity to strengthen relationships or forge new ones thus improving your social aspect of life and also touching on the third and fifth Principles of Not, Relationships and Community.

A body in motion stays in motion. It is critical that we stay active. The need to remain active becomes even more important as we get older.

February 8 – Physical Nutrition

Today's entry may be one of the most difficult of all to address. Physical nutrition is a topic with a tremendous amount of confusion and controversy.

However, we believe that just as it is with spiritual nutrition, there is not a physical nutrition plan already in existence that is perfect for you. You have to make your own.

We recommend that you do your own research and pay close attention to how different foods make you feel and what they do to you physically.

Again, simple but not easy. For instance, you may feel bad after eating something that tastes really good. This can be extremely difficult to reconcile internally. For instance, *"How can something this good make me feel bad?"*

You can do research and you can ask around about how other people handle physical nutrition but the bottom line is that ultimately you and only you will be able to tailor a plan that works best for you.

As with the other aspects of your journey, a journal can be very useful in sorting out the things that work for you and the things that do not work for you.

Just remember that more than any other source, you should trust your own gut feelings and inclinations when choosing a path.

FEBRUARY 9 – PHYSICAL REST

Physical rest is critical for your body. The amount of rest needed will vary for each person but generally speaking eight hours of uninterrupted sleep per night is recommended for most people.

Physical rest will provide more than just rest for your muscles. It also allows for emotional rest and a mental rest as well. A night of good sleep can act as a complete reset for your entire body and psyche. This reset can be tremendously helpful. (See also, *A Day in the Life*).

But sleep is not the only way to rest. Other ways to provide physical rest for your body are to just sit down where it is calm for a few seconds or a minute and rest. If you are out and about, you can find some shade and drop to one knee for a few seconds. Just standing and not moving can even be restful. Unfortunately, there is a need to balance how you look in public with how you feel. Just standing in a public place doing nothing for more than a minute may start to draw unnecessary attention. Sad, but true.

One of the tricks to finding rest is to engage mindfulness while engaged in a relaxation technique. Rest is not just a state of activity but it is also a state of mind. For instance, you might be riding a bus and have a few minutes where you are more or less stuck in one place. Even if you are standing on the bus, you can use this opportunity to turn this period of relative inactivity into rest for your body. Be aware of which muscles can be in a relaxed state and allow them to feel relaxed.

Once more, meditation can be tremendously helpful. There are many relaxation techniques available for mass consumption. Most of them are free and easy to employ at your leisure.

February 10 – Social Media

Social media is a bizarre new addition to human civilization. The impact social media has made on humanity has yet to be fully realized. For that matter, the impact hasn't even finished. You might say concussive waves are still radiating out from social media's initial impact.

For some people, using social media can be a great way to network with other people and get a sense of their own community and their place in that community.

For some people, using social media can be a draining experience that causes depression and anxiety.

And for some people it can be both good and bad.

People's use of social media ranges from people who have never used it, to those who have used it but quit, to those who use it sometimes, often or "all the time."

Not unlike most anything else that is controversial and certainly addictive, each individual person must ascertain for themselves whether or not social media adds value to their lives or causes damage.

Without making a statement as to the value of social media in the world, I can safely say that there is a big difference between being social and using social media.

Today's meditation is to consider what role social media plays in your life. Ask yourself if you are receiving valuable benefits from social media relative to the amount of time you spend using it. Or perhaps an easier approach is to honestly assess your feelings during or after using social media. Do you feel happier or not? Then adjust your use according to your answers.

February 11 – Social Fitness

You have probably heard the expression that "humans are pack animals." (That is to say, "running with the pack," not 'carrying supplies'). While I would have to disagree on the animal part (see also, *Are Humans, Animals?*) I cannot argue the pack part. Almost all people need a social connection of some kind to feel complete. Some people need more, some people need less. But there is no denying that we all need each other.

Social fitness covers relationships which harkens to the third Principle of Not (which is Relationships), but also includes everything else external to you.

Social fitness includes your involvement in the community and in social groups such as churches, clubs and associations as well as your immediate neighbors.

Social fitness is also how you appear to other people. This is what clothes you wear and whether or not they are clean or dirty or have rips in them (and whether or not the rips are intentional) or are well kept. It is the cleanliness of your house and yard or your apartment and patio or deck. How you clean your vehicle. Even how you park your vehicle.

It is how you carry yourself – whether you smile or scowl, make eye contact or avert your eyes. Whether you avoid people or seek them out.

February 12 – Social Exercise

Exercise in this domain will depend vastly on where you want to strengthen your social aspect. Do you need to reduce the amount of time you spend socializing? Do you need to increase it? Do you want to make a better impression at work or in your neighborhood?

If you want to change the way you are seen by others you can start implementing those changes as a form of social exercise. You can change the clothes you wear or change the way you get around (bicycle instead of walk, walk instead of bicycle, etc.)

There is also the possibility that you are not happy with your social aspect of life and want to change it but are not sure what it is you are unhappy with. If this is the case you can also implement changes in how you appear to others and take note of how those changes affect your social standing. As with most aspects of your journey through life, trial and error is often the best teacher.

The most important aspect of trial and error is maintaining awareness of the trials, the errors and keeping track of the results. Again, journaling can be a very useful tool to track what kinds of changes you make bring what kind of changes to your life.

FEBRUARY 13 – SOCIAL NUTRITION

Social nutrition comes primarily in the form of social interaction, but not exclusively. This can be accomplished through group activities, going out with a friend or friends, or even just going to a place where there are other people around.

Just being around people – even people you do not know – can help feed the need to be social.

This may seem counterintuitive, but sometimes the most nutritious choice for your social life is to spend an evening home alone. First of all, spending time with yourself may be a healthier choice for your entire being (E.g. the other four aspects of self) and therefore the net effect on the social self is a positive effect. Secondly, it may be that a night without you demonstrates to your social group how valuable you are to them. After all, absence makes the heart grow fonder.

Finally, a break from your social group may enlighten you as to the real nutritional value that social group is actually bringing to you. If you realize it is truly socially nutritious, great! Keep it in your life. If you realize it isn't, then now is the time to change it.

February 14 – Social Rest

Of course rest is necessary in this aspect of life as well as all of the others. Social interaction, like everything else, should be moderated. Too much social interaction can overload the emotions and the mind and cause unnecessary anxiety over time.

In order to rest from social action, you should find a place to be alone. Ideally, when you find this alone time, you should disconnect from streaming and social media so that you can really feel the effects of being alone.

You may not be surprised to read that meditation can be a good thing to do to fit this bill. Sitting in silent meditation is excellent "alone time."

Taking a walk, or going for a swim, jogging or taking a bike ride or a drive in the car are all things you can do to gain some alone time. A lot of these activities may take place where other people are nearby but far enough away that you can still feel alone. If that is not the case, you should try to find somewhere more isolated to enjoy the experience of just being with yourself.

February 15 – Relationships

At the end, when you are lying on your death bed and you look back over your life, that which will matter most will be the relationships you have had. Those that you have garnered, those you have squandered, those you have broken up or helped create. Thus the next most important thing to life and staying fit are your relationships. This discussion on relationships is almost exclusively reserved for relationships between living things.

It is possible that relationships between living and nonliving things is also important. For instance, the relationship between a living person and a dearly departed person (or even between a person and a soccer ball). But the relationships between living beings are more important than relationships between non-living beings or anything inanimate (even Wilson).

If you look deeper into important relationships with the inanimate, you will find a life-connection at the root. That connection may even be your own connection with yourself. In other words, the inanimate object will likely be a proxy for something that either is, was or will be animate.

In fact, the most important relationship to garner is your own relationship with yourself. We will talk about this more in the future, but loving yourself is paramount to maintaining a healthy self, finding fulfillment in your life and building all other relationships.

The thought for today is relationships. (See also *Necessitudo*.)

February 16 – Self and Life

Is any single relationship more important than another?

The most important relationship you can garner is your own relationship with Life. You should spend some time feeling your connection to Life and understanding it. You should know that this relationship with Life is an unbreakable bond that can carry you through any hardship.

As paradox is prevalent in truth, it may not surprise you to see that your relationship with Life is paradoxical. The term "relationship" implies the interrelation between two distinct entities or things and you are not separate from Life. But nonetheless, you have a relationship with Life. Just like you are not separate from yourself but you have a relationship with yourself.

Understanding that you are not separate from Life is one of the milestones in spiritual growth that you should strive for. As you proceed with this journey of exploration into your own relationship with Life, you will come to understand that, because you are not separate from Life, the truth of this journey is "self" discovery. It is the understanding that self is Life and that you are interconnected with everything else and everything else is interconnected with you. And I do mean *everything* else - not just other living things. The mountains and valleys are made of warm, light, active presence and you are made of warm, light, active presence.

FEBRUARY 17 – THE LOVE-SPARK

The reason it is so critical to cultivate your own relationship with Life is that in so doing, you will ultimately experience love for yourself.

Having, feeling and giving love is not a mandate in having relationships with other people, but nonetheless love is something we should all strive for and you cannot truly love other living beings until you first love yourself.

The good news is that you do not have to love yourself unconditionally from the start. Just a tiny spark of love is all it takes. Once you have even the tiniest glimmer of love for yourself (Life), you can immediately start sharing that love with others.

In fact, like blowing on a fire to feed the flames more oxygen, sharing that tiniest spark of love with others will cause it to grow. Once it grows anywhere it grows everywhere and the fire within you that began as a spark, will grow larger. The nurturing of the spark of love is what is referred to as a virtuous cycle. It is the beginning of the path to liberation from the chains of old paradigms and social locking that has come, in part, from the mistaken adoration of economy instead of society.

Once you have established even the barest beginnings of this love relationship with yourself, you can then spend some time and energy on fostering other relationships.

FEBRUARY 18 – YOUR FAMILY IS WHATEVER YOU SAY IT IS

The term "family values" has become cliché and lost its meaning over the decades but it is something you should hold high in your value system. The "family value" concentrates focus on the immediate family first, then ripples out from there.

As a child, your parents and your siblings should come first. This carries on through young adulthood until you find a partner. Your relationship with your life-partner should then come first as this creates a new nucleus of a family unit. And then, to close the circle, your children should come first (but never at the expense of yourself).

The life-partner relationship is a special relationship. It is stronger than family relationships and stronger than relationships with friends. The life-partner relationship is the strongest relationship because it is a friend relationship that has transcended the boundaries possible with friend relationships and has become the progenitor of an entirely new family. Once this happens, it has now become both a family relationship and a friend relationship combined into one. The beginning of a life-partner relationship is the seed for the growth of a new family. As the life-partner relationship grows, the family becomes stronger. Whether or not the relationship creates or adopts progeny, the creation of a new family is a beautiful thing.

It is not uncommon for a friend to become so close as to be considered "family." Something important to understand is that your family is whatever you say it is.

FEBRUARY 19 – GIVING TIME

Time...

Time is a commodity that each of has.

Time is something we all have the same amount of. We each have 24 hours each day with which to live our lives. What we do with that time is up to us. The difficulty in life is choosing what to do with this invaluable commodity.

If you want to show someone you love them, besides giving love itself, time is the most precious thing you can give to them.

Who we give that time to is our choice.

Do not give your time to a relationships that brings you pain. It is a violation of the second Principle of Not (Fitness) in that giving time to a relationship that causes you harm is counter to remaining mentally, emotionally and spiritually fit.

Give your time to someone you love. Even if that means yourself. If it is you, do something nice for yourself. Give yourself a nice bath or a walk in the woods. Let yourself sit for a few moments unassigned and unpressured.

You can give the same thing to someone else or just be there for that person. Hang out with them for a few minutes just being. It is not necessary that you even speak.

Today, consider giving some of your time to someone you love.

FEBRUARY 20 – CULTIVATING RELATIONSHIPS

Cultivation can take the form of nurturing, encouraging, supporting or helping someone or something (if the relationship is with a pet, for instance).

A relationship is an interchange between you and some other entity. You must put some energy into the relationship in order to get some energy out of the relationship.

The fascinating thing about a relationship is the "third person."

When you and I form a relationship a third entity is formed. There is you. There is me. There is us. If I put energy into the relationship and you put energy into the relationship then there is something that has just received energy from both of us. That something is the actual relationship itself. The relationship becomes an entity in its own right which radiates its energy back to us. (See also, *The Collective Conscious Imperative*).

Therein lies the secret power of relationships. This radiation of love energy seemingly from nowhere. The energy from the relationship can warm us and comfort us. The relationship energy is something that cannot really be explained using logic and reason but it is because of this "magical energy" that relationships have such incredible value and are so important.

Cultivate a relationship today.

February 21 – Pruning Relationships

Perhaps just as important as cultivating relationships is the importance of pruning them.

What kind of energy are you getting out of the relationship? Is it good energy? Is it positive energy?

If it is not good energy, you should consider doing some pruning. Perhaps today you should put less energy than you have been into a relationship.

You see, if the relationship is radiating negative energy then adding more energy from your own being is not going to be good for you and it is not going to change what the relationship is emitting. Pull back on how much energy you are putting in.

You should see a change.

If you notice the relationship is now giving off less negative energy, it may be time to end this relationship.

All relationships are important but they are not necessarily all good for us. If you find a bad one, it is best to get away from it as soon as you can.

Today consider, are there any relationships you are feeding that may need to be pruned?

February 22 – Creating Relationships

You + Me = Relationship.

Notice in that equation there are only two things being added but there are three things total.

The relationship that forms when you and I add our energy together becomes its own entity.

This entity (relationship) is sometimes known as "the collective conscience." It is the sum total of the varying energies being fed into it. You can witness this in a classroom, a tour, a theater, a bus, etc. Anywhere more than one person gathers you will find the energies of those persons combining to form this third entity which can be considered the collective conscience of the group that formed it. (See also, *The Collective Conscious Imperative*).

So you might ask, "How do I create a relationship?"

The answer is shockingly simple. You need only interact with another being. Even saying hello to someone you have never met before is instantaneously creating a new relationship. Granted, a hello in passing may create just a tiny relationship that almost immediately fades away but it is nonetheless creating a relationship.

Even if you create only a tiny relationship today that goes away as soon as it is formed, it is still worth the effort. After all, there is always the possibility that the relationship does not fade away entirely. It could be that the spark you used to generate the relationship at some later date it fanned into a fire.

February 23 – Non-Love Relationships

Shouldn't all relationships be bursting with love?

In a fairy land where unicorns and puppies slide down rainbows and dance on happy clouds, that would certainly be the case.

But in the world we live in, it is often difficult to continuously emanate love for our fellow beings. Also, there is justification for maintaining relationships that are not "love-relationships."

For instance, that person you randomly said hello to yesterday. There is no reason to try to quantify the love you might have for that random person. If you meditate on it long enough, you can probably find a way to love them, but there are likely going to be far more non-love relationships in your life than love-relationships.

The mail delivery person, your auto mechanic, the clerk staring hate daggers into you from behind the counter… These are all people you may "form a relationship with" that will not necessarily be a love-relationship. (See also, *The Opposite of Love*).

It is okay to not love everyone! Even a non-love relationship is worth having. And love is a tricky concept. One never knows where love energy might form.

February 24 – Immortality

As long as your influence affects the world, you continue to exist.

Besides the fact that the atoms that comprise your being will not go away, even if, some 400 years after your death, someone notes your position in a family tree, listens to something you recorded, reads something you once wrote or looks upon a work of art you created, then you are still alive.

Do not fear death because as Life, you cannot really perish.

Warm, light, active presence cannot become cold, dark, static emptiness.

February 25 – What is Moral?

How do you know if you have good morals? How do you know what is morally right or wrong?

Authorism simply defines morality as "A moral person will endeavor to prevent harm to themselves or others."

Today you should ask yourself these questions and consider your answers:

1. Am I doing something that is harming myself?
2. Am I doing something that is harming others?

If you think you might be causing harm to yourself or others, you should start thinking of a way to change your behavior or actions such that you can prevent this harm.

February 26 – Your Personal Code

As you move through life, learning more about yourself spiritually, mentally, emotionally, physically and socially, you learn to love yourself and you develop relationships and become more at peace with yourself in all aspects of life.

Over time, as you analyze the varying paradigms that you find on your journey, you will collect these splinters of truth and start to form your *personal code*. Everyone has a personal code that guides them though many people do not realize they have constructed one.

Your personal code helps define you as a person (though who you are is actually deeper than your code). (See also, *Deeper than Belief*.) Your personal code is part of your *structure of belief*. And your structure of belief is built on top of your *foundation of belief*. If bricks of belief are used to build your foundation and structure of belief, perhaps your personal code is the mortar that keeps all of the bricks together. That is not entirely accurate, however, as *the bricks* in your foundation and your structure of belief may also be considered elements of your personal code.

For instance, "I have integrity" might be an element of your personal code. Or you may think of yourself as a warrior, a seeker, a student, a follower or a leader. Your code may contain statements about you such as, "I always pay my debts," "I'm an honest person," or even something like, "I want to find myself." Also things like, "God is love," "Prayer heals," or "Jesus saves."

Each of those expressions can be a part of one's personal code and each of those expressions can be a brick in one's structure or foundation of belief. (See also, *Codice Personalum*.)

FEBRUARY 27 – ARTICULATING YOUR CODE

Write it down.

If someone asked you to, could you write down some bullet points that outline your personal code?

If you cannot articulate it (or perhaps even if you can), today is a good day to sit down and think about what some of your bullets would look like.

Make a list and after you have written down five to ten bullet points, look them over and see if you feel they are worthy being part of your structure of belief.

FEBRUARY 28 – CENTER YOURSELF

You should identify yourself with your code. Relationships may come and go. Jobs may come and go. You may even change religions. But your code cannot be broken or taken away from you. Though your code can change, it can only be changed by you and therefore even in flux your code is your island in the chaotic storm of everyday life.

You can center yourself around your code. On your code. And therefore no matter what happens all around you, you will not be lost. You will always know who you are – where you are – what you are. You can always find yourself. Even if your entire personal code is just the six word sentence, "I am building my personal code."

Today, I am balanced and centered.

February 29 – How should I act?

How should I treat other people? What should I do? Which path should I choose? How should I act in any given situation?

You can also figure out where to go and what to do based on your personal code. Your personal code is from whence comes "external" authorization. The paradox in "external authorization" is that even though we desperately seek it, the comfort and approval which we hope to derive from it can only come from within ourselves.

Your code also tells you what not to do. Or at least helps you figure out what not to do.

Your code becomes your compass and can guide you in moments of calm and through the most turbulent storms.

If you are ever perplexed about what to do, write down your question on one page and write down your code on another page. Your code will guide you.

Look to your personal code to guide you today.

(See also, *Splinters of Truth* and *How Do I Be?*)

MARCH 1 – HEALTHY SKEPTICISM

Would you be surprised to find out you were wrong?

I hope not.

Growth and flourishing is all about finding out you were wrong. Over and over and over again.

Each time you make a leap to the next level of understanding about the world around you it is often after discovering that you were wrong about something.

Or, contrariwise, after making a leap to a new level of understanding about the world around you, you will often see that you were looking at something all wrong before.

Because of this, you should always maintain a healthy skepticism about what you are seeing and what you are being told. (See also, *The Garden.*)

Could what you are being told be all wrong? Yes. Could it be all right? Yes. Is it likely somewhere in between those two extremes? Yes!

Use skepticism to test the bricks in your foundation of belief! Is there a brick you have not tested in a while? See if you can break it today.

March 2 – Shake Your Foundations

Is your foundation of belief strong?

Is it strong enough to build a structure on?

How do you know the foundation won't shift?

Test the bricks.

Take a brick (which is an individual belief you hold as true and right) and see if you can break it. Can you find something wrong with it? If not, hand it to someone else and see if they can find something wrong with it.

This is most easily accomplished by just stating your belief as a fact and then standing back to see what happens. Does the other person argue with you or agree? If they argue, does their argument hold water? If they make a good argument then perhaps your brick is not a good one to keep in the foundation of your beliefs. In that case, either move it up to the structure (which is an easier place to make changes in your beliefs) or get rid of it altogether.

If they cannot crack or break it, keep it in your foundation but also keep letting people try to break it when you have the opportunity. The longer you can go without it being broken, the more solid and unshakeable you can know your foundation to be.

You should try to shake your foundation but it should never budge.

MARCH 3 – SUPERSTRUCTURES

Why build just a meager *structure* of belief when I could build a *superstructure* of belief!?

Actually, there is a good reason to keep your structure of belief humble and relatively small.

Recall that your structure of belief is sitting atop your foundation of belief and that those two combined with your personal code, essentially define you as a person.

This may seem counterintuitive but the larger and more complex your personal code is (or your structure of belief), the more difficult it will be to make decisions about "right action."

A superstructure may have so many hallways and rooms that too many choices becomes just paralyzing as no choices, leaving you frozen with indecision.

A more sensible and defensible structure will be smaller and have an unshakeable foundation. From this kind of structure, you can quickly and decisively make "right choices" (right for you).

MARCH 4 – CODE SEEKING

If I were starting from scratch, what would I put in my code?

Why don't we just start with some words?

I think a good personal code might contain the following: Wisdom, reason, skepticism, critical thinking, gratitude, fortitude, kindness, generosity, self-examination and personal fulfillment.

Turning that into a personal code can be done by writing the words in a sentence. For example:

"Wisdom, reason, skepticism, critical thinking, gratitude, fortitude, kindness, generosity, self-examination and personal fulfillment are all very important aspects of who I am."

Are there any other things that you would want in your code?

March 5 – Personal Fulfillment

Today we will focus on personal fulfillment.

Do you feel fulfilled?

If so, it is time to sit down for a moment and bask in this feeling. Give thanks to yourself for making decisions in the past that have led to the fulfillment you are feeling today.

If not, perhaps you need to ask, "What does that even mean?"

To feel fulfilled, you will feel you have achieved something. It is the feeling you get after having accomplished a task or after the attainment of some goal. Or the feeling you get while working on accomplishing some task or attaining some goal.

If you do not feel a sense of personal fulfillment today, one of the best things you can do today is to give yourself a goal. Think of something you would like to achieve.

Do you want to learn a new language? Would you like to learn to play a musical instrument? Maybe you would like to learn to paint? Take a class in something? Become a black belt in some martial art? Learn a new sport? Visit a new country?

Today, think of something you would like to accomplish.

Now, write it down somewhere. That is all you have to do today.

Well done!

MARCH 6 – TAKE A STEP

We were talking about personal fulfillment and having goals for your future.

If you do not have any goals for your future, how will you be able to get to your desired destination?

If you do not take the wheel and direct the vehicle, the vehicle will just careen around and there is no telling where you will end up.

You must decide where you are going to go. This begins with a single goal.

And once you have a single goal, in order to attain that goal all you have to do is take one step.

"A task begun is a task half done."

Starting it is the hard part.

Today, take one step toward one goal. What is the step you can take, today, toward your goal?

March 7 – Self Actualization

Self-actualization is essentially the fulfillment of one's own potential.

This can be tricky for people especially if they do not realize their potential or if they think their potential is far greater than it could possibly be. Here I am not talking about an overinflated ego but rather a mistaken assumption that one is responsible for far more than they are or that is even realistic. (See also, *Your Higher Power*.)

How do you measure your potential? Just how much can you achieve in this life? How much should you achieve?

Answering these questions starts taking us down the rabbit hole of the great mysteries of life. These mysteries pose questions that have remained unanswered for millennia. (See also, *The Mysteries : Album Mysteria Non*.)

Why are we here? What is the point of human existence? What is the purpose? What is *my* purpose?

We must consider these questions in order to reconcile our potential. Do we have the potential to achieve our purpose?

I would argue that we do. I would further posit that you may find self-actualization in the realization that the universe is indeed unfolding as it should. This is meant to be. You are meant to be. You belong here and what you have done needed to be done in order for the universe to become what it became just now. Further, you need to be, as you are, right now, for the universe to become what it is moving toward becoming.

Each moment of the past was a moment in history where everything was exactly as it needed to be in order for the present to become what it is. And from the perspective of the future, every moment of our present is exactly what it needs to be for the future to unfold as it is supposed to.

MARCH 8 – THE UNEXAMINED LIFE

Before we move away from the discussion of personal code, we should discuss a controversial quote attributed to Socrates: "The unexamined life is not worth living."

This quote generates a lot of argument among people but it could make a great addition to one's foundation of belief. Well, not exactly as stated perhaps. Authorists would argue that if taken literally, this statement would directly violate the first Principle of Not (and probably the second Principle as well). But this statement should not be taken literally. The statement should probably be reworded, "The unexamined life is at risk of stagnating."

The point of bringing up this quote is that it can make an excellent brick in one's foundation or structure of belief.

Authorists believe that one should constantly be checking one's own structure and foundation of belief for any breaks, cracks or signs of weakening. More than that, we should try to shake the structure – try to shake the foundation – to see if there is any need for fortification or maintenance. (See also, *Shake the Foundation*.)

The following sentence is another good example of something that might appear as a brick in one's foundation of belief: **There is only one absolute: it is the statement, "There are no absolutes."**

As we have mentioned before, *paradox is prevalent in truth*, (a statement which, could also be a brick in the foundation of one's belief).

MARCH 9 – COMMUNITY

We have talked about Life, fitness, relationships and the importance of personal code. There is one more thing we need to consider in the list of "that which matters most."

Community.

After all, humans are communal beasts. We are tribal. We need each other. Even if just a small group, we still need a community of some kind in order to feel belonging and fulfillment.

We talked about this before when we talked about relationships. The relationships we develop in the community end up sustaining us with their own unique energy. And each community that we are a part of becomes its own individual group consciousness. (See also, *Cultivating Relationships*.)

It is important that we belong to a community but that belonging is a two way street. In order to get energy from the community we need to give energy to the community.

But 'community' is an expansive word. It can cover many different groups, subgroups or even relationships within groups. So what do we mean by it?

The first community to consider is your immediate family, roommates, building mates, etc. It is the little group of people closest to where you spend most of your time.

What is the communal mind of that group like? What kind of energy can you feel from it? What kind of energy do you give to it? (See also, *Civitas*.)

March 10 – Communities within Communities

The question we considered yesterday was about what kind of energy we get from and give to our immediate community.

Today we consider this on a broader scale. Today we consider the broader community and the little communities we are involved in within the broader community.

For instance, are you part of a club? Do you meet with a small group of people semi-regularly? A large group? Do you work out? Do you work from home or somewhere else? Do you go to church? The people you interact with regularly are part of a community you are involved in.

What kind of energy do you give to that community? What kind of energy do you get from it?

March 11 – Neighborliness

You live in a community. It may be a very small community spread out across a great area (rural) or it may be a very large community with many people living very near each other (urban). Either way, you live among your neighbors.

Just like any other collective consciousness, this community-of-neighbors-entity you are in a relationship with needs energy from you and gives energy to you.

You should be part of it. You should add to it. Be an active part of your community. In order to get what you need from it, you'll need to give to it. In turn, what you give to it dictates, in part, what you get from it.

As you can see, this "relationship thing" is significant.

What kind of neighbor are you?

March 12 – Take Care!

A common expression added to saying good-bye in the USA is, "Take care of yourself!" This is also often abbreviated as "Take care!"

But you *should* take care of yourself.

What does this mean? Does this mean that you should constantly pamper yourself and shower yourself with gifts?

No, that would be spoiling yourself. To spoil something is the opposite of taking care of something.

Taking care of something means loving it. In order to take care of yourself, you need to love yourself. This means loving you, and most everything about you. And when I say "about you" I actually mean "around you."

You should take care of your belongings. Keep them clean and in good repair. Take care of your property. Keep your room clean. Keep your lawn in order and keep your house clean and in good repair.

There is a surprising effect from this. You barely even notice it but it has a huge impact. As time passes and you continue to take care of yourself and your property, you will feel good. You will feel like you are being taken care of. You will feel loved.

Is there something you can do today to take care of yourself?

March 13 – Pick-up Sticks

Listening to people argue over things like politics, smartphone manufacturers, sports or even religion at times makes me think of "the pick-up sticks analogy."

Imagine a game of pick-up sticks has just begun. The sticks have fallen and are arrayed all over each other in a well-mixed, multicolor pile. Somewhere underneath the pick-up sticks are some tiny little people. They do not know what the pick-up sticks are but they think these giant colored sticks crisscrossing above them as far as the eye can see must be very important. They have no concept of the people who put the pick-up sticks there or why the pick-up sticks are there.

One of these tiny persons points to an orange one about three sticks up and says, "That orange one is the most important thing there is. It is obviously the key to all of existence. We should focus on the orange one. We should worship the orange one."

Another person, points to the closest one and say, "No, of course this red one is most important. It is the closest to us." Another person points higher and says, "No, the green one is above the others. It must be the most important one of all."

The people form factions and create divisions among themselves based on the pick-up sticks, never knowing anything about what they really are or why they are really there.

This is what I see when I see divisions among us. What is important is life, Life, fitness, relationships, your personal code and our community of living beings. The pick-up sticks just *do not* matter. Today, stop looking at the pick-up sticks and focus on one of the things that actually matters in the world.

MARCH 14 – YOUR AVATAR

To take the pick-up sticks analogy a little further, imagine you are visiting some friends and there are some of you talking in the kitchen, some of you playing a board game in the dining room and a few more hanging out in the living room.

You decide to join in on the board game. It doesn't even matter what the game is because for this analogy, the game is *life* here on earth. The avatar (game piece) you use on the board is your flesh and blood body here on Earth. The soul or consciousness of that avatar is you (the person visiting friends who is playing the game). You are the spark of animation in the avatar. You are the avatar's spirit. The avatar knows only the game board and the other avatars but you (as the animating spirit) know far more.

As time passes and game play goes on, each time you touch your game piece on the board, the avatar "feels a connection to the divine". The avatar feels the connection from the player and maybe even gets some kind of abstract sense of the player's thoughts, motives, desires, intentions, etc.

Now let's say some time passes and you end up getting knocked out of the game. Your avatar is removed from the board and you can no longer play out the rest of that game. For your avatar, this is what we mortals call "death." For your avatar, it is over. The avatar is dead. It is final. That avatar, with you animating it, is gone (tossed back in the game's empty box top (which is to say, placed in a coffin and buried six feet under)). But you - the part of that avatar that was animate - are still very much alive. You may go into the living room and talk with some of your other friends until the game finishes. After the game is over, you may decide to start again or you may not play again that night. Can your dead avatar imagine you sitting in the living room talking with friends?

To the other avatars in the game, they've lost a friend, family member or colleague. They experience the death of the avatar differently than you (a real person) and your friends (real people) that are still playing the game.

Now do you see how the avatar cannot even begin to fathom the living room, the kitchen or the world outside? How can the game board avatar imagine you going home after the party or what your room looks like? Or the thoughts you are having about taking a trip or buying some new lawn furniture? The gulf is so vast that there is absolutely nothing the avatar can do to bridge it. There is no context that the avatar can muster to even begin to comprehend your world or your concerns.

Perhaps this is the case with us, here, now, on this game board we call "life."

How can we fathom what is in the beyond? There is no context for it. The only context we have is that of the game board, the other pieces and the occasional contact with the animating spark, (our spirit-consciousness).

Is it any wonder nobody comes back from "the other side?" In the game board analogy, nobody ever comes back because the game ended, the avatar was tossed in the box and the player went on to do something else. Perhaps a similar reason prevents us from hearing back from avatars that are tossed in the box here (placed six feet under).

What does this mean for the rest of this game? It means if being an avatar in the game of life is the objective, we should be the best avatar we can be.

MARCH 15 – MAKE THE WORLD A BETTER PLACE

Some people argue that there is something inherently wrong with that statement. They point out that it assumes the world is not the best it could be at any given time.

Is that true? Can the world get better than it is right now?

Is there something you can do to make the world better?

There is. You have one of the most valuable commodities in the universe and nobody else has it. *Your* time. Other people have their own time that they can contribute to the world, but nobody else has *your* time. Only you have that.

You can make the world a better place by giving some of that special and rare commodity to the world. Give your time. It may be that giving your time to another person is all you can manage, and if that's the case then you are giving a wonderful gift. But if you have some time you can give to the greater community, you can add a bit more *you* to the world, thereby making it a better world for you.

One of the quickest and easiest ways to give some of your time to the world is through volunteering. By volunteering, you give your time and energy to the world and even if the world was pretty darn good already, you make the world a better place.

But there is another way to give your time to the world. Create something. Music, literature, art. Anything. Add something to the world and the world will be better for it. Even if what you make is only criticized, ridiculed and torn apart, you have still caused events. You have created action in others. (See also, *Creation and Destruction*.)

March 16 – Financial Independence

This book of meditations is about deeper thinking and richer meaning and as such I try to avoid discussing "the pick-up sticks" but money is one that really must be addressed. (See also, *Pick-up Sticks*.)

Debt slavery is one of the greatest plagues of modern society. As long as you remain in debt, you remain a slave to a system that does not lift you up and set you free but rather holds you down and exploits you for a few nickels and dimes.

Don't buy into it. It is remarkably simple but sometimes not easy. If you have debt, eliminate that debt as soon as possible. If you do not have debt, do everything in your power to keep it that way.

You can still play the game, but do so on your terms. Get a credit card in order to build your credit but know that you are using the card as a move in the great game, not because you need leverage to purchase something you can't afford with cash.

Strive toward financial independence. Do not let money become a cold master that makes you work for it. Instead, use money as a tool to get where you want to go. You should own the money. The money should not own you.

Today, take another step toward financial independence.

MARCH 17 – MONEY DOESN'T EXIST

When humans first began to engage in economic trade, we think it was done through barter. The goat farmer would trade a goat for a certain amount of vegetables from the vegetable farmer. The spear maker would trade spears for cloth from the cloth maker, and so on.

This system could not scale with larger populations and eventually money was invented. The idea is that we make some little pieces of metal called coins and we all agree that 100 coins equals the value of a goat. 10 coins equals a bag of potatoes. 15 coins equals the value of a spear, and so on.

Money only has value because we all agree to allow it to have value. This is why entire economies can collapse overnight. The money that holds the economy up is ethereal.

As you can see from this extremely simplified explanation of economics, there is no intrinsic value in the actual pieces of metal. Or pieces of paper when you consider cash. Or data representations of cash when you consider wire transfers online bank balances and crypto currency.

Money does not exist. But the idea of money is very real. Can an idea have much sway in dictating how our lives will be?

Consider this: If, through pure thought, I can manifest changes in physical reality, can I also use thought to manifest changes in conceptual realities? In other words, if I can manifest a new job or a new car, shouldn't it be easier to manifest this ethereal construct of "money" that doesn't even really have a basis in reality?

MARCH 18 – THE TESSERACT

If you attempt to draw a three dimensional cube on a piece of paper (which is effectively a two dimensional plane) you would essentially draw two overlapping squares (each square of course having only four lines in it) and then connect the corners from one square to the other using one line for each corner (this would take another four lines). Twelve lines in total.

If there were a two dimensional being that encountered your drawing, that 2D being would be fine with what she saw, but she would not be able to fathom what the actual 3D cube looked like. The being would only see lines – like everything else in her world – she would only see the second dimension and everything she saw would be two dimensional. She would understand forward, back and side to side. She would have no conception of an "up and down."

Another way to understand this is to imagine the 3D cube is semi-transparent or made of toothpicks. Now hold it over a piece of paper (the second dimension). Shine a light on it and look at the paper. The shadow being cast down onto the paper will look very much like the drawing you made earlier. In short, the drawing of a 3D cube on paper is the shadow of a 3D cube as seen in the second dimension.

We cannot fathom a fourth dimension. Well, we can fathom that there is one but we cannot fathom what it looks like, where it is, or how to get there.

Just as the 2D person cannot imagine "up or down," we cannot imagine ... well, whatever the words would be to get us into the fourth dimension.

However, the tesseract is a great model for showing us that there probably is a fourth dimension. The tesseract is also sometimes called a "hypercube" and it is basically the shadow of a four dimensional cube here in the third dimension.

In other words, if a 4D person held a semi-transparent 4D cube "over" the 3rd dimension, the shadow of that 4D cube as seen here in the third dimension would look like a hypercube to us.

One could almost make the assertion that because the hypercube exists, a 4D version of the thing must also exist in order to cast such a shadow into our dimension. If so, a fourth dimension must also exist.

Imagine the 2D person and that all they see are varying lines across an infinite horizon. If you could lift them up from their 2D plane and show them the third dimension, imagine how much more world they are then exposed to with this new concept of "up" and "down."

Today, ask yourself how much more world would you see if you could be [lifted up to/brought to/transported to/shown] the fourth dimension?

MARCH 19 – NOTHING TOUCHES ANYTHING

The fact that nothing touches anything provides a solution to Zeno's Paradox. Around 450 BCE, the philosopher Zeno of Elea noted that in order for an arrow to reach the target it would have to travel half the distance before it could travel the whole distance. But in order to travel half the distance, it would have to travel half of that distance first. But in order to do that, it would have to travel half of that distance first. And so on and so on until you realize that mathematically the arrow can never reach the target because you can keep cutting the distance in half forever.

Is this true? Is it true the arrow can never reach the target? Well, of course not. But maybe it is…

On the one hand, we see the arrow trike the target and we know it has completed its journey. Zeno was wrong. Or perhaps we just finally hit our effective bailout value. We say, "Yeah, yeah, the arrow never hits the target but – forget about it! BAM! It's now in the target."

On the other hand, if we look really closely – I mean – really, really closely – down at the atomic level, we will see that true enough, the atoms are not touching each other. The "arrow atoms" do not actually make physical contact with the "target atoms." The arrow really does never reach the target.

When we look closely enough, we see that nothing really touches anything else.

March 20 – Time Cannot Pass

Much like the discussion from yesterday on nothing touching anything, today we consider the prospect that time cannot pass.

We think of time as line. A vector. We think it is moving straight and forward. You read this sentence. Then a second later, you read this sentence. A second passed in between. You are moving forward in time.

But for a single second to pass, a half second has to pass. And for a half second to pass, a quarter second has to pass. But for a quarter of a second to pass, an eighth of a second has to pass. Before that, a sixteenth. It is the same as Zeno's Paradoxes.

Looked at in another way, you could let most of the second pass before you start looking really closely at it. Let's let 90% of a second pass before we start looking really closely at the passage of time. Ninety percent of a second is 0.9 seconds. Before 0.9 can turn into 1.0 (a complete second), it must increment to 0.99 seconds. That is to say nine one hundredths of a second has to pass. But before nine one hundredths of a second can pass, nine milliseconds have to pass. The new time looks like this: 0.999 seconds. But before that, the new time must look like this: 0.9999 seconds.

And then this: 0.99999
And then this: 0.999999
And then this: 0.9999999
Etc., and so forth, forever…

This number cannot change to 1.0 until we stop adding a nine to the end. In other words, this passage of time will not be a full second until we let it change to 1.0. We can keep adding nines to the end for as long as we want. We can go on adding nines to the end forever. And as long as we keep adding nines to the end, the second will never pass.

You see, a single second can never pass. And if a second cannot pass, then time cannot pass.

But if a single second cannot pass and therefore time cannot pass, how do we explain the fact that things change states? How do we explain that water evaporates, that the sun warms the rocks throughout the day or that trees grow?

The fact that things change state implies the passage of time so we know that time *can* pass.

The next logical assumption then, is that it isn't that "time cannot pass," but rather that *we do not know how to measure the passage of time.*

MARCH 21 – THE VERNAL EQUINOX

Spring! In practice we think of the Vernal Equinox as being the transition point between winter and summer. "Equinox," denotes that day and night are of equal length today but the days continue to grow longer as we move toward summer.

Today we celebrate the first day of spring! The cold, dark, silent emptiness of winter has passed and the fresh, warm, light, active presence of new life abounds. Spring is the ultimate celebration of Life and life! (See also, *Life (big "L")*, and *life (little "L")*.)

As is mentioned in the NR&C, this day also marks the transition from the six months of the Rites of Not to the six months of the Rites of Life.

Today is a day to celebrate. If you cannot perform the Vernal Equinox ritual, then at least find a sign of spring outside and bring it in to your altar. There you can set it in the center and light a candle to honor spring.

Today's meditation is on spring, new life and new beginnings.

March 22 – The Mainstream

Within society at large there is a sea of thought and action. The commonalities in thought and action gravitate toward each other and flow in a current of their own. This current of thought and action is commonly referred to as "the mainstream."

Within the mainstream there are certain themes which naturally develop. You can see this in "mainstream diets", "mainstream fashions", etc. On social media you will see the mainstream is called out as "trending."

The mainstream is not led by any group. It is not controlled by any entity. It is an organic ever-changing stream of dogma that flows through society. If you are picked up by the mainstream, you will just "go with the flow" unless you take the wheel and direct your vessel's course with intention.

That can be okay. It is certainly easy. And sometimes it may be necessary to just let go of the wheel and let the flow take you until you see something you want. Until you see something you need. When the time comes that you do see something you want, you then need to grab the wheel and go to that thing with full, intentional control of your vessel.

What are you going to do today? Are you going to just go where the mainstream takes you or are you directing your course today?

March 23 – Veer Away!

Should I flow along with the mainstream or veer away? That is usually an easy answer. Veer away!

While the mainstream does not necessarily have an agenda or a conspiratorial master plan, it is still not necessarily a good thing. The mainstream has the mental and emotional acuity of the mob. What this means is a lot of thought and action with little direction or intelligence. Don't be fooled into thinking that because there is thought there is also intelligence. Thought and intelligence are not always the same thing!

Looking back through history you can plot the course that the mainstream has taken and you can often see the mistakes made by the mainstream thinkers. In short, ignorance, bigotry, fear and hate are among the chief offenders.

In order to live a healthy life as an active member of your community, you cannot help but splash around in the mainstream from time to time, but be your own person. Think your own thoughts. Ask your own questions. Do not follow the crowd without having your eyes wide open.

You owe it to the universe to emanate your own uniqueness. Do not let the other crabs pull you to the bottom of the bucket. You are a star shining in the black. Burn brightly and light the way for others! (See also, *Achievement*.)

MARCH 24 – GO WITH THE FLOW

Why not just go with the flow? If everyone else is doing it, it must be the right thing to do. Right?

The mainstream can be very wrong but it can sometimes be right also. Only you can know what is right and wrong for you. This is the burden of self-authorization.

Often the difficulty in life is figuring out what you want. Once you are handed something or shown something you can usually fairly quickly make a decision as to whether or not you like the thing. In other words, just as it is easier to destroy than it is to create, it is easier to decide what you do not want than it is to decide what you do want.

Maybe going the opposite direction from the mainstream is a bit extreme. Maybe a more balanced approach is the best idea. In other words, if you don't know where to go, maybe going with the flow is not a bad idea.

Going with the flow is a fine approach as long as you keep your eyes open and maintain an awareness that this is what you are doing. In the meantime, since you are keeping your eyes open, you can look for opportunities to seize along the way.

If you know what you want, keep your eyes on it and go get it. If you don't know what you want, go ahead and go with the flow until you see something you want. But when you see it, be ready to leave the mainstream if you must in order to grab it! Carpe diem!

MARCH 25 – IS RELIGION GOOD OR EVIL?

Religion has been used for good and evil but religion itself is neither of these things. And both. Religion has been used to control the population and to help govern the masses. Religion has been used to justify actions. Have the actions been ethically good? It depends on the case in question. Sometimes yes, definitely. Sometimes no, definitely not.

When used to govern and control the masses, religion is just a tool. When used to justify crimes against humanity religion is a dangerous weapon (but could still be used for evil or (arguably) good). When used to give us an example of something greater than ourselves toward which we can aspire, religion is a savior. When used to explain the mysteries around us through metaphor and allegory, religion is a salve. When used to bring love and goodness into the world, religion is good. When used to stop scientific reason and exploration, religion is evil.

Because good and evil are human constructs and because religion was created by humans, religion is both good and evil.

You must choose whether or not you will give religion a place in your life. You should know before you choose that any religion, no matter how it is presented on its website or in its scriptures, may be used to distort realities, control behaviors and justify both good and evil actions including immoral and evil crimes against humanity and life in general.

It is the individual human, through self-authorization, that must choose how the individual human is going to act. Do not worry too much, because just as you can always change your behavior, you can also change your religion. But do not be mistaken that the more important of the two is your behavior.

MARCH 26 – DEEPER THAN GOOD AND EVIL

When discussing religion, ideology and philosophy the concepts of good and evil are usually at the core of the deepest discussions. And rightly so. What could be more important?

Not.

Not is deeper than good and evil. In fact, Not is at the very bottom. There is nothing deeper. Once you remove all warmth, light, activity and presence, you are left with Not.

This breakdown of everything else is necessary. We must deconstruct the entire cosmos, (good, evil, religion and gods included) in order to find the baseline. What is underneath it all? What does the canvas on which Life is painted look like?

When we look at this deepest core we see this absolute and true perfection which is Not.

From there, we begin construction again and realize the basis for Alchemy 2.0 – the fundamental building blocks of Life. This fundamental basis for all of existence is also deeper than good and evil. Warm, light, active presence does not comply with our labels of good and evil. It is better that we just call Life, "nature," and realize that nature is outside of the constraints of good and evil.

It is only later, when we begin building the Principles of Not on top of Life that we begin to understand the concept of good and evil and how those two necessary models must exist together within us and around us in order for us to flourish.

Philosophy and religion are deep. Good and evil are deeper. Underneath these two distinctions is Life and underneath everything that ever was, is or will be, is Not.

March 27 – The Gradient Yin-Yang

Good and evil. We talk about these as if they are opposing forces which are distinct from one another. Like a yin-yang, we like to imagine good and evil as two different forces which are in a constant struggle (or perhaps a balance) but that one day good will triumph over evil.

In real life, the "opposing forces" are not distinct. In fact, they are not even opposing. Opposition implies that one force may will-out over the other. That cannot happen. None of us would wish that.

If everything and everybody were "all good," there would be no strife. There would be no opposition to good. There would be no way to leap forward; no way to grow. You cannot have growth without strife. Hindrance is a necessity for progress.

Good cannot exist without evil. Light cannot exist without darkness. Day cannot exist without night. Etc.

The reason "opposing forces" appears in quotation marks is because these two forces are not really opposing each other. They are instead joined in unity. We are not good or evil. We are both. In The Book of Not, we draw attention to the image of a double helix (think of a strand of DNA). The two legs of the ladder are good and evil and we mortals are the genes stretched between the two legs. When two forces combine, much like the religion and scientific reason of Authorism, the resultant force is stronger.

Thus instead of Life being represented by a yin-yang, we must instead use a *gradient yin-yang*. The gradient yin-yang has no pure black and no pure white but is represented only in shades of gray like the "opposing forces" experienced by mortals in daily life. This hazy image of a yin-yang also illustrates the hazy, gray ambiguity that is Life. Where good fades into evil and evil into good can sometimes be a hazy ambiguity. It can be a fine line. (See also, *Fine Lines*.) If it were not this way, life would be simple. In fact, maybe too simple.

March 28 – Good Mandates Evil

What is *good* if it is not defined by "that which is not evil?" Since there are many ways the word 'good' can be used, before we go on we should clarify that when we discuss "good" relative to "evil" we mean "ethical goodness."

The average Jew, Christian or Muslim will tell you that anything their god does is good. E.g. "God is good" and therefore everything God does is good. But their god does many things which most people would consider evil. Including *creating* evil itself (See Isaiah; KJV).

Just by way of example (and there are countless to choose from) most people will agree that burning people alive (Genesis, Leviticus, Numbers, Etc.) and having children torn to shreds because they teased someone (2 Kings) is not "good" behavior. So we cannot define 'good' as "anything their god does."

From merriam-webster.com:
good noun
Definition of good (Entry 2 of 3)
1a : something that is good
b(1) : something conforming to the moral order of the universe
(2) : praiseworthy character : goodness
c : a good element or portion

It looks like definition b(1) is the one we are after. But, what is 'the moral order of the universe?' Who can describe what that means? So for our philosophical definition of 'good' we are going to stick with "that which is not evil."

As such, by its very definition, in order for us to have good in the world, we must also have evil in the world.

MARCH 29 – EVIL

What is *evil* if it is not defined by "that which is not good?"

Yesterday we discussed the fact that we cannot use traditional religious definitions of good and evil because of how often they intermix through the various scriptures those religions define themselves with. In other words, trying to depend on religious definitions becomes confusing and contradictory and prevents us from isolating a clear and concise definition.

In fact, in order to define 'good' we had to compare it to evil. We said that good is "that which is not evil."

In order to define evil, we will have to invoke the same logic. 'Evil' must be that which is not good. But for 'evil,' I think that definition is not quite good enough (no pun intended). Especially because we are using 'evil' to define 'good.' Also, we need to expand a bit on what evil is so we can actually identify it in the world and try to avoid it.

We could define evil as "that which intentionally causes harm to life."

As you can see, due to the root word "intention," in our definition, nothing can be evil that does not have intention. The sun burning the face of Mercury is not evil. The lightning that starts a forest fire which burns people and animals alive is not evil. It is *awful*, but it is not *evil*. There is no intention there.

But this is still not quite right. There are many times where intentionally hurting someone else might be ethically good. For instance, if some evil person is hurting someone else or you and you defend that person or yourself against the evildoer, by intentionally harming the bad person you are being good.

We will have to add a clause to our definition. To be 'evil,' the person inflicting the harm must also be malicious and have some ulterior motive such as personal gain or personal pleasure.

With that in mind, we now have this definition:

Evil — that which causes harm to life through malicious intent and has some ulterior motive or derives some reward from their actions such as personal gain or pleasure.

MARCH 30 – WE NEED BOTH

A couple of days ago, while discussing the gradient yin-yang, we alluded to the need for both good and evil. Picture heaven, as described by the religious devout, and ask yourself how desirable that really is.

Is heaven to be relaxing on a cloud while playing a harp all day? Of course, that is a simplistic image painted for children, but what would eternity without evil really be like?

How could you progress without strife? Without pain, how would you be able to distinguish pleasure? Heaven is supposed to be a place where even a stubbed toe is not part of the equation. Could you learn anything? Could you advance? Could you become better than you were the day before or is everything just perfect? (See also, *Not, Perfect?*)

If you are perfect, you cannot get better. Perfection cannot change. When you truly think it through, it seems pretty dreadful. Your perfect self could not get better and the perfect world you lived in could not get better. For all eternity you would just be happy and perfect.

For the sake of conversation, I will grant that maybe things are different enough there that our earthly rules do not apply. But here, now, in this non-heaven world of ours there is no doubt that strife and discord are necessary for us to grow and advance.

Pain teaches us the value of pleasure. Discord teaches us the value of harmony. Evil teaches us the value of good.

MARCH 31 – DON'T BE EVIL

Just because we *need* evil does not mean we should *be* evil. In fact, we should be quite the opposite.

Perhaps it is strange that we should endeavor to eliminate this thing from our world right after we have established that it is something we really need in our world.

I am loathe to draw a comparison between evil and Not for many reasons (not the least of which is that because Not has no intent it cannot be evil), but I need to reference Not, in order to help explain why we should not be evil.

Ethical goodness is part of our heritage. As members of a pack, a tribe, a community – verily – a race – we need to work together for the common good of humanity at large. We, life, are reflections of Life. We are warm, light, active presence. Being "good" is good for life, Life, and for the advancement of our civilization.

Just like Not is contrary to Life, being evil is contrary to the advancement of our civilization. In this way Not may be compared to evil. Of course, Not is not evil because Not does not have malicious intent. Nonetheless, Not is Anti-Life. And evil is "anti-good."

"But you said we *need* evil!" Yes, we do. But there is plenty of evil in the world already. The amount of evil that exists in the world today is quite sufficient to maintain a balance of good. We do not need to add more evil to the world! In fact, in order to maintain "the balance," it may be that we need only a very small amount of evil. It seems clear when we see it that a little evil goes a long way. As such, try to avoid creating any!

April 1 – Not, God?

As long as we are talking about Not and evil, as I mentioned yesterday: Not, is not evil.

But does that make Not, good? The other day we said that 'good' is anything that is not 'evil.' Perhaps that was being rather broad in trying to define 'good.' It might have been better to say that actions which are not *evil* must be *good*? Maybe. It seems more likely that it would take longer than a single day to do justice to 'good' or 'evil.'

At any rate, to answer the question "Is Not, good," the answer is no. Not is not good either. And Not is certainly not God. Not is not an entity. Although I can see where someone might mistakenly compare Not to God. After all, Not is *inherent perfection*. (See also, *Not, Perfect?*)

The perfection of Not may be worthy of adoration but certainly not worship. What would be the point? You cannot curry favor from cold, dark, static emptiness. You cannot curry anything from it.

April 2 – Introduction to Not

The basis for Not was discovered around 1995, during a deep philosophical discussion which was focused primarily on a search for the meaning of life.

As it happened in the original discussion then and there, in attempting to root out the meaning of life, here for the reader, we will break down all of existence into the most fundamental core concepts. There are four of them and we generally refer to them as the core precepts. In breaking existence down into these four precepts we discover what we refer to as absolute purity. The term purity is used because these four precepts cannot be broken down any further and because it is upon these core precepts that the fundamental building blocks of all of existence may be reflected into manifestation.

It is because this is so fundamental to all of existence, all of life, all of everything we have ever known or will ever know, that the original *The Book of Not* was written and the Church of Not was brought into the world.

What are these fundamental core precepts upon which all else is built? To talk about them further we may need to think of them as *states of actuality* rather than general precepts.

In brief, Not is not warmth, it is not light, it is not active and it is not present. Therefore, Not must be the polar opposite of those things. Thus, Not is cold, dark, static emptiness.

April 3 – Coldness

There is no such thing as cold.

"What?" you respond, "Of course there is! Snow is cold. Ice is cold! It is cold at night. Space is *really* cold!"

True, but technically coldness is a state you can only arrive at by removing heat. In any given system, if you remove some heat from that system, that system will become colder. As more and more heat is removed the system becomes colder and colder.

If you remove all heat from a system, you will be left with the ultimate in cold. In science, this theoretical state is called "absolute zero." But coldness, by itself, does not exist. You cannot add or remove coldness to or from a system. There is no "coldrowave" (opposite a microwave) which you can use to "cold your food." The closest thing we have to that is a refrigerator or freezer and those machines *remove heat* from the inside, they do not *add cold* to the inside.

If we could arrive at this "absolute zero," we would have achieved a perfect coldness. With absolutely no heat whatsoever in the system, the system would be *the perfect form of cold*. We say it would be "perfect" because there can be no cold that is colder. It is the pinnacle of coldness! Perfection in coldness.

Heat transfer is the process of something becoming cold. If you touch ice, and leave your finger there too long, it will start to hurt. This is because the heat is transferring from your finger to the ice and as more and more heat leaves your finger, your nerve endings will become damaged. If you leave your finger there too long, you will get frostbite. The body needs warmth to live. The pain is warning you to stop what you are doing before the damage becomes irrevocable.

The colder something is, the faster the heat will transfer. For example, you could leave your finger in cold water a lot longer than you could leave it on ice. This heat transfer is one of the reasons nobody could live in the vacuum of space. It is so cold in space that the heat from your body would transfer into the surrounding space within seconds. You would freeze to death almost instantly. (There are other reasons we cannot live in space without a spacesuit, but all we are discussing right now is "coldness.")

Most people think that the temperature in space is absolute zero. Technically, it is not. It is really close, but it does not actually get all the way down to absolute zero in space. Perfect cold would be even colder than space. The pinnacle of cold would be the pinnacle of pain if one were to touch it. The reason I draw out this point about pain is because it becomes an important point to consider later when we discuss Not and Life.

We need to consider one more thing before we move away from the topic of "coldness." In fact, this last consideration is the reason we cannot achieve absolute zero. If you were to try to measure the temperature of the perfect coldness, your thermometer would introduce warmth to the coldness. There would be some amount of warmth in the thing measuring the coldness and that warmth would immediately start to transfer into the cold thereby "infecting it" with some warmth. It would no longer be a perfect cold, but instead it would be just really, really close to perfect. So if there could be a perfect coldness, it would not be something humans could detect. And if there is something we cannot in any way detect, is it safe to say that that something does not even exist? This is why I begin today with the thought, "there is no such thing as cold."

In logical discourse, we can prove there is a perfect state of coldness, but in reality I suspect there cannot be. Perhaps it is both: There is a perfect state of coldness. Humans can never *know* it.

Coldness is the first of the four core precepts that make up "Not."

April 4 – Darkness

There is no such thing as darkness.

"What?" you respond, "Of course there is! It is dark when you turn off the lights. It is dark at night. It is dark inside the refrigerator when the door is closed.

True, but like coldness, technically darkness is a state you can only arrive at by removing light. In any given system, if you remove some light from that system, that system will become darker. As more and more light is removed the system becomes darker and darker.

If you remove all light from a system, you will be left with the ultimate in darkness. Perfect darkness. Perfect black. Perfection is subjective, but I can still safely say that this darkness I describe is perfect because there can be nothing darker. There can be no darkness that is darker. In being dark, this darkness where all light has been removed is the ultimate achievement in darkness. Thus, it is perfect.

Like coldness, you cannot carry darkness around with you and insert it into a system where there is light thereby making that system darker. The only way to make a system darker is by reducing the amount of light in that system. By removing light, you make a room darker. Adding light, makes the room lighter (less dark).

It is as if darkness is the canvas on which the room is painted with light.

Nowhere in all of existence is there such thing as this perfect darkness I describe. The reason it cannot exist is because there is always, somewhere, a stream or wave of photons (particles of light). Even if it is just a single photon, there is technically light there.

In order to see the perfect darkness I describe here one would need to setup some kind of photon detector. The human eye, of course can detect light, but for the sake of conversation let us imagine a device someone builds in order to detect photons. If this device is placed anywhere in the known universe, there will be starlight visible to the device. Thus, it cannot reside in total darkness. Contrary to what one might think, space is filled with light, not darkness.

If someone were to construct a device within which there were no photons, then theoretically that someone would have created the perfect darkness I describe. But it still could not be detected by the human eye. It could only be known to us through some readout from the device created to detect it. Even so, I would posit that where there is molecular activity one will find a photon. Therefore the detecting of perfect darkness in and of itself would "infect" that darkness with photons thereby making it no longer a pure and perfect darkness.

Like coldness, darkness is not something we can manipulate directly. Only through light can we understand darkness. And a perfect darkness cannot exist. For this reason, I begin today's thought with, "there is no such thing as darkness."

Darkness is the second of the four core precepts that make up "Not."

April 5 – Stasis

There is no such thing as stasis.

What is that supposed to mean?

First, what I mean by 'stasis' is a measure of activity. Or, rather, in this case, a measure of inactivity. An active system is not a static system. A system with no activity would be a static system. It would be a system in perfect stasis. Imagine an empty room that has a layer of dust in it. There are no objects in the room and there is no movement whatsoever in the room. It is completely still. Or is it?

This room is not really in stasis. Inside each speck of dust is a cosmic explosion of molecular activity. Within the trillions of molecules in each single dust speck are countless trillions of atoms binding, spinning, attracting and repelling each other. Within the atoms are quintillions more subatomic particles in a quantum dance with each other zinging and whizzing around and these particles have bindings and associations with other particles possibly trillions of miles away in quantum entanglements and other quantum sub-arrangements we have yet to comprehend.

In short, like cold and darkness, stasis is a concept but not a "thing." In other words, you cannot add stasis to a system. You can remove activity from a system to arrive at a static system, but you cannot add inactivity to a system to make it less active.

Complete and utter stasis is something that cannot be achieved in actual existence. And like coldness and darkness, if it could be achieved, a state of absolute stasis would represent a form of absolute perfection.

Why can we not achieve true stasis? A system that is perfectly static would be a system with no molecular activity whatsoever. It would be a system with no atomic activity. A system with no subatomic activity.

Not, Daily Meditations

A group of atoms or molecules that have no subatomic activity whatsoever is a theoretical concept at best. It is a state of existence we cannot create or measure. Just like cold and darkness, an attempt to measure a completely static system would introduce an active measuring device, thereby causing activity to enter the system. This theoretical state of perfect stasis would be "infected" with activity and no longer be a state of pure stasis.

Just so, we cannot take stasis and deliver it to a system. We cannot "hold" it or manipulate it directly.

Stasis is the third of the four core precepts that make up "Not."

APRIL 6 – EMPTINESS

There is no such thing as emptiness.

That sounds a little bit mystic, a little bit cosmic and a lot bit metaphysical. But if you have followed along from the previous discussions on the four core precepts that make up Not, you will see immediately how this must be the case.

There cannot be a pure state of emptiness because there must always be something present to discern the emptiness. (If no presence is there to discern the emptiness, how can one know that there was emptiness there to begin with). And as soon as some presence is there to witness the emptiness, the system is no longer empty.

For this discussion we consider a "presence" to be some conglomeration of atoms. A rock, a tree, a flower, a sun or a person are all things considered to be a "presence." But even smaller groupings of atoms are a presence. Any warmth, light or activity must necessarily also be "a presence." You see, if nothing else, there would exist the *presence* of warmth, light or activity.

Like coldness, darkness and stasis, one cannot take emptiness and deliver it to some system of presence to make the presence be gone. You can only remove presence from a system to arrive at emptiness. You cannot add emptiness.

If you could remove all presence from a system you could then achieve a state of absolute and perfect emptiness. The perfection of the emptiness is implicit because a system that contains absolutely no presence is the ultimate in emptiness. It could not become emptier. If it cannot become emptier then it is perfectly empty. If nothing else can be removed it is the pinnacle of emptiness. In this way, it represents a certain perfection.

Emptiness is the last of the four core precepts that make up "Not."

April 7 – Not

There are four core states of actuality that underlie all of existence. These states of actuality we consider to be core precepts underlying all of *existence* itself. They are:

1. coldness
2. darkness
3. stasis
4. emptiness

Not is cold, dark, static emptiness.

The reason these states of actuality are unique is because in a very real sense, none of these states exist. Or, rather, they can only exist if their counterparts do not exist.

We can infer their existence, but we can only arrive at these states by virtue of the taking away of their constituent counterpart forms which later we will see exist as life affirming building blocks.

The ultimate states of cold, dark, static emptiness mean instantaneous non-existence to life. Not, in essence is Anti-Life. Nonetheless, Not is ultimate purity. When everything else is removed, the only thing remaining is absolute perfection. In fact, Not may be the only true state of perfection.

What do you think pure cold, dark static emptiness would be like? (See also, *Introduction to Not*.)

April 8 – Not, Perfect?

When everything else is removed, the only thing remaining is absolute perfection. Not may be the only true state of perfection.

How can Not be perfect?

Because there is nothing there to critique. True and absolute perfection is a subjective concept.

What one person considers perfect another might disagree with. But in the case of Not, there is nothing to examine. One cannot make the case that Not could be more cold or more dark or more static or more empty. Not is truly the pinnacle of perfection in being what it is.

Clear your mind and envision this state of absolute purity. This clear, icy, black, silent emptiness that is completely unblemished. While we know it could not be experienced, imagine what it would be like nonetheless.

Perhaps this is what some mean when they consider "divinity." (See also, *Not, God?*)

April 9 – Not to be Seen

Of course, Not cannot be seen.

As discussed a few days ago with the core precepts, if Not could exist, in order to see it, one would necessarily render it no longer the pure cold, dark, static emptiness it had been before it was "corrupted" by that which beheld it.

In varying fields of science, the observer effect is the theory that the mere observation of a phenomenon inevitably changes that phenomenon. For instance, when you use a tire gauge to check the air pressure in your tire, you can hear the sound of air hissing out of the tire when you apply the tire gauge. You have changed the air pressure just by virtue of measuring it. It was 39 PSI before you took the measurement, then after you finished, it was 38.5 PSI. You were not able to accurately measure the pressure without changing that which you were measuring.

The very presence of an observer renders Not, not. In other words, if you posit Not, then try to observe its existence, you must – by the very nature of observation – introduce something warm, light, active or present into Not, in order to observe it. Once you have done this, Not is no longer pure. It is no longer cold, dark, motionless and empty but instead there is now something there which can make an observation.

I can take this a step further using the same arguments and assert that not only can Not not be seen, but it cannot be experienced at all. Again, to experience Not would be to introduce into Not the thing that has the experience thereby making it no longer the pure, cold, black, static emptiness it had been before being experienced.

Thus, Not cannot be seen.

April 10 – Not must not Exist

If Not may not be observed or experienced by Life, for all intents and purposes it does not exist.

This is similar to the ontological argument that deep within space orbiting a star we cannot see, in the center of a galaxy where we cannot see, there exists a subatomic all-powerful blue kitty cat and this kitty cat is the origin of all things. Just because I say the kitty cat exists does not make it so. And even if the kitty cat really did exist, since you cannot see, touch, feel, discern or in any way connect with or experience the subatomic all-powerful blue kitty cat from the center of the galaxy, then for all intents and purposes, the blue kitty cat does not exist. Or at the very least, "may as well not exist."

Even though I can infer the existence of Not, it may as well not exist.

This is yet another reason it is referred to as, "Not."

And even though I state plainly here that it cannot exist, I still infer its existence through reason and I still insist that it does exist. Recall that cold exists, darkness exists, stillness exists and emptiness exists. So Not exists. However, to be more precise, I should say that a perfect form of Not cannot exist. Or to be even more specific, this perfect Not exists ideologically, but not actually.

Through reasoning we establish this perfect and pure Not. But in real life, it cannot be.

April 11 – Nothing isn't Not

Not is not the same thing as "nothing." When one thinks of "nothing" one generally envisions one or more of the building blocks of Life missing but the others still present. To be more accurate, in reality one envisions reductions in the elements of Life, not a complete removal of one.

For instance you may envision an empty room and say "There is nothing in that room." While that is generally true and most anyone should agree with you, of course we know there are things in the room. There is air in the room. If you can see that it is empty then that means there is light in the room. The room is probably at "room temperature" which means there is some degree of warmth in the room. And because there is molecular activity in the air, walls, floor, etc. that means there is activity in the room.

If one could somehow transport one's self into Not, the result would not be good. The prospect is terrifying. (Consider that being locked in a pitch black freezer would be like warm sunshine compared to experiencing the cold, dark, static emptiness of Not). However, as opposed to Not, "nothing" can actually be a safe place. Sometimes it is nice spending a few minutes in a room with nothing in it. In this case, "nothing" may be peaceful. Also, for example, in meditation many practices ask you to clear your mind of all things (make it so that "nothing" is in your mind). Clearing your mind such that "nothing" is in your mind can be a very peaceful exercise.

The reason I call out the difference between "nothing" and Not, is that while "nothing" may be good, as a being of warm, light, active presence, Not should invoke terror at the very thought of it. The reason one should feel terror is because of the completely alien and unfamiliar nature of Not. It is not death. It is worse than death. It is the antithesis of all of existence. The antithesis of Life. It is Anti-Life.

April 12 – Not isn't Everywhere

Many people, when introduced to the idea of Not, think that Not is everywhere, mixed in with Life. After all, isn't there a lot of empty space out there?

Speaking of space, isn't space supposed to be so cold that is called "absolute zero?" Isn't the space between stars absolute cold, dark, static and empty?

As a matter of fact space is not Not. While space is mostly cold, dark, static and empty, it is not completely cold, dark, static and empty. There is energy in space. In every square meter of space there is energy. But the fact that a stray atom or subatomic particle may exist in a section of space is not the final test of whether or not an area of Life should be rebranded as "Not."

The real test is to mentally put yourself in the area of space in question and ask yourself, "What can I see from here?" From where you are (sitting/standing/existing) in your imagination, if you can sense any warmth, light, activity or presence (besides yourself of course), then you are not in Not. You are in Life.

And anywhere you teleport yourself, somewhere, at some distance, you will see stars. If you can imagine not seeing or sensing anything warm, light, active or present, then you have achieved a meditation on Not.

APRIL 13 – WHAT ISN'T NOT?

I think we have been pretty clear on what Not is. But now that we know what it is, it might be useful to ask, what it isn't. "What is not, Not?"

The answer is pretty straightforward and easy: everything else is not Not.

"Everything else" we break down into two major groups: Life and Anti-Not.

How we explain Life is something we will go into here in this book but we'll have to come back to that on another day. (See also, *Life (big "L")*.)

Anti-Not is also theoretical and could never exist other than through logical inference. Anti-Not is essentially Life taken to the extreme. (See also, *Anti-Not*.)

April 14 – Paradox is Prevalent in Truth

Yes, *truth* is paradoxical. This means that when you discover something that you feel is really true – something that gives you that tingling down your spine or that rush of revelation of having found a real truth – there will inevitably be a paradox involved.

For example, the statement, "There is but one absolute, and it is that there are no absolutes." For many, this statement feels like truth. And perhaps it is because this statement is a paradox. Another example (taken from The Book of Not) is that life must destroy life in order to live. We should value life, right? We should not take life, right? But we see throughout all life (at least all animal life) that life must destroy other life in order to live. Whether the life that is destroyed is plant life or other animal life, either way, life consumes life in order to thrive. Another truth. Another paradox.

Finally, I will plant a seed here that perhaps can grow to be discussed in more depth later on: "All of the religions of the world are wrong, and all of them are also right."

When you read that last sentence you probably felt the sting of truth in it. And of course the paradox.

The reason both statements in that sentence are correct is explained in detail in *The Book of Not* and in this work as well. We must, however, save that discussion for another day.

April 15 – Not in your Mind

Perhaps that which separates us humans from the rest of the animals is this thing we call consciousness. Can the other animals think like we do? I guess, considering that we don't even understand how we think, we cannot really know the answer to that.

Did Not exist prior to The Big Bang? Is Not what the quantum singularity was sitting in before it exploded? Sitting in? Existing in? Being in, perhaps?

If so, is Not surrounding the expanding universe? Of course, we have already established that we could never know. I can claim that Not surrounds the universe with just as much certitude as I can assert the existence of the subatomic blue kitty cat at the center of this galaxy that is the creator of all of existence.

In other words, we cannot prove or disprove the existence of Not.

However, consciousness, whether or not we understand it, is capable of logic and imagination. And through logic and imagination we can deconstruct existence all the way down to the four core precepts of Not.

In our minds, we can envision Not. Is Not the canvas on which Life is painted? Is Not the purest form of perfection and Life is the invader? Is Life a cancer that has infected Not? Or is Not just a theoretical construct that has no basis in reality? (See also, *Life, The Disease*.)

Even if Not may not exist in actuality, there is one place Not may exist with certainty: Not may exist within our minds.

April 16 – Warmth

There is no such thing as cold, but there is definitely this thing called warmth.

In our lives, warmth brings to mind comfort and even belonging. We think of campfires or a living room fireplace in the cold of winter. Warmth brings to mind images of a yellow-orange square in a house on a cold, dark winter night.

Other images of warmth are being wrapped under a warm blanket in a soft bed. Or the warmth of an embrace, whether that be from a pet, child, sibling, parent, family, friend or life partner.

There is also another important warmth. It is the fire that burns within each and every one of us. This fire is warmth. The Chinese call it dan tien. It is in the center of your body and it may very well be the energy ball that is your spirit-consciousness. If you could see past the body that covers it, you would see that each of us is a blazing star shining brightly in the black.

You can connect with this warmth through thought and meditation. You can stoke this fire with thought and it can strengthen your resolve. Like a virtuous circle, you can feed the fire with thought-energy and the fire can then provide power for your thoughts.

Without warmth, there can be no activity. Without warmth there can be no energy. Without warmth there can be no spirit or consciousness.

Warmth is the first fundamental building block of Life.

April 17 – Light

Light is often thought go hand in hand with warmth. Indeed, they are very much connected in Life and life.

We almost always think of light when we think of warmth and we almost always think of warmth when we think of light. There is good reason for this. The subatomic particles that make up light also cause vibration and this generates heat.

Although I did not mention this in describing warmth, it may be noteworthy that warmth (heat) is actually "light" that we cannot necessarily see. Thus it makes sense that we connect warmth and light in our minds.

Because humans are conscious and because human spirit-consciousness is what we are discussing in this book, we separate warmth from light and cold from darkness as these bring very distinct feelings and impressions to our bodies and souls.

Light, as distinct from warmth, is associated with intelligence. A light bulb over a cartoon character's head shows they have an idea. Light shows us the way to go. Only with light can we find our way and avoid dangers that lurk in the darkness. Because of the extreme significance of light, it is associated with the divine. Like the sun they were patterned from, most gods are associated with light.

Light is more than just the opposite of darkness. Light is the second fundamental building block of Life.

April 18 – Activity

The third building block is perhaps a necessary byproduct of the first two. Activity is the opposite of stillness. Action is a necessary element of life and Life.

Or perhaps instead, I should have said that warmth and light are necessary byproducts of activity. It is the action of the subatomic that creates the warmth and light that we can ultimately feel and see.

It may not be surprising to find that they are all three tied together along with one more which we can discuss tomorrow.

First thing in the morning, we become active! Ready to go about the business of the day. But of course activity is present at all times, even in times of stillness.

Our bodies are always alive with internal activity. Each cell in your body is constantly dancing with molecular activity. Every molecule everywhere (in or outside of our bodies) is dancing with atomic activity. And each atom is alive with subatomic activity. Each subatomic particle is alive with internal activity that we can only speculate on. And each sub-subatomic particle is alive.

Look around you. No matter how still something appears to be on the outside, deep within that thing is a cosmic dance of energy and action. Warm, light, action!

Activity is the third of the fundamental building blocks of Life.

April 19 – Presence

As mentioned yesterday, warmth, light and activity are all bound together where each one is a byproduct of the other. But these three building blocks are also consequences of the fourth. There is a fourth and final fundamental building block we need to discuss.

Presence.

When we talk about presence, we could be referring to the presence of any object, but what we are usually thinking about is the presence of some kind of being. Something animate. A consciousness.

When there is a consciousness present, there is automatically warmth, light and activity. Consciousness likely cannot exist without it. I say "likely" because humanity is still not sure what consciousness is.

But regardless of whether we are specifically calling out a consciousness, presence is the opposite of emptiness. If there is something there, there is something present. If there is nothing there, there is emptiness. Again, in order to observe emptiness, there must be a presence and once there is a presence, there is no longer emptiness.

Presence is the fourth and final fundamental building block of Life.

April 20 – Life (big "L")

Life, as written with a capital "L," is the combination of the opposite of each of the core precepts of Not. In other words, Life is warm, light, active presence. This warm, light, active presence does not necessarily mandate a spirit-consciousness but it can.

Life encompasses *everything* that isn't Not. Life with a big "L" includes stars, rocks, planets, dirt, lakes, clouds, etc.

Life, being built from warm, light, active presence, is the most basic level of existence. It is the first layer of reality that is not Not. Even though there is activity at a molecular level, this "Life" we would consider inanimate. A better word might be "stuff," but we use the word Life to describe it because deep down at the molecular level it really is the same. A rock is warm, light, active presence and you and I are also.

This "Life" is essentially the substrate of existence. Anything that ever was, is or will be is included in the single word Life with a capital L.

This may seem extremely human-centric (and later we'll discuss how and why that is certainly the case and why it's okay) but Life is extremely significant because without it, nothing could have importance. Nothing would matter. Nothing could matter.

Because if not for Life, there would be only Not.

April 21 – life (little "l")

Yesterday we discussed Life with a big L. There is also life with a lowercase "L" and that life is a subset of "big" Life. This "little L" life more or less follows the dictionary definition of "life."

Anything that eats, grows and reproduces is called "life" with a little "L." As advances in artificial intelligence continue, we may need to alter our definition of "life," but for now (the year 2020) we are still looking only at these things that autonomously grow, consume and reproduce to be considered "life."

Life and life are both opposites of Not and both of these variations of "the opposite of Not" are warm, light, active presence.

From the substrate of Life we discussed yesterday, comes the life that we as humans know and are concerned with. Our lives and all the other life we know of are what we consider "animate life."

As mentioned already, this life is also made from the four fundamental building blocks of warmth, light, activity and presence. But this is the life that matters most!

We will discuss this more in the future, but for now suffice it to say that I can say with ease and with absolute certainty: nothing is more important than this life.

APRIL 22 – LIFE, ROCKS

The comma is in the right place. We are saying that rocks are considered to be Life. How can rocks or a single rock be considered "Life?"

What we call Life is anything that contains any single one of the four fundamental building blocks of life. So by our definition, pure light is considered Life. Also, raw energy is considered Life. A planet, a star, a brick, a piece of chalk, a burning match (or a match that is not burning, for that matter)… All of these things we consider as Life. This book is Life.

You may ask how a rock could be considered Life. A rock is composed of quintillions of atoms and they are all in motion. The atoms themselves and the subatomic particles within them are all engaged in a complex song and dance that creates "a rock." Because of this, despite how it may look and feel to human touch, the rock is also generating light and heat. And of course, because the rock is taking up space, it has presence.

What about a beam of light flying through the vacuum of space? Yes, all four building blocks are present there. First of all, a beam of light is composed of ***light*** (which is a fundamental building block of Life and life). Other than in very specific and possibly strange and unusual lab conditions, light cannot exist without moving. Photons are similar to other subatomic particles in that they are in ***motion*** (another building block). Due to the internal movement, there is also an emission of energy, or ***heat*** (another building block). And of course the beam of light is present (wherever it exists) therefore it has ***presence*** (the last of the four building blocks).

Imagine a barren landscape on a planet in a different solar system that has never been visited by any lifeform. Despite the seeming desolation of the scene described, that landscape, the planet and the suns in that planet's sky are all Life.

APRIL 23 – DEATH IS LIFE

Discussion surrounding life or Life cannot really be complete without discussing death. If everything in existence is Life and death is part of existence, then would not death also be considered to be part of Life? Or is death the expression of Not onto Life? I could go on with intense and scary questions about how death is cold and dark, but to cut to the chase, death has nothing to do with Not but rather it is a transformation that takes place within both life and Life.

It is somewhat tricky to discuss death in these terms. On the one hand, we have to be perfectly clear in what we believe, but on the other hand, it may sound as if we are in denial. Death is certainly real, but death is also literally only a transformation of Life. It is literally warm, light, active presence transforming from one form into another.

Thus we can say this and mean it: "Death is Life."

Or, rather, death is a part of Life. And we do not mean this in the normal sense where to console someone in mourning I say, "I'm sorry for your loss, but death is an inevitable part of life." Yes, of course that is also true, but death has all of the component building blocks of Life and therefore something dead is the same as something alive when it comes to how we define Life. All of the fundamental building blocks of Life are present in the living and the dead. In the animate and the "inanimate." (Truly, nothing but Not is actually inanimate).

Not unlike the rock we discussed yesterday, a dead body is composed of atoms which are in ***motion***. Because of this the body is also generating ***heat*** (and technically, heat cannot exist without some associated wavelength of ***light***). It might be argued that the heat generated by the dead body or the brick is on an atomic scale and not something you could feel as emanation by holding your hand over it but there is warmth inside. And of course a dead body is ***present***.

This does not mean we have a cold indifference to death. On the contrary, we hold life in the highest regard. So much so that we expand that respect and reverence to Life, not just to living things. Our reverence and respect for life is, in fact, the most important and highest held tenant of Authorism.

Death is a real transition from being alive to being something else and the impact on the people still living when someone dies is tremendous. We respect that and take every measure to comfort those living who mourn the transformation of a loved one.

But we also know that death is Life. Your loved one may have undergone this most incredible and significant transformation, but I can assure you, they are not "gone." As something that holds attributes of Life, they cannot "go" anywhere. Life must continue to thrive as Life and the dead are part of Life!

In this regard all of Life is immortal.

April 24 – Life is not Death

Let me rephrase that: "Life cannot experience death." At least not in the sense of cessation of activity.

On the one hand Not is the ultimate antithesis of Life. And Life may be horrified by the thought of Not. Yet still, Not may also be the ultimate catharsis. Life is constant striving. Even death is part of this striving as death is just a transformation of Life. Death is transformation, not release. Life and death are an endless cycle and in truth, Not would be the only true release from this endless cycle.

This may remind the reader of a religion like Hinduism or Buddhism where an endless cycle of life and death is described and the purpose of life is to break that cycle and achieve transcendence - or Nirvana.

For better or for worse, however, even Nirvana is trapped within this cycle of the transformation within Life. Because Nirvana would exist in warm, light, active presence, Nirvana would exist within Life and therefore would be bound to the dictates of warm, light, active presence.

There can be no warm, light, active presence that exists outside of Life. Thus, even a soul transcendent must exist within Life.

Perhaps it is bad news that life must always exist within Life. But on the other hand, the good news is that Life cannot experience death! Life is truly immortal.

April 25 – Life, Not and Life (Not and Space)

Many people, when introduced to the idea of Not, think that Not is everywhere, mixed in with Life. After all, isn't there a lot of empty space out there? Isn't cold, dark, static, empty space the same as Not?

No, it isn't.

Space is vast, cold, dark and seemingly empty, but it is not what it seems. There are atoms and little bits of warm, light, active presence like tachyons and photons flying around in space. In fact, it seems space is "filled" with activity like this. There is likely at least one subatomic particle in every cubic meter of what we would otherwise accurately call "empty space."

As I have already mentioned, Not may not exist.

In order to observe Not, there must be that which is warm, light active and present. In other words, "Life."

Or at the very least the observation of Not must require some attribute of Life in order to make the observation. There would need to be some light, some warmth, some kind of activity or some presence to take the measurement or make the observation.

Once Life or an attribute thereof is introduced to Not, Not is no longer "pure." It becomes not. Not becomes not.

Can Not exist between Life and Life? In other words, could one who is in the bubble of Life look across an expanse of Not and see another bubble of Life on the other side?

No.

In order to see across Not, light would need to go through Not and once light enters Not, it isn't Not anymore.

Although, theoretically Not could exist between two "bubbles" of Life as long as the two Life bubbles could not sense each other. As long as they never sense each other, Not could exist between them. If they did sense each other in any way they would represent connected Life. Once connected, they would both just be "Life" again and Not could not exist between them.

April 26 – Life is Death

Life by its very nature is destructive. Life thrives only by destroying other life. Life, in fact, cannot thrive without destroying (transforming) other life. This seems paradoxical, but perhaps this is a self-correcting problem.

For if life were left unchecked it seems it would continue to consume other life until there was only one living thing left. Perhaps it is fortunate that life destroys life so that life is always striving. As such, no single life can become the All-Consumer since there will always be other life that must consume the All-Consumer in order for life to thrive.

So, how is it that Life is death?

The absolute destruction ("transformation") of all else seems the natural tendency of life. Life is transformation through destruction. Recall that death is also considered "transformation." If life is transformation and death is transformation then,

"Life is death."

April 27 – Anti-Not

Earlier in the year we established that the perfection of Not exists ideologically, but not actually. Through reasoning we established this perfect and pure Not.

There can be no equivalent in Life.

There may exist Not, this pure and perfect absolute, but there may not exist the extreme opposite – a pure and perfect absolute warm, light, active presence. Such a thing would necessarily assure the destruction of all of existence with the exception of one thing: itself.

Imagine a star. Start by picturing the sun. Now imagine that star expands to engulf everything in its "warm, light, active presence" until it becomes infinite in size and mass. It must be so bright that nothing else can be seen except pure white. You are blind as you can see nothing but whiteness. Opposite of pure black. Opposite of Not.

It must be so hot that nothing else can exist except its own fire. All else is consumed. It is infinitely hot (whatever that means). It must be so frenetic that within itself there is nothing that is not moving at maximum speed relative to everything else. It is infinitely active. It must be so present that nothing else may coexist with it. There is no room for another presence. It is infinite in its presence.

Perhaps what I have just described is what the quantum singularity feels like from inside before it bursts into becoming the universe. Some might say that what I have just described is their god. Perhaps this is "divinity." From a physical standpoint what I have described is obviously not possible.

Although no life could exist inside of it, this infinitely hot, bright, frenetic presence is not the antithesis of Life but rather the antithesis of Not. As such, what I describe here we call "Anti-Not." I have mentioned how terrifying Not is to consider. I suspect that this ultimate white-hot, infinitely frenetic energy presence is equally terrifying to Life.

But do not worry about that because as we have already established: neither Not nor Anti-Not may exist in perfect actuality. If they did, it would not matter to Life because Life could not discern them or exist in any way near or around them. Ideologically, however, they certainly exist.

Today consider the ultimate white-hot, infinitely frenetic energy presence. And since your consciousness is the only consciousness that you can be certain exists, if such a thing as Anti-Not did exist, it must be you.

APRIL 28 – THE ULTIMATE EXPRESSION OF LIFE

Yesterday I introduced the idea of "Anti-Not," and how if life were left unchecked it might consume all life. Can it be that Anti-Not is the ultimate expression of Life?

No, it cannot be.

Life cannot become this all-consuming infinite mass called Anti-Not.

Consider that Life by its very nature is destructive. As discussed previously, life thrives only by "destroying" other life.

If life were left unchecked it seems it would continue to consume until there was only one living thing left and then this last remaining consumer would become Anti-Not.

This is all well and good except that at this point there would no longer be life. With life having been consumed completely by Anti-Not, there would only be two theoretical possible actualities: Not and Anti-Not.

And by the very definition of each they can never coexist. It is for this reason that we cannot make the mistake of saying that Anti-Not is the ultimate expression of Life.

April 29 – But Anti-Not Cannot Be

Besides being opposites, there is one big difference between Not and Anti-Not. The difference is that we can actually describe and imagine the existence of Not. Just take away light. Take away heat. Take away activity and remove presence. Now we have Not. However, it is more difficult to imagine the opposite.

How does one fathom infinite light? Infinite heat? Something infinitely active and infinitely present? Especially "all in one package."

It cannot be infinitely hot because we can always imagine that it can get a little hotter. It cannot be infinitely bright because we can always imagine it getting a little brighter. It cannot be infinitely frenetic because we can always imagine it getting a little more active. Finally, it cannot be infinitely present because we can always imagine it getting a little bit bigger – thus a little bit "more present."

Not may not exist in real life (forgive the expression), but we can certainly imagine Not. But Anti-Not cannot exist in real life or in our imaginations.

What does it mean to us if neither of these polar opposites can exist?

April 30 – Walpurgisnacht

Today and tomorrow is the time for the celebration of Walpurgisnacht! But why would even celebrate an obscure holiday such as this?

It is because we wish to honor our roots. We wish to acknowledge where we came from. The solstices, equinoxes and various other times of year were extremely significant to our early ancestors and then became even more significant to humanity during the age of agricultural. These holidays marked the times we would sow, plant and harvest. The times of year for planting and harvesting were extremely significant because our food depended on it!

The Walpurgisnacht celebration is a ceremony of dance! If you can dance around an open fire, then you should do that instead of the ceremonial practice described in the NR&C. Understanding that the opportunity to dance around an open fire is not afforded everyone, you may instead choose to perform the ritual described there. Walpurgisnacht is another spring ceremony but other than the Vernal Equinox, this could be considered *the* spring ceremony. For instance, if you could only celebrate spring one time in a year, Walpurgisnacht would be an excellent choice for that one time.

It is celebrated on the night of April 30th and on the day of May 1st. It is the celebration of transitioning from spring to summer though summer is still almost two months away. This night of Walpurgisnacht has a dark aspect whereas the day celebration tomorrow has a bright and cheery aspect. Both rituals are described in the NR&C and of course you may elect to do either or both.

May 1 – Only Life Exists and it is Eternal

Going back to the fact that Not cannot exist and adding in the fact that Anti-Not cannot exist, there is only one conclusion that we can come to.

In actuality, only Life exists.

If this is true then truly there is nothing to fear.

We, as life and Life, cannot not be. We must exist. In fact, as a result of this line of reasoning we must conclude that not only does Life exist, but it also must always exist.

Life cannot stop existing.

Life is eternal.

May 2 – Pain and Suffering

It is hard to imagine a life without pain and suffering. Like most people, I do not like pain. And because I dislike pain so much I really hate to say this, but I have to wonder if a life without pain would be a life worth living.

The thought of 'no pain' is so completely foreign and alien to my existence that I cannot really fathom what a life without pain would be like.

Would I still be able to feel pleasure? Are pleasure and pain on a metered scale where the top is pure pleasure and going down from there are varying degrees of pleasure until it changes into the "pain range?" And then as you continue to drop down the scale you reach maximum pain on the bottom (whatever that might mean). After all, pain and pleasure do actually share a strange relationship. They can intermingle. As such, could one really completely remove pain?

Pain can be compared to evil just as pleasure can be compared to good. Good cannot exist without evil. Pleasure cannot exist without pain.

Just because we need evil doesn't mean we should be evil. Likewise, just because we need pain doesn't mean we should seek it. Do your best to put 'good' into the world and do good when and where you can and evil will still find you. Likewise, (unfortunately?) do your best to avoid pain in the world and pain will still find you.

MAY 3 – AUTHORIZATION

You are reading this right now. Who authorized you to do this? Who gave you authorization to read this page?

Ultimately, no matter what your circumstances, you are the one that authorized the action of reading.

It is a trick question really. I don't need to know your circumstances to know that you authorized the action because we are the only ones that can authorize any of our own actions.

Authorization for action comes from within ourselves.

Perhaps you might say, "Why should I need approval for my actions? Why should I even need authorization for my action?"

At the risk of being flippant, there are entire fields of psychology devoted to those questions.

The bottom line is that many of us seek approval, validation, acceptance and authorization not just for our actions but for our very being. Many people experience guilt just for existing.

There are many reasons for this and the degree to which people seek acceptance, authorization or experience guilt can vary from a little to a lot. In the worst cases it can be almost debilitating.

The irony here is that the solution to this problem of seeking authorization is right there in the core of the individual who is seeking it. People seek external authorization but authorization comes from within. And it can only come from within.

MAY 4 – EXTERNAL AUTHORIZATION

Humans are all searching for truth, meaning, purpose, acceptance, validity and ultimately for authorization. We are trying to find our path. We are trying to find ourselves. In that search, some of the most precious treasures we desire are acceptance, validation and authorization for our existence.

This need for authorization is so fundamental and so deeply embedded in our psyches that it would be futile to consider life without it. It is truly important and it is part of what makes us human.

Where can we find it?

As toddlers we learn to seek it from our guardians. As we grow from toddlers into children we begin to understand that authorization for our being comes from outside of us. We see that it comes from our guardians, then later our siblings and peers, and so forth. All the while many of us are also taught that the ultimate authorization for our being comes from a supernatural higher power we are raised to believe in. (This would be some kind of god or gods.)

This need for external authorization is real and it is not going away anytime soon. But there is a dichotomy in the term "external authorization." It is thus: The need for authorization is real, but it cannot be found externally. Stated another way, one can find external authorization and be content, but that authorization is not really coming from an external source.

May 5 – Authorization Loopback

The following steps are the typical progression for the receipt of external authorization:
1. A person needs authorization for some thought, feeling, action, deed or state of being.
2. Having been taught that they can only find authorization for themselves externally, they implore the heavens for the authorization they seek.
3. Authorization is granted in the form of a thought, a sign, a portent or some other symbol that the person interprets as divine or universally discharged.

In real life, the "external authorization" described in the above progression is actually from the same person that requested it to begin with. This is called an "authorization loopback:"
1. A person needs authorization for some thought, feeling, action or deed.
2. Not believing that they are capable of authorizing their own actions, the person creates a deity or imagines one that has been taught to them then proceeds to implore the deity for the authorization they seek.
3. Authorization for their action (deed, thought, dream, etc.) comes forth from within themselves (but is not yet granted).
4. Ignoring the source, the person then projects this granted authorization "out" to their god, then loops it back to themselves (through their god) so that it appears to come from without thereby attaining the external authorization they originally sought.
5. Thanks can then be sent to the god for the authorization the person has granted themselves.

As a side note, this proffered thanks is also looped back to the original sender (the person that just authorized their own action by invoking an imaginary external authority). As such, giving thanks to your imaginary external authority is certainly a good thing to do. The gratitude is not lost on yourself and ultimately this helps add goodness to the world.

May 6 – Self-Authorization

If authorization is something we seek and need and external authorization does not truly exist, then the authorization we receive is authorization that comes from within. This is self-authorization.

To summarize: You're going along with life from day to day and all of a sudden you have this need for "external authorization." If you are used to getting this authorization from a god, you will then implore your deity for the authorization you seek. If you are used to getting this authorization from peers, colleagues or your partner you will try to get it from them. If you are used to getting this authorization from yourself, you will look within yourself for the authorization you seek and then grant it to yourself.

There are countless applications for "authorization," but just to give you an example, we'll use a self-esteem issue.

Someone very close to you says something extremely hurtful rather out of the blue. It would be hard not to take such a thing personally. This is a good example of when one might immediately feel the need for authorization from some external source. Or from within themselves.

Once you realize that you are the one who grants all of your authorization for being, you can start reinforcing yourself from within yourself. When something happens outside that makes you feel the need, you will instinctively reach inside for the authorization (validation, acceptance, etc.) that you need to get you through the crisis.

MAY 7 – SELF-WORTH

Various anxiety disorders, narcissism and people pleasing are some of the many negative side effects that come from a damaged sense of self-worth. These and many other personality problems are in part the result of a failure to acquire the authorization one seeks.

When we say "authorization" we are really referring to a host of emotional basics. Validation, acceptance, love, belonging and recognition just to name a few. In self-help literature there are countless works devoted to your "inner child." The inner-child is the deeper part of yourself that actually grants the emotional needs the "outer-adult" has in day to day life.

In New Age literature there are countless works devoted to the "divinity within." This is the same thing as the inner-child. And both the divinity within and the inner-child are the same thing as what most religions call "the soul" and what Authorism calls the "spirit-consciousness."

All of these are ways to reference your inner self – the inner self that loves you whether you understand it or not. (In fact, this is why the self can grant authorization to begin with.) The self wants you to be authorized. And the truly magical but ironic truth is that the inner self doesn't need validation because it already knows it is completely valid. Your deep-down unadulterated, crystal-clear spirit does not need authorization because it knows it is authorized to be here. It has a perfect knowledge of, "I am."

It is ironic because a lot of self-help work is ultimately involved in authorizing the inner self. But what really needs to happen is the other way around: the inner self – which needs no authorization from you or anybody else – is the only one that can grant you (the "outer you") the authorization you are seeking.

Western culture has a history of damaging people's self-worth from an early age. While this is almost exclusively the fault of theistic religions in western culture, at this stage there is little value in trying to point the finger. Instead, you need to understand your own self-worth or how to build it up to where it ought to be.

It is all well and good for me to say "Just understand that you are ok," thereby trying to grant you external authorization, but the bottom line is that you, and only you, can truly understand this. And the understanding must come from within yourself.

While I cannot give you the authorization you might be seeking, I can show you one of the many ways to find it by yourself from within yourself. However, since that would take longer than we have to discuss today's meditation, I will have to just tell you where to find it. A good beginning is recorded in "Cinereo Ascensus" in *The Book of Not*. (See also, *Cinereo Ascensus*.)

In the meantime, today's meditation is on self-worth: the understanding that your true self does not need authorization from anyone but can grant authorization to you when you need it.

May 8 – Rejection

Yesterday's meditation brought up you (inner) and you (outer) and we need to address this, but first we should talk about rejection.

Imagine you open your arms to embrace someone and they punch you in the stomach. Awful, right? This is what rejection can feel like. Especially when we feel the rejection coming from those closest to us.

The reason for this is that authorization is probably the thing that we value the most in our collection of emotional treasures and rejection by others is the opposite of being authorized.

When we seek external authorization (instead of understanding that the "divinity within/inner child/soul/spirit-consciousness" is the only one that can truly authorize us) we open ourselves to rejection. And the irony here is that the rejection usually isn't even there. Most often, the alleged rejection is actually just the other person reacting from their own motives without trying to anticipate or calculate how this may be interpreted by others. But even if the rejection is real, it should not have so much power to affect you.

If I want to give love to someone and they do not want it, this should not make me feel bad for me. Perhaps I can feel sympathy for them, but this does not make me less of a person. If I want someone to like me and they do not, I need to accept this and move on. The rejection I experience from the world around me is a signal to me to do something else. It should not make me curl up in a ball and wish I were dead. The wellspring of love (spirit-consciousness) that sustains me is my validation and authorization, not the world around me.

I am like a sun, or a rock, or a tree. I am the brilliant warm, light, active presence of Life shining in the black of Not. Does a sun need validation? Does a rock or a tree need to prove itself or ask forgiveness for being? Do stars and rocks feel guilt?

You too are like a sun, or a rock, or a tree. You are the brilliant warm, light, active presence of Life shining in the black of Not. You need not seek external authorization because you are already authorized to be. *Being* is the authorization for being. And no one (especially not you) can deny the fact that you are currently *being*.

May 9 – The Soul

Does all this talk about you granting authorization to yourself or you receiving authorization from yourself seem confusing? How can you know which of you I am referring to when I say you or yourself?

How do I know which self I am referring to when I am reading to myself or listening to myself reading to me? Is it myself that is reading to me or is it me reading to myself? It would seem there must be two very distinct entities within each and every one of us. Am I really two different entities?

Yes I am. But the how's and what's of this vary depending on who you ask about it.

A devout atheist will tell you that you are both your mind (just raw brain activity) and that you are also your consciousness and that consciousness is a superset of properties that result from the complex synaptic network within the brain. The consciousness is therefore a property of the brain just as swirling water is a property of a stream. A stream of water is a complex system and swirling water within the stream is a complex system and they are two different things but they are of the same thing.

A devout theist will tell you that you are both your mind (just raw brain activity) and that you are also your spirit and that your spirit is the animated soul that some divine being breathed into your body to animate it.

There are hundreds of variations in between the two explanations I just provided. Many of the explanations have roots that go back into the religions or sciences that birthed them. Some have no explanations at all. Do you think we are two entities within one construct? (And which of "you" thinks this?)

MAY 10 – AUTHORIZATION FOR CRIME

If authorization for our being comes from within ourselves and that is truly all we need, then can't I just authorize myself to do whatever I want? For instance, if I see something I want, can't I just authorize myself to steal it? If I don't need external authorization, then surely I can just go around the world doing as I please, right?

No. You are not allowed to do that! The Principles still apply. First of all, Life may not be harmed. Second, your own fitness needs to be considered. This includes all five aspects of the self: spiritual, mental, emotional, physical and social fitness. (Getting arrested for criminal behavior would infringe on some of these.) Your personal code comes into play – hopefully 'not stealing' is part of it. Finally, there's the Principle of Community. In order to build and maintain an advanced civilization there are certain rules and laws that we must all abide by.

Even if you are not an adherent to the Principles of Not, your own morality and community laws apply here. Most criminal activity ends up harming someone and we should all strive to do no harm to others.

So you see, authorization for action *does* come from within but action itself must be mitigated by your principles. Self-authorization does not mean authorization to do as the self pleases. It means validation and self-love. It means knowing deep within that you belong here.

May 11 – I am God?

If you search online for "the divinity within," you will find a plethora of varying results. Authors from nearly every religion and spiritual practice use this same language to explain their own spiritual practices.

Through self-authorization, can't I authorize myself to be god? Or at least god-like? Can I overinflate my ego? Doesn't 'divinity within' mean that I am godlike already?

Authorism does not actually use the 'divinity within' language though we also take no issue with it. Like countless other approaches, there is validity and value in pursuing spiritualism that uses that kind of language. (See also *Splinters of Truth, The All-Truth* and *Paradigms of Truth*.)

Just as self-authorization may not be used to sanction criminal activity, nor may it be used to pump one's self up into being a narcissistic, arrogant egomaniac.

You could not use self-authorization to tell yourself that you are great and wonderful anyway. That kind of thing comes from the ego. Self-authorization comes from a place much deeper. It is the love one mistakenly seeks from outside themselves. I do not say "mistaken" because the mistake is seeking love. I say "mistaken" because the love is already inside yourself.

Seeking love externally is a necessary part of life and critical to fitness, relationship building and strong community. But finding someone to love is not the same as trying to find someone to give love to you. Love that you give to yourself is part of self-authorization.

May 12 – Comparing Yourself to Others

Role-playing games are games in which players advance through a make-believe story adventure for which their character or party of characters gain experience which improves the character's various attributes and abilities. It is interesting to look at this in terms of building our own character. Each character in a role playing game is made up. And when making up a character one must establish values for their character's various attributes such as strength, bravery, dexterity, charisma, etc. In the old book and paper role playing games players would use dice to establish random values for their character's traits. In modern times, computers generate random values for these character traits.

Imagine if you could write out all of your character traits, attributes and aspects and assign a value to each. For instance, on a scale of 1 to 100, maybe your strength is around 70. For intelligence, let's say 85. Maybe for charisma, you are a 90 (wow, you are *very* charismatic!).

There are hundreds of traits you could rate yourself on. And the values for those traits will likely vary depending on the day, the time of day, how you feel during that day or time of year, time of month, etc. For the sake of conversation, imagine your list of traits has one thousand entries. Now imagine that everyone you know or meet also has a list of one thousand character traits with various values for each trait.

What I want you to take away from this mental exercise is how all of these numbers will be literally all over the place. Especially with these numbers changing in real-time based on how people are feeling and reacting throughout their day.

Someone you compare yourself to might have a higher intelligence, charisma and kindness score than you. But those numbers might be different tomorrow. But even if they aren't, there will still always be people with some higher values than yours and some lower values than yours.

So if you see someone you think seems really dull, ignorant or particularly irritating, know that those values are temporary and that you might be dull, ignorant and irritating to someone else.

And of you see someone you think seems smarter, better looking and more gracious than you, know that those values are temporary and that you might be smarter, better looking and more gracious than someone else.

There is always someone, somewhere who is better than you at something and you are always better at something than someone who is somewhere else.

Truly we are all varying degrees of all kinds of character traits all the time. (That's a lot of "all's" but it is really true.) This may seem extremely non-intuitive but it is sound advice: you can compare yourself to others but do not let that comparison change how you see yourself. Instead, anchor your own value on the authorization for being that comes from deep within you. Only that deeper self truly knows you and that deeper self cares more about you than you can ever know. That deeper self loves you unconditionally.

May 13 – Choosing a Religion

I have decided I want god(s) in my life. Now, which religion should I choose? Spoiler alert: we do not actually address this specific question until we talk later about *Becoming Religious*. Now, back to the question at hand: Which religion should I choose?

Wait. I get to *choose*? How is it possible that I get to choose? Does that mean there are many gods? Can I pick an old god? Maybe I should pick a new one… I heard that there is a new religion that offers *general artificial intelligence* as a deity. That might be better. I wouldn't want to pick the wrong religion! What if the one I pass up has a vengeful, jealous god that will torture my soul and cause me agonizing pain for all eternity because I made a mistake? That would be awful!

But wait. Does a god choose me or do I choose a god?

Imagine this: God exists. God created us all. God loves us. God presents itself to us, and says, "Child, I love you. Please be part of my religion." Isn't this a wonderful fiction?! If this were true, there would be only one religion on this planet. (And it would be the exact same religion on every other planet in the universe, too).

But there are hundreds and hundreds of religious and spiritual practices and variations to choose from (including Authorism!).

Some of them claim that you can choose one and not worry about making the wrong choice. Some of them claim that if you choose poorly you will suffer eternal anguish. Some of them say they are the only correct one and that all the others are wrong.

The conclusions most people come up with are that either "only one of them is correct" or "all of them are wrong."

That's not quite right. As paradox is prevalent in truth you should not be surprised to hear that in actuality, all of them are true (in part). And all of them are wrong (in part). We will go deeper into this aspect later.

But one thing is certain: Gods do not choose who will follow them. Gods cannot choose because gods are not actually there. Instead, humans choose which gods to follow. This is true because humans are actually here. This has been the case from the beginning. This is still the case today.

So back to the original question of which religion to choose if you are looking for a religion to join. I'm afraid we're going to have to come back to this question in a few days. (See also, *Becoming Religious*.)

Today's thought is around the idea that if there were really just one true religion, there would be no confusion on this matter. But there is confusion. A lot of it. And this, alone, is indicative of a manmade construct. That being, religion.

May 14 – All Religions are True

If a person believes in something strongly enough, a person can literally manifest their thoughts into reality (not every thought and not every time). For some people this may be an abstract and difficult to accept concept. But there has been a lot of research in the field of quantum mechanics which indicate that subatomic particles change their behavior based on whether or not they are being observed. There is even supposition that subatomic particles can travel back in time due to the presence of an entity observing them in the present. These complicated notes on quantum physics are being mentioned only to highlight the fact that the study of how consciousness can alter reality is a serious concept that the religious and various fields of science are trying to comprehend.

What we do know is this: If you hyper-focus on a single event that you want to occur in your life, there is a very strong probability it will occur. Many people have many theories as to why this is but there are countless references to it in success literature and other literature whose focus is on getting what you want from life. E.g. manifesting your own reality. The method is tried and true and dates back hundreds of years.

Today it can be found under headings such as "the law of attraction," "the power of positive thinking," "manifesting your own reality."

How does this relate to religion?

Pick a god, any god. If you hyper-focus on this god and you determine that you believe in this god beyond all else and further you convince yourself that the deity is supernatural and can change reality in the way you want because of your prayers, and then you pray fervently for some event to occur, there is a very strong probability it will occur. (See also, *Authorization Loopback*.)

This is why, for all intents and purposes, it does not matter which religion, way, path, etc. that you choose. But you must choose something.

Part of the power of religion is in the religious (as in repeated and consistent) re-affirmation of the existence of this external focal point that can be used to align your thoughts. Repeated affirmation that this thing (god, or magic, manifestation, etc.) exists makes it easier to use in times of need and removes the seeds of doubt that can interfere with manifestation.

So the religion you select may not be "true" for everyone, but it can be true for you if you determine to make it true. Now you can see why people become so unfalteringly convinced that their god is the one true god. To them, it really can be. But other people's gods can be equally real to them. Thus, all religions are true (to those who believe them to be true).

May 15 – The All-Truth

The all-truth is the promise that one day we will know the mind of god(s) and understand not just how all of existence came to be but also the meaning and the purpose of it all.

Is there an all-truth? It surely seems unlikely. Whether there is such a thing is one of several mysteries that have endured since before humans could write. But for the sake of conversation, it is useful to imagine there is such a thing as the all-truth. For our purposes, let us imagine that the all-truth is the explanation for everything. Any mystery as yet unsolved will be answered by the all-truth. All questions of origin, meaning and purpose can be answered by the all-truth.

The reason this is a useful construct to imagine is that we can better explain the splinters of truth as long as we pretend there is such thing as the all-truth. But before we go into the splinters of truth, we should look a little more closely at the all-truth. This "all-truth" I describe is essentially philosophical in nature in that it solves all philosophical quandaries and unites all religions, ideologies and philosophies under one colossal all-truth.

If the all-truth was discovered, there would be no more fighting. We would all understand everything and this would amount to an intellectual bliss for everyone. (Do you see why it seems unlikely that such a thing could exist?) While I am primarily talking about philosophy here, there is an equivalent search going on in science right now. The scientific version of this all-truth is called "the general theory of everything."

In a similar way, the general theory of everything would unite all scientific fields and answer most of the mysteries that current operating theories of science can only partially answer. The thought for today is the concept of the all-truth. (See also *Splinters of Truth* and *Paradigms of Truth*.)

May 16 – *The* Truth

You may have heard people talk about seeking *the truth*, or trying to find *the truth*, or that their religion, science, philosophy or ideology *is* the truth.

The truth is often discussed as if it is a single thing (like the all-truth (see also, *The All-Truth*)). As if you could be flipping through a magazine one day and stumble on a paragraph which is *the truth*.

There is not a single thing which is *the truth* all encompassed.

There are truisms, there are truths and there are things which are true, but there is not one thing somewhere which could be considered "*the* truth."

Here's another sneaky thing about *the truth*. What is true for me is not necessarily true for you. Does that mean that truth is subjective? Well, yes, but it can be objective too. For instance, 2+2=4 is a mathematical truth. Nowhere can you have two, then add two more and someone argue that there are not now four.

But a devout [_____] (fill in the blank with your favorite religious devotee) may swear to you that their religion is true (or their atheism in the case of those who are devout atheists). In fact, they may have such a deep and profound knowledge of this "truth" that they are willing to die or kill for it. Does this make their religion true for you?

There are many truths in this existence and I suspect you have already discovered some. But for better or for worse, we will not be able to find *the* truth.

May 17 – Splinters of Truth

Have you ever read something that rang so true in your mind that you had a physiological reaction? That feeling upon reading or hearing something that rings as an absolute truth to you is the experience you have when you encounter a splinter of truth.

There are two reasons I use the term "splinter of truth." One is because the truth that you encounter is obviously true (for you at the time) and as such is likely part of this imagined construct we talked about yesterday called the all-truth. If the all-truth were deconstructed, or broken up, it would be a thousand splinters. These could then be called, "splinters of truth." This is one way to consider where a "splinter of truth" might come from.

The other reason is in considering a different source for a splinter of truth. Instead of the (nonexistent) all-truth having splintered into a thousand pieces, consider instead a large construct such as an ideology or a religion. Then imagine that that construct is made of many splinters of various kinds: some truths, some not. In this case, a "splinter of truth" may be derived from the large construct.

Let's say you had that physiological reaction when someone was explaining their religion to you and they told you "God is love." You suddenly had a "Whoa! That is so profound!" experience. For you, "god is love" is a splinter of truth. The larger doctrine of that religion likely has things in it that you do not believe or things that you feel are even contrary to advanced civilization (like inequality among the sexes, encouragement of slavery, etc.) In this way, the religion itself is not something you could embrace but the splinter of truth "god is love" is nonetheless very real to you.

These splinters of truth are everywhere and each one is valid and real and true. It is truly awesome when you find one. It is deeply fulfilling. In fact, it is during those times of revelation that the idea of an all-truth becomes something you could actually imagine *could* be real.

These splinters are often fragments of entire paradigms of thought. Or sometimes a splinter of truth is itself an entire paradigm of thought.

Often times a splinter of truth can be so powerful that it convinces the person hearing it to accept countless other splinters of, well, not-truth, that are wrapped up in the dogma surrounding the splinter that was true. Thus the validity of the splinter of truth is so profound to the person hearing it that they are inclined to consider all of the dogma surrounding the splinter as true also.

As a result, the person becomes a convert. For a while. Over time, all of the non-truths and broken truths of the surrounding dogma begin to surface and the person becomes disenchanted and realizes that this thing they thought was the answer to their prayers is, in fact, just another false start.

But do not be disheartened if this should happen to you. When you find a splinter of truth, clutch on to it and embrace it! Keep it. Add it to your personal code or philosophy of life or put it in your journal. These splinters of truth are wonderful and they are real. Just because everything around it might be wrong doesn't mean the core truth that spawned all that non-truth was wrong.

Once you have collected enough splinters, you will have an actual bundle of truth. Once you have a bundle of truth, time and patience will allow you to figure out how the splinters all interrelate and you will then have this experience of finding yourself. (See also, *Finding Yourself*.) It is an "Ah-ha!" moment. And from there it just gets better as you discover more splinters of truth from this religion or from that ideology or even from movies, songs and other works of art that you can add to your bundle.

If you have not started already, today consider tying together your bundle of truth. (See also *The All-Truth* and *Paradigms of Truth*.)

May 18 – All Religions are False

Wait a minute. Just a few days ago I said that all religions are true. How can they all be false if they are all true?

Well, the reason we determined that a religion could be true was because we saw how the religion worked in the life of the religious devout. In other words, the devout believer puts so much energy into the belief that they literally manifest changes in their reality which they attribute as having come from their god(s).

Recall that if you hyper-focus on a deity and absolutely believe that deity is causing changes to your reality, you will manifest those changes in your reality through sheer power of belief.

But this external thing that is being hyper-focused on is not actually there. Herein is the paradox of religion, the confusion that comes with it and why even the most intelligent and free-thinking scientist can still be a religious zealot. The god is not really there but the power of the god can be made manifest in the life of the believer.

Thus, all religions are true (the power of their gods can be made manifest by the believer) but they are all false (there are not really hundreds of gods floating above the Earth glancing around the CNN and AT&T satellites looking down on us and vying for "likes.")

There are no gods, thus the religions that exalt them are inherently false.

MAY 19 – BECOMING RELIGIOUS

If you are going to join a religion, it will not be for their god(s). The fact that all religions are true in that each has a splinter of truth and that these splinters of truth all represent true aspects of various paradigms notwithstanding, what does this mean for someone seeking some kind of clarity?

Today we circle back to the question posed a few days ago, "How do I choose a religion?" (See also, *Choosing a Religion.*)

The answer of course, is dependent on answers to some other questions that come up when trying to answer the first question. Why are you seeking a religion? Are you looking for community? Are you looking for belonging? Are you looking for answers to the age-old mysteries of *life, the universe and everything*? (See also, *The Mysteries : Album Mysteria Non.*) Are you looking for a way to give back to the world which you feel has given so much to you?

Religion often does promise to be the answer to all of those questions but now that you have read about the all-truth and the splinters of real truth that might comprise an all-truth, you should realize that the only solution that can satisfy all of those wants and needs is the mystical and pretend all-truth. I'm sorry to say, there is no one place that can provide everything you are looking for. Each religion, mystical society, magical community or spiritual practice may be able to satisfy some of those desires but there is not one complete system that can satisfy them all. At least not without introducing some contradictions or generating some nagging doubts that make one wonder if they are going in the right direction.

The best religion is the one where you collect your splinters of truth, tie them into a bundle and then piece them all together into a coherent working structure of belief that brings you success, happiness and fulfillment in your life. In other words, the best religion for you is going to be the one that you create for yourself.

I cannot deny, that sounds really hard to do. And unless you're predisposed to this kind of thinking already, it probably is fairly difficult. On the other hand, I believe that ultimately that is what everyone really does anyway, they just don't call it that. I have met many religious people who, when discussing the deeper aspects of their belief, reveal that they think of their god very differently than their scriptures describe it.

In the meantime we recommend that unless you really feel the need to choose a god for your focal point, instead you use the tools presented through Authorism and unify your own core such that you can manifest your reality through your own thought and willpower which fuels the energy that emanates from you like a sun.

This is not the same as saying "you become your own god," because we actually *do not* recommend that you do that. Instead, you realize that you do not need a god.

We can't get into this today, but not having a god is not the same as not having a higher power. We believe that having a higher power is critical to mental, emotional and spiritual balance and those that deny the existence of a higher power are making a dangerous mistake. There are higher powers than us. They just aren't giant supernatural white men with beards or giant multi-armed, elephant-headed immortals.

If you are looking for a religion, today ask yourself what it is you hope to find in the religion you are seeking.

May 20 – Good God!

If there are no gods isn't it a bad idea for over half of the entire world to go about claiming there are some? More simply put, if there is no god isn't it bad to say there is one? I'll even take this all the way into the atheist camp and say, "Isn't it irrational, delusional or even borderline insane to claim there is a god?"

No. In fact, god(s) *can* be really good.

A god can provide a focal point for the manifestation of thought and desire into reality. This is where prayer comes into play. There has been a lot of work in recent years on the idea of the manifestation of reality at a quantum level through pure thought or consciousness. We mention this because there is certainly a basis for belief in the power of prayer, magic, and manifestation of reality through thought. Many religious people use prayer to put goodness into the world. A god can be an excellent focal point to use for this kind of manifestation. Even though the goodness actually comes from the person themselves, not a god. Nonetheless, for this reason, god is good.

If you believe in a benevolent god and when you pray to this god, good things happen in your life then that is wonderful! How each of us chooses to manifest our own reality is part of our personal journey and the best way to do it is something each person must find for themselves.

Gods can provide an object for adoration and worship. How is this a good thing? Why should we adore or worship something external to ourselves? Is it not dangerous to put something on a pedestal? Yes it can be, but let's talk about that tomorrow when we discuss higher powers in more depth.

For some people, there is something humbling about a sentient being that is more powerful than us that might take measures to keep us in line. I'm not talking about just fear, but the presence of an entity that knows what we are thinking or planning. This can be good in that it might guide us toward more civility than we might otherwise exhibit if we thought we were the highest power. If aliens that were smarter and more powerful than us came to Earth to become our benevolent overlords many people would welcome this.

Finally, a god can provide and an easier to construct conduit to the love and acceptance that flows from within ourselves out to ourselves (even if it is just an authorization loopback). (See also, *Authorization Loopback*.) This feeling of love can embrace us with validation, acceptance and belonging and of course with authorization for our being.

In all these ways a deity can be good.

When looking back through human history and considering the evils that religion has wrought on humanity it is quite evident that most often it was not the gods that did terrible and evil things to people in the name of god(s). It was the people that did terrible and evil things to people in the name of their god(s). This is still our truth in 2021.

I think it is okay for us not to blame the gods but instead to acknowledge it was the people.

With all that in mind, if you are going to make a god or use one that someone else has made, be sure to only use the good parts. The god might be great, but don't let the religion take you places you do not feel comfortable going.

MAY 21 – YOUR HIGHER POWER

Some might argue that if you do not believe in god(s), then you do not have a higher power.

Others might argue, "So what?"

There are two things that must be pointed out here. One, you do not need to believe in some supernatural entity that cannot be proven in order to have a higher power in your life. Two, it is very important that we acknowledge a higher power than ourselves.

Why should we adore or worship something external to ourselves?

The adoration or "worship" of something external to ourselves is a good thing. Acknowledging a power greater than ourselves is an intelligent approach to personal growth. There are many reasons to acknowledge there is a power greater than yourself.

If you do not think there is anything greater than yourself, it is human nature to naturally assume you are the greatest thing. The danger here is that you do not even realize you are doing it. There are two major problems with this. First, it gives you an overinflated sense of self which can manifest in egotism and other undesirable behavior. In other words, you can become arrogant, overconfident, self-serving and just generally unpleasant to be around.

Second, if you think you are the highest power, whether you know it or not, you take on the world's problems as your own and this can be completely overwhelming. When things go wrong, the believer can just point their finger at a deity and say "It's God's fault!" But if you are the *highest power*, when things go wrong you feel like you should have or could have done something to prevent it. Over time, this weight can be overbearing and lead to intense mental, emotional, and spiritual anxiety. It gets worse because it is exceedingly difficult to pinpoint the source of the anxiety in order to fix it. Psychiatry and psychology will often run around and around your mind searching for a scientific explanation that is just not there. (In fact, this is why religion can sometime be the only answer to save people from spiritual, mental or emotional maladies that science was unable to remedy). Acknowledging a higher power can help us understand that we are not the source of *all* creative energy in the universe (just some of it).

Collectively, we have always placed ourselves (humanity) as the highest power and that has not been a great thing for our advancement as a civilization. Consider the way we looked at the world as early civilization (earth-centered universe) then even when "waking up" still put ourselves in the middle (sun-centered universe) and perhaps we are still doing it with the idea that there is only one universe - the one we are in! And as long as there is no evidence of intelligent life beyond our little blue spheroid, most of us will continue to place ourselves as the highest power in the cosmos.

I find it amusing that we should assert there is only one universe and that it is infinite and that it is the universe we are in. But at the same time, I completely understand why we think this way. We have awoken in the middle of something that is so mind-blowingly inconceivable that we have to put our foot down at some point and say, "Instead of being completely overwhelmed into inaction by this incredible existence, we are going to choose a starting point and take a step." So for that, I applaud humanity in our ability to carry on despite the inconceivable vastness of our surroundings in macro, micro *and* inter-dimensionality. (See also, *The Linear Spiral.*)

MAY 22 – WHAT IS GREATER THAN HUMANITY?

Not, Life and Anti-Not can all stand-in as higher powers.

My higher power is Life, but it is all Life - especially including life and this spirit-conscious pool-connection that I sometimes feel so strongly.

As we have established, Life is warm, light, active presence. Placing Life on a pedestal seems a safe choice. Without it, there would only be Not. Of course there is great risk in putting anything or anyone on a pedestal. If you regard someone or something with such reverence and awe and then discover you were wrong, the after-effect can be devastating to your morale and psyche. In this case, however I am hard pressed to imagine a time when having reverence and awe for Life could ever be seen as a mistake. After all, if Life goes away, we won't be here to be disappointed.

What could be more deserving of our adoration and worship than the warm, light, active presence of Life? There is nothing richer, deeper or more remarkable than living life (which is, of course, part of Life). There is nothing more awe-inspiring, astounding or breathtaking than experiencing lucid reality. There is nothing more rewarding, fulfilling and gratifying than engaging in the action of life within Life. Life is that power greater than ourselves. Life is what sustains us and provides us with meaning. Life is everything. Nothing is more important than Life. We do not need to have faith in Life because we know Life exists and we can prove that Life exists. "Life exists," is an axiom! We experience our Life fully and we interact with our Life constantly. Better yet, we do not need to kill other people in the name of Life because, as we hold Life supreme, our very belief in Life prevents us from making this mistake. Not even death is greater than Life because death is just a part of Life.

May 23 – The Power of Prayer

It is highly improbable that there are several hundred gods orbiting the earth staring down at us hoping we *like* and *subscribe*.

It is equally improbable that there is only one god floating around up there hoping for our *likes*.

Nonetheless, it is evident that prayer can absolutely make real changes in people lives. There is no doubt that one can manifest reality through prayer, meditation and/or pure intention.

Prayer - even directed at a god of your choosing or one that does not exist - can focus your thoughts and direct an outcome. Ultimately prayer is the power of intention and that power is very real.

If you are able to use prayer to manifest changes in your reality, that is a wonderful thing and you should embrace it and use it! I would like to go a step further and say that if you have not experienced the power of positive thinking, the law of attraction or "the power of prayer," you should give it a try. In other words, is prayer something you would rather try than just thought or meditation?

The way you bring your own power of manifestation into reality is not nearly as significant as the ability to actually do it. Do first. Adjust the process later. If nothing else has worked for you, and you would like to try prayer, pick a god (there is a list of over one thousand religions to choose from in *The Book of Not*) and start praying to it. Why not? If this brings manifest changes into your life, then it might be working! Stick with it! Or realize that it is all coming from within yourself.

May 24 – Size and Scope

I suppose it is fitting that today's meditation takes up more pages than most any other in this work. We are, after all, talking about size and scope!

If you have never taken the time to examine this, today is the day to do so. If you *have* taken the time to examine this, your mind has already been blown by it, but today is a good day to revisit this because each time you really consider this it will blow your mind again. And having your mind blown on occasion can be a good thing.

I'm talking about the size and scope of "it all."

I am not going to go into the distance statistics to try to make my point. You can find that information quickly and easily online or in a book. What I am going to say is that the size and scope of our solar system is truly unimaginable. Well, perhaps it is more accurate to say that it is inconceivable. Only in a very limited way can we get our minds around the vastness of our solar system. It is far larger than most anyone truly comprehends. Our average sized star has gravitational and light affects which emanate out to distances we cannot comprehend. In fact, there is a sphere of influence that the sun has in the space around us and the distance across this sphere of influence is not something the average person can comprehend. Ok, I am going to use some statistics. Some estimates place the size of our solar system at approximately 287 trillion kilometers across (178 trillion miles).

Scientists estimate that there are about 100 billion stars in our galaxy. And that there are approximately two trillion galaxies in the observable universe (did you catch that? "Observable"). That should be enough for you to realize that we cannot comprehend the sheer size of this universe. And, how could we when 1. We cannot see it from outside of itself. 2. We still don't know how much bigger it might be than what we can see so far.

Now, real quick, let's go the other direction. Did you know that there are an unfathomable number of atoms in the average human body? Estimates place the number around 10,000,000,000,000,000,000,000,000,000 molecules. Molecules are collections of atoms. So one more number: The number of atoms in the human body? There are approximately 7,000,000,000,000,000,000,000,000,000 atoms in a human body.

One last statistic just to drive home this point: A single drop of water is estimated to contain 5,000,000,000,000,000,000,000 atoms.

These are very real estimates I am providing here, but as you can see, the numbers involved in trying to quantify the large and the small are completely ludicrous.

So as you look out into the universe, you should be filled with wonder at the sheer magnitude of what you see. And glance down at your hand sometime and imagine zooming in to a point on your skin. Keep zooming in deeper and deeper and again, the magnitude (minitude?) of what you envision should be somewhat overwhelming.

And here we are, in the middle. Or are we? Hasn't that always been the mistake of humanity? To place ourselves right in the middle when we are not actually in the middle. In fact, there most likely is not a middle.

Because we think in a linear fashion, it is easy to imagine all this on a line. We start our line by placing the pencil point down on the paper at "the smallest thing in existence." The we draw the line, and as the pencil moves away from the "smallest thing in existence" point, it goes further and further "out" until it reaches our scale ("normal everyday stuff"), then keeps going out to galaxy, galactic cluster, super cluster then known universe, then multiverse perhaps, and so forth.

But what if we thought in a circular fashion instead? Instead of drawing the line straight away from the "smallest thing" point, what if you traced an arc instead? And as the arc continued, things got larger and larger including the universe, then multiverses, interdimensionality, etc. until the arc you were tracing came back to meet at the original point you had started on?

And then, maybe even though it looked like a circle at first (as seen from above) when you tilt your perspective you realized that what you were drawing was actually a spiral… Is that the shape of things?

Finally, today I would like to end with these questions:

Can we really find a beginning? In other words, is there really a "smallest thing?" (See also *The Elementary Particle*.)

As we trace our line away from the smallest thing toward the largest thing, does the line ever end? In other words, is there a "largest thing?"

May 25 – We Are not the Center of it All

When we talked about size and scope, I noted that looking up into the sky things just get bigger and bigger and grander and vaster until the magnitude of the scale becomes incomprehensible.

And when we look down – when we zoom into the cells and eventually the molecules, atoms and subatomic particles things just get smaller and smaller until similarly, we lose our ability to comprehend the infinitesimal tininess of it all.

And it seems like somehow we are somewhere in the middle of these differing scales of vast and quantum. But then I also pointed out the warning that we as humanity have often made the mistake of thinking we were in the middle of it all. It is a very human thing to assume that we are at the center of everything! Each of us thinks this way. And collectively we think this way.

But how do we know we are not the center? When looking out into space, how do we know that Earth is not the very center of the entire cosmos?

The answer lies in raisin bread.

Imagine a big lump of raisin bread dough. Now imagine that you are standing on one of the raisins somewhere inside the dough. You'll have to pretend you can see through the dough to the other raisins. Now the bread is placed in an oven and starts to bake. As the bread bakes, the dough expands. As you look out at all the other raisins, they are all moving away from you. Without any more information to go on, it would be natural for you to assume that you are at the center of the raisin bread universe because all of the other raisins are moving away from you. In fact, it would be very convincing evidence.

A few hundred years ago it was quite obvious that we (Earth) were at the center of the cosmos because everything revolved around our planet. The sun, the moon, the other planets and all the stars moved around us. There could be no dispute because all one had to do was look at the evidence (e.g. look at the sky).

Then we discovered that the Earth is actually the one turning in the cosmos, not the cosmos turning around the Earth. We still call it sunrise and sunset but the sun does not rise and set. It is not the sun that is rising and falling, it is the Earth that moves around the sun. If our ancestors had known better, they would have called it "Earthrise" and "Earthset" or "Earthroll," etc.

Looking out at other galaxies, it appeared our galaxy was at the center of the universe because all the other galaxies were moving away from us. The raisin bread scenario demonstrates how we could have made the mistake of assuming we were at the center of the universe. The galaxies were moving away (and still are) because the universe itself is still expanding. The center of the dough is where we think "the Big Bang" occurred and everything continues to move away from that center. As it all continues to expand, the galaxies will continue to appear to move away from us.

But we now know that we are not at the center.

When we consider other paradigms of thought such as mentioned in the entry titled *Size and Scope*, we should keep in mind this lesson of us not being the center of everything. In fact, anytime you find yourself thinking "I am at the center of everything," it is probably wise to stop and ask yourself, "Am I *really* at the center, or does it just look that way from where I am standing?"

May 26 – The Occult

The occult is "that which is obscured." In this day and age, with the full library of all human knowledge just a web search away, it is tempting to think there is nothing obscured from us anymore. But there is much that is still obscured. As long as the great mysteries remain unanswered, there will be obscurity and the occult. (See also *The Mysteries*.)

Let's trace the roots down and see what kind of ground they go through. As we follow the roots down we also go through time tracing back to the origins of occult practices.

On the surface, the occult appears to be essentially divination, witchcraft and ritual magic primarily used by the practitioners to make better their lives or the lives of their loved ones. (This is not unlike the primary use of prayer.) If you are looking for the "spooky side" of the occult, it is at this most shallow level that you will also find anything related to Satan or "the dark arts."

Looking deeper into the occult, we find some older texts regarding angels and demons. We still have not gone very deep or very far back. Angels and demons take us back only a few hundred years where Christianity is still the prevalent religion in western civilization.

Going much further back (and deeper still), we are now about three thousand years back in time where we find occult origins stemming from Jewish mysticism. This is where the oldest angels and demons originate as well as the Kabala. Most occult practices cannot trace their roots deeper than the Jewish mystics of old. It might be noteworthy that during this time there are polytheistic religions in most of Europe and Judaism as a religion is relatively new.

Going even further back, the roots go deeper still (about five thousand years) and we find Egyptian mysticism and the earliest human writing. This is where gods such as Thoth come from. Tracing roots deeper than Egyptian mysticism takes us into the vague records cobbled together from Sumerian and Akkadian cuneiform. We cannot really see deeper than that because written history did not begin until about five thousand years ago. Everything prior to around 3000 BCE is essentially guess work.

However, without having to guess at the religions of the time or the mystic origins of the gods of their gods, or the gods that came before those gods, I can tell you that Alchemy 2.0 traces its roots even deeper than Akkadian and Sumerian mysticism and the gods of their foregods. I know this because the roots of Alchemy 2.0 go all the way to Not, and there is nothing deeper. In fact, for the roots to even reach Not, they have to drop through the substrate of existence where they then leap across this boundary (which must exist and cannot exist) between the real and the reflected.

Each of the four fundamental building blocks of Life has an antecedent core precept which is but a reflection of the building block. Actually, perhaps to be more accurate, it is the other way around: the fundamental building blocks are the reflections of the core precepts. At any rate, the opposites of those building blocks must *be* in order for the building blocks themselves to be. Warm, light, active presence cannot exist without cold, dark, static emptiness.

There is nothing underlying the four building blocks of Life but this inferred reflection, so truly warm, light, active presence is the deepest we can go in our search for the origins of the occult (and everything else, for that matter). This is why the four fundamental building blocks in Alchemy 2.0 replace the four elements from Alchemy 1.0 (those being fire, air, water and earth).

When we cross between Life and Not, we reach this perfect base of cold, black, silent emptiness. We have reached the "bottom." The very core.

May 27 – Modern Humans

In this age of quantum computing and artificial intelligence it is easy to be fooled by the moniker of "modern humans" in reference to ourselves. We feel modern and we certainly feel like we are incredibly advanced compared to our hundred thousand year old ancestors.

To be more accurate, our technology is far more advanced, but in truth we are not much different.

While civilization has advanced far beyond the age of agriculture, humanity itself has not really made any significant advances since the first *Homo sapiens*. All other things being equal, a child raised in the wild today would differ very little from a *Homo sapiens* child raised in the wild 300,000 years ago. The difference only becomes clear and present when you introduce our technology into the equation.

We call ourselves "modern humans," but do not forget that the 300,000 year old *Homo sapiens* is essentially the same as you or me. In other words, the humans from 300,000 years ago, 100,000 years ago, 10,000 years, 200 years ago and everyone alive today are all humans that future humanity will look back on as "early humans."

May 28 – Future Humans

Continuing from yesterday's meditation on "where we came from and what we are," it might be useful to consider today, where we are going.

I said that future humanity will look back on those of us alive today and call us "early humans."

If that is true, what will finally distinguish these future humans from us early humans?

Nobody can really know that yet, but the answer will probably be a combination of gene manipulation and integrated technology.

The future human will need to be born with technological enhancements. I suppose they might be something along the lines of "cyborgs" unless the technological enhancement is a biological enhancement. This would be essentially biological machinery that we are born with. Or perhaps technology which is interlaced with our DNA.

Whatever it is, the real distinguishing feature between future humans and early humans (us, now) will be in the actual genesis of the embryo. All other things being equal, a future human child raised in the wild will be a more advanced human than one of us born in the wild.

May 29 – Magic

The evil wizard raises his wand and blasts a blinding, red, lightning looking arc of raw energy at the good wizard and the good wizard raises his staff and counters this attack with a blinding, green, lightning looking arc of raw energy. The two zigzagging streams of raw energy meet in the middle and create a massive explosion of energy that knocks over the nearby bystanders.

Is this the kind of magic you are looking for? We are sorry to inform you that you will not find that kind of magic. You will not find it anywhere. Magic is real but it does not look like that. If you find someone who tells you that that kind of magic does exist, we would implore them to demonstrate that magic for the world to see. For as long as it is kept in secret and never demonstrated to anyone, like the gods that created the planet or the blue kitty cat at the center of the galaxy that is the source of all joy, it may as well not exist.

Understanding magic is just about as easy as understanding religion. This actually stands to reason since for the most part they both came from the same place and are both used to accomplish the same ends.

Why would we compare magic to religion?

Let us look at two major components of each: origin and purpose.

Please forgive me as I summarize fifty-thousand years of human evolution in a few short paragraphs. We can summarize the origin of religion by saying that a time came in the ancient evolution of humanity where humans began asking questions that their science could not answer. (This was not difficult as we did not yet have science). What is the sun? What is the moon? Why can't I touch the moon, even from the tallest tree? Why does it rain? Why do animals have fur? Where did all this come from? What is the purpose of life? And so forth…

In order to answer some of these questions, it was natural to make some assumptions. Since we make our huts and other things out of mud and sticks, then surely someone long ago must have created us from mud and sticks. That creator must be more powerful than us and have a greater understanding of everything than we do. Thus was born the first god. Barring other facts, the logic in this supposition is quite sound so there really is no way to argue against this proposition that "gods exist" and "gods created all of this." That logic worked five thousand years ago and it still works today.

"God did all this."
"Prove it."
"Prove He didn't."

Adding a new dimension, weather and other natural disasters terrorize the people and the people wish for some kind of explanation and a modicum of control. What could cause such devastation as a flood or a hurricane? Only a god. It was probably a god that caused the hurricane or flooding and therefore it only makes sense that another god must be able to stop the flooding and redirect the hurricane. Or we just need to appease the god that is causing these disasters. Appeasing the gods was thus the progenitor of the first religions.

How do the gods affect change in the world? They must use powers that we do not possess. They must use powers we do not understand. Those powers, we called "magic." Thus, magic was born into the world. Anything we didn't understand was called, "magic."

In this way, both religion and magic were used to explain things we did not understand. Wait. Little has changed. So, let me restate that: to this day, both religion and magic are used to explain things we do not understand.

Religion and magic have the same origin and the same purpose. They were created by humanity to explain the world and to give us an avenue by which we can affect change in the world.

They are both there to give us some kind of sense of control over forces we cannot fully understand. Through religion we implore the gods for help and guidance and we direct the gods to act on our behalf thus affecting change in the world around us.

Where does this power of the gods come from? It comes from deep within the person who implores the god for help. It starts deep inside as a need or a plea. The person shapes it in the form of a prayer and focuses their energy intensely on the outcome. They then emanate this energy in a wave or stream through a direct connection to their god. Mentally and spiritually they envision their god affecting the change they have requested in the world around them.

The religious call this prayer. We call this magic. Does it matter that the religious person uses an imagined god to relay their power into the world around them? Not at all. We applaud anyone you can affect change in their world through the power of belief whether that belief be in magic, Zeus, Allah, Jesus, Kali or Ahura-Mazda.

Myth: Through magic, we implore unseen forces for help and guidance.

Truth: Through ourselves – by emanating power from within – we affect change in the world around us for help and guidance.

Because the method by which we do this cannot yet be fully explained scientifically, it receives the label "magic."

May 30 – A Visual Aid for Manifestation

Truly, magic is unnecessary. The actual manifestation of thought into reality is taking place at a deeper level. It is the power of manifestation from pure spirit-consciousness directly into reality. I take the liberty of calling this "magic" because neither science nor religion can yet explain it.

When you manifest your own reality directly into the world you do so through self-authorization. If you use a god or magic, the Authorist believes this is accomplished through Authorization Loopback. (See also *Authorization Loopback*.)

Let us use healing magic as an example. In the book, *Not Rituals & Ceremonies*, there is a Ritual of Healing. In the Ritual of Healing, the practitioner wishes to manifest healing energy into a person they love who is very far away. This can be done merely by thinking it.

However, a visual aid may be helpful. By envisioning a direct line of energy leaving the practitioner and entering the loved one, the healing energy may be more easily broadcast.

The practitioner, however, may not be ready for this kind of power. If not, the practitioner may wish to invoke a god or use ritual magic. Magic, in short, is a visual aid we use to help us manifest our desires into reality.

The same manifestation of power into the world may be accomplished through the use of thought, gods, magic or religion.

MAY 31 – HOW DOES MAGIC WORK?

Magic works from the inside out. Magic, just like authorization for being, comes from within you. Always, it must start from within and flow outward.

This is not so hard to imagine when you consider that everything you know about the world is only a sensory copy of actual reality that is being recreated in your mind.

You see a bird fly from the bush to the tree. The bush, the bird and the tree exist outside of you. They seem to be separate from you. But you do not really know that.

Why? Because the bush, the bird and the tree that you saw only became real to you when your mind recreated the ideas of them in your mind's eye. Your mind imagined these things when it processed sensory data, but even this processing all took place within your mind.

In other words, your senses captured "bush, bird, tree" and passed them to your mind. Your mind then recreated what the senses passed to it so you could react to "The bird flies from the bush to the tree." No matter how hard you try you cannot get passed the reality that the bird flying from the bush into the tree took place in your mind. Did this event also take place outside of your mind? Maybe. But the point I want to make here is that the final rendition of this event was akin to a movie playing in your mind for the benefit of the spirit-consciousness.

The bush, bird and tree in your mind is the one that is real to you. And it is all in your mind. This is the basis for "mind over matter." This is the basis for how we manifest our own realities. This is the basis for the power of prayer that comes with religion, the basis for magic and why both prayer and magic actually work.

Everything you know is a reflection of the real thing that exists only in your mind. And whether you fully understand this yet or not, you have control over what takes place inside your mind. Who controls your mind? Your spirit-consciousness. So when you want to perform magic, you must start inside your mind or spirit-consciousness and work outward from there.

Once you have made the changes you want internally, you can then focus on emanating those changes outward over and over and over in waves, out into the universe and you will see that these changes begin to take effect externally.

Let's go through an example. In our example, let's say that you wish you had a job with better pay where you worked less hours.

First, you internalize this as a directive instead of a plea. "I want a new job where I have better pay and work less hours." You close your eyes and you realize inside your mind there is a whole complete copy of the entire universe. This is your universe. It is the universe you understand to exist.

In this copy (which is really the only universe you truly know), imagine yourself having a different job with more pay where you work less hours. Know that you have achieved this goal already. Feel that sureness.

Feel the relief you have when you switch jobs and realize you have affected this change in your world. Think about what you do with your extra time. Think about what you'll do with the extra money. But mostly, focus on that feeling of having achieved this goal.

Once your internal-universe-self (you, actually) feels really good about the new job and having achieved this goal, feel that good energy and start to release it into the universe that exists outside of yourself. Let it flow from you in waves or shoot from you in beams. Use your imagination to emanate this feeling into the universe.

You only need to work on this one to five minutes at a time and you should do this at least once a day but ideally two or three or more times a day.

What I have just described is what real magic is. And adding ceremonies and rituals to the above thought exercise can magnify the power of this magic tremendously.

Why do you think magic is still practiced in the world? Because it works. It is not as easy as the wizards on television make it look with magic wands and energy blasts, but it is nonetheless very real and it can be very effective.

Again, this is the same as religion. If you had a god that could just give you the new job that might be easier. If you can create or find a god like that perhaps you will not need to do magic yourself. (But you would probably need to pray a lot instead.)

For those of us who do not have gods that will do our bidding, it must come from within. (And, for those of you who do have a god that will do your bidding, it is still actually coming from within you).

June 1 – Authorization for Magic

You may wonder what use an Authorist could possibly have for magic when each of us knows full well that the power of manifestation comes directly from within. There are several answers but two that I will bring to the forefront.

Doing something religiously reinforces that thing in our minds and hearts – in our spirit-consciousness. By practicing "magic" religiously we reinforce those things we hold true and important to us.

Another reason is that just thinking something into existence is sometimes challenging with all of the other distractions of thought which are continuously competing for mind-space. By holding a ritual and invoking certain rites we are able to completely focus on a specific task or end goal with little possibility of distraction.

Ritual magic brings us clarity of focus. It is an effective method of sharpening the edge in spirit, mind, emotion and intellect. It teaches us focus and helps sharpen the skill of intention.

Rituals and ceremonies literally improve our overall health much like meditation and prayer have been shown to do in those who practice either or both of those things religiously. During a ritual, one can be completely present and focus on the task at hand thereby letting the worries of the rest of the world slip away.

Daily, weekly, monthly, etc. rituals can become touchstones in our lives, allowing us to reconnect with parts of ourselves that might otherwise drift.

Of course it is also enjoyable and gives us something to share with each other but at the same time it provides something deeply personal that we need not share with anyone.

You can change yourself and your universe through the power of thought. And it does come from within you. You are the Author of your destiny.

JUNE 2 – ASPECTS OF THE SELF

Humans are complicated beings. We have feelings and emotions, conflicting paradigms of belief, passions, desires, hopes, dreams, inner and outer needs, the ability to communicate in metaphor and analogy, physiological drives that may conflict with mental and spiritual desires and spiritual and mental drives that may conflict with physiological and social mandates.

In order for us to talk about ourselves we need to agree on a working model of "a person" that can be used to talk in-depth about some of these deeper aspects of ourselves.

The model I use when writing about Authorism is "the concentric self" model. It breaks the self down into five distinct but completely interconnected aspects. You can draw this out on paper by drawing a circle and writing the word "spirit" in the middle. Then drawing a larger circle around the first one and writing the word "mental," in that circle (but outside of the spirit circle). Then drawing a larger circle around the first two and writing the word "emotional," in that circle (but outside of the mental circle). Then drawing a larger circle around the first three and writing the word "physical," in that circle (but outside of the emotional circle). Then drawing a larger circle around the four and writing the word "social," in that circle (but outside of the physical circle). You should end up with five concentric circles and each one should be labeled with an aspect of the self.

(((((spiritual) mental) emotional) physical) social)

The deepest and inner-most aspect of self is the spirit-consciousness. This is the spiritual aspect of self. Outside of this but also very close to the core is the mental aspect of self. This is also referred to as *the mind*. It is what is reading these words to your spirit-consciousness right now. Whether or not you are listening is dependent on a great many variables in your life! The next layer out (which may have just experienced a jolt from the previous sentence) is still inside you but less "core" and that is the aspect of emotion. This is where feelings arise and also where certain needs exist such as the need for love, validation and acceptance as well as the need to love, trust and respect others. Finally we reach the outer layers with the next aspect which is the physical body.

Many schools of thought place the mind in "the body" not the brain and we do not take a position on this. Think of it how you will. In any event, the body is crucial for the self and the physical aspect of self is extremely important. Finally we have everything external to the physical body that still matters to the self. This includes self-image (because how we see ourselves is a hodge-podge of our own interpretations of how we interpret the reactions of others to ourselves). Meaning, other people matter to us even if we do not want them to. This aspect of self also includes external things to the self that we integrate into the self-image such as material items that may be important to us and of course this also includes love, familiar and platonic relationships. This also includes our self-image as it is affected by how we think others perceive us.

Truly we do not pretend that the self is so easily dissected into neat little concentric ovals such that we could remove one and work on it exclusively or that we could operate in only one of these rings without affecting another.

These rings are drawn only to give a general framework of the idea that we are complicated and that we have many aspects which are interconnected. It is likely one could redraw this model with a hundred ovals and go into much more detail about each one. However, this could result in one or many large books and is not the subject matter we wish to discuss here.

June 3 – Never in the Same Place Twice

You will never be in the same place twice. Nothing will.

Imagine yourself standing in a meadow on a nice, sunny day. There are no clouds in the sky, the butterflies are fluttering and the daisies are slowly waving back and forth in the nice, flowered breezes.

Now make a duplicate of yourself right there on the spot but make the duplicate be a translucent single colored copy of yourself. Let's say it's a translucent blue.

The duplicate will remain fixed in space and time. It is a snapshot of you at that very moment and will never change. The camera that is witnessing all of this will stay fixed on the translucent blue you.

What does the camera see?

It sees the blue you remaining in place while the real you, the meadow, the sunshine and the butterflies, all fly away as the spinning earth continues to arc around the sun. The sun continues to arc around the center of the galaxy as it turns and all of this keeps moving away from the translucent blue you that remains fixed back there in space and time.

You can and will never overlap with that translucent blue you. You can never be in the same time or place again. You are constantly being reborn in a new time and place!

June 4 – The Spiritual Self

When I talk about the spirit or the soul or make reference to consciousness or the spirit-consciousness, I am referring to the same thing.

Without explaining spirit-consciousness (since I cannot), I define it as the "other you" in the awareness of being aware. One of you is aware and the other is aware of that awareness. In this way, it seems we are two. Perhaps we are two. Or even three if you posit that the mind (awareness) plus the spirit-consciousness (that which is aware of that awareness) equals you. And to make "you" be a third entity we would need to stipulate that "you" can only exist as a complete person (or intellect) when the other two aspects (mind and spirit) are combined. This idea would be something like [engine + chassis = car].

The spirit is the part of your being that follows you into dreams. Your mind may be asleep during a dream, but your spirit-consciousness is still there. It is the part of you that just rolls with whatever is happening. "Oh, I'm in a submarine deep within the ocean. Now I'm walking up sunlit stairs in a dark forest. My friend is in the backseat and the car is driving really slowly through the blue and red snow." The *mind* would balk at such things and refuse to accept what you were experiencing as reality. The spirit-consciousness, however, has no trouble just rolling with it.

The spirit is the real-time you. It is the you that exists only now. It is, I think, the you that your mind is reading this to.

June 5 – The Mental Self

The mental aspect of self is the mind and intellect. This is the "automatic self." This is the part of you that can be an automaton. When you drive for a couple minutes then realize you have no recollection of having done it because you were off in thought, it was your mental self that was making the steering adjustments, looking for obstructions in the road and working the pedals while your spirit-consciousness was lost in thought.

Of course this mental self is also the part of you that stores memories and does some of the thinking. The thinking the mental self does is different from the thinking the spirit self does. The mental self is more of a calculator.

In fact, your mental self can work on problem solving while your spirit-conscious self is preoccupied with other things. This is why you can all of a sudden have an epiphany about something or suddenly realize a solution to a problem completely out of the blue! Your mind – your mental self – works out solutions while your spirit-conscious self runs the show. Just like your mental self can run the show while your spirit-conscious self drifts around in fantasy and day dreams.

A healthy mental state is critical to overall health and wellbeing. Of course, all of these aspects interact and overlap, so a poor state of mental health will emanate out to the other circles causing emotional, physical and even social and spiritual problems.

June 6 – The Emotional Self

The emotional aspect of self is all about "feelings." There are hundreds of feelings one can have and there are thousands of things that spark a feeling. Here is a very short list just to give us a baseline of what we mean by "feelings:"

Amazed
Foolish
Overwhelmed
Angry
Peaceful
Proud
Loving
Anxious
Relieved
Ashamed
Happy
Hopeful
Sad
Hurt
Satisfied
Comfortable
Scared
Silly
Jealous
Joyous
Lonely
Worthless

People talk about "getting control of their feelings" but this is a dangerous way to think.

Feelings are real and having feelings is not something you can really control. What you can control is how you react to your feelings.

There are countless approaches to exercising the emotional self and emotional self-control is definitely something we should all spend time working on.

Clearly, emotional health is just as critical as spiritual and mental health. If you are an emotional disaster, the "disaster" part will affect all of the other aspects of the self creating disharmony and unease.

A great meditation for today is to sit still for a few minutes and feel the feelings that you have. Feel the feeling, then let it go. Do not react to it. Just allow it to come, to saturate you then to pass away from you.

JUNE 7 – THE PHYSICAL SELF

In philosophy and religion, the physical self is often the most ignored and disregarded aspect of self. The main reason for this exposes an interesting division. Philosophy is primarily an intellectual pursuit reserved for those who not only take the time but who also have the luxury of spending time on the thought and contemplation necessary for such pondering. For many, it is difficult to contemplate the origins of the universe and the meaning of life when you are struggling to find food, water and shelter for yourself and family. Because this is primarily an intellectual pursuit it is relegated to "the mind" and over the centuries a myth has developed that the mind and the body are two separate entities. Further, western culture assumes that the mind is located only in the brain (instead of an aspect of the entire body). In other words, many people believe their mind is separate from their physical body and that of the two, the mind is more important.

Taking a different route but ending up in the same place, most religions have spent the last few hundred years trying to convince humanity that their physical bodies are irrelevant and that the only part of self that truly matters is the spirit-consciousness (E.g. the soul.) After all, your time here on Earth is but the tiniest of flickers compared to the eternity that follows for your immortal soul.

But here and now matters, and the physical self is an extremely important aspect of self. In fact, depending on your perspective it is easy to argue that the physical self is the *most important* aspect of self. For instance, brain matter is physical and even with the mind (or mind and soul) spread throughout the entire body, without a brain you can't really appreciate any of the other aspects of self or enjoy life at all.

Like all aspects of self, the condition of the physical self affects the other aspects of self. It has a direct effect on their condition. A severe physical injury can cause emotional, mental and even spiritual scarring and has social implications as well. For instance, one's job might be in jeopardy, one may need to alter the way they interact with society while recovering from the injury, etc.

Physical wellbeing is critical to an all-around healthy self. Just as emotional depression can cause physical sickness, so too can physical sickness cause emotional depression.

It is worth noting that when you are tired and feeling sick, it is difficult to force yourself to exercise or eat healthy. This makes it all too easy to continue to lay around and eat unhealthy foods. This is called a "vicious cycle." Fatigue begets fatigue.

The opposite of a vicious cycle is a virtuous cycle and it works (in opposite) the exact same way. Eating healthy and getting exercise and a healthy amount of rest makes you feel better which encourages you to eat healthy, exercise and get healthy rest. Good health begets good health.

June 8 – The Social Self

The social aspect of self is everything external and societal. This encompasses your jobs, your associations, clubs, schools, gym memberships, churches, etc.

This also encompasses the rules and laws of society and the sub-societies you are involved in. For instance, your apartment complex rules, your HOA or even the "Etiquette for Behavior" at the local recreation center.

Another big ticket item that is part of the social aspect of self is money and all of the things that go with money and the economy. Consumerism, shopaholism, debt, taxes, overspending, underspending, etc., are all encompassed in the social aspect of self. In this consumer-culture, money has a significant impact on us. For instance, someone who is suffering from a major financial crisis will feel that as stress in all of the other aspects of the self.

Of course social media falls into the social aspect as well. How much time you spend on social media, what kinds of things you monitor, the things you post, the things you like, the people you follow, friend, unfriend or unfollow, etc.

When we talk about "community" we can have some flex in the definition. You define what the boundaries are of your community. How you interact with your community affects your other aspects of self.

In short, if you want to love yourself and be a healthy person who enjoys their life, you need to love your community and be a healthy member of that community and enjoy your community.

June 9 – Scarcity & Abundance

There are entire books dedicated to scarcity or to abundance and also to the interrelationship of scarcity *and* abundance.

Some philosophies or ideologies might argue that scarcity and abundance are frames of mind. While we cannot deny this truth, it is nonetheless very real to people who are suffering from extreme poverty or a scarcity of water or other natural resources.

It is true, the power of positive thinking *can* change your life. You *can* manifest a new reality for yourself. But these changes are not overnight events. It often takes time, and usually (not always) the more radical the change you seek, the longer it takes to manifest that change into your reality. In other words, *manifesting* water into your reality when there is a scarcity of water may not always work right away.

The dance between scarcity and abundance is the primary source of contention and strife in human civilization. If you recall, we discussed the need for *evil* and *pain* and that those terrible things must exist in order for us to have *good* and *pleasure*. Thus it is also such with *scarcity* and *abundance*. We cannot have one without the other. (See also, *The Gradient Yin-Yang*.)

JUNE 10 – THE PEBBLE IN THE POOL

When you drop a pebble in a pool of water, the ripples go out in every direction. The ripples are waves and they will keep traveling across the surface of the pool until they reach the edges. A single pebble can affect the entire pool.

There are so many applications of this metaphor in life. The first and most obvious is that "All it takes is one small action to change the world." The action is *the dropping of the pebble* and *the changing of the world* is the ripples which spread across the entire pool.

Today, take action. The action can be smiling (even if it is not "at someone," just a smile all of a sudden will cause the ripple effect). It could be doing something nice for someone or looking in the mirror and saying, "I love you." It could be as simple as sweeping the porch or hugging a pet or a friend – or even yourself. Any action you take will have intention behind it and will cause the ripple effect in the world around you.

Needless to say, this cuts both ways. Negative actions can create negative ripples, so another thing you could try today instead of performing a simple action to change the world for the better is to omit a negative action that you might have normally performed. If you were going to react angrily to something, at the last minute, change your reaction. If you were going to lie about something, think of a different way to react where you do not have to lie. If you weren't going to let that car in front of you, change your mind and let them in today.

Remember, we cannot control having feelings but we *can* control how we react to them.

June 11 – The Self, Connected

Over the last few days we have discussed how each of the five aspects of the self are connected. Today's meditation is to consider that this connectedness of the selves is not just a linear progression. It is not simply that the spirit connects to the mental and the mental connects to the emotional and the emotional connects to the physical and the physical makes the final connection to the social self, all in a straight line.

Instead, each of the five aspects of the self interconnect with the other four. If you draw five circles (each one being an aspect of the self) and then connect each one to the other four with a straight line, you will have 20 lines when you are finished drawing, not just 10. But just because they are all interconnected does not mean that each single aspect always influences all of the others. In other words, a spiritual experience can be *just* a spiritual experience, and an emotional experience may sometimes be *just* an emotional experience. A physical injury may be small and insignificant enough to only affect the physical self.

But because these aspects are all interconnected, an impact on one may affect any number of the others. For instance, a more serious physical injury might also impact the mental and the emotional aspects of the self. An even more serious physical injury might affect all four of the other aspects of self.

Likewise, a spiritual pleasure might only be experienced in the spirit-conscious self. But a more intense spiritual delight might flow out to be experienced in the physical and the emotional self. And a spiritual epiphany might be experienced throughout all five aspects of self.

This all seems fairly straightforward but there is another layer of complication I want to highlight. An impact in one area of the self may cause impacts in other areas of self (we have already said this). But these secondary impacts caused from the first impact can also act as new impacts on the areas of self they affect, thus causing their own impacts on yet other areas of the self, sometimes even on the area of self that initiated the waves of impact to begin with. There is a reverberating affect that can take place when something happens to you. Your experience of an event may initiate a chain of multiple impacts/waves of experience that reverberate throughout your entire being.

Merging these ideas with the metaphor of "the pebble in the pool," we can imagine this reverberation effect as multiple pebbles. First you have to envision the five aspects of self as circles drawn over the top of the pool (or on the bottom of the pool if you were going to really create this construct). The first pebble is the initial experience you have in the world. The experience happens and the waves go out in every direction. Now for each aspect of the self that is impacted by that initial experience toss a pebble into that circle. Let us imagine that three other aspects of the self were affected so you toss in three more pebbles. The waves go out. Let's say that from those three impacts, four aspects of self are affected, thus you throw in four more pebbles. Also, these impacts can all take place almost immediately or can take place over periods of time. If you're following along in your mind, you can see that there may be hundreds of little waves all intermixing and flowing out and among each other almost like a scattering of pebbles were thrown into the pool.

As a person living in the world, you already know all this through your own experience. You have already seen how complicated people are and how tremendous a single experience can be in a person's life.

The point of today's meditation is to consider that experiencing something in the world (or within yourself) or making a change in just one area of ourselves can have widespread and long lasting changes to our entire self.

JUNE 12 – EVERYTHING IS CONNECTED

Today we will take yesterday's meditation on the interconnectedness of just the self and extrapolate out to the rest of existence.

This interconnectedness with all of existence we have already alluded to in many of the preceding meditations in that 'manifestation of reality through thought' most certainly takes advantage of the interconnectedness of everything. In metaphysics, interconnectedness is a given. In the hard sciences there is no single definitive explanation but there are clear allusions to the thought/reality connection in quantum physics and chaos theory.

For instance, the Butterfly Effect from Chaos Theory implies that the flapping of a butterfly's wings in your backyard garden effects the winds on Saturn. Whether or not this can be proven or measured in any way is not something I am going to get into here; I mention it only to point out that there are some scientific precedents for the idea of the interconnectedness of everything.

While I cannot explain the science behind this interconnectedness of all things, I can explain the Authorian philosophy behind it.

How is it that we are all interconnected?

Humans can see an extremely tiny sliver of the spectrum of energy in the cosmos (this spectrum is called "visible light"). If we could see the entire spectrum, I daresay we would see only pure white. It would be like looking at Anti-Not. (See also *Anti-Not*.) This is because, with no filter, we would see all energy equally bright. And looking into the cosmos, it really is *all* energy.

But if we could see these various spectrums of energy in layers – perhaps only a few layers at a time – we would be able to see the strands of energy that literally connect all things. In the mind's eye, these energy strands may be actual energy that is easy to locate and follow here in this dimension or perhaps it may require us to "move up" one dimension (or many). (See also *The Tesseract*.) But these suppositions are more along the lines of the science behind it, not the philosophy.

Authorian philosophy fully supports the idea of the interconnectedness of all things because of the Authorian definition of reality and the "inverted" "reflection" of reality that is Not. What is reality? It is warm, light, active presence. At the deepest level, the stars, planets, alien landscapes, trees, life on worlds unknown and everyone and everything here on Earth are all warm, light, active presence. What Authorism calls, "Life," with a capital "L."

It is through this substrate of warm, light, active presence that we are all connected. (See also *We are All Connected*.)

JUNE 13 – AWARENESS OF YOUR AWARENESS

Who are you?

I mean, deep inside, who are you?

Are you reading this *to* you or are you listening to this being read *by* you?

The fact that *you* can read something to you and that both *you* and you can be aware of this happening is what we mean by the awareness of your awareness. If you have ever felt crazy or insane because of this, relax and join the club. How could you not feel crazy when you are talking to yourself while simultaneously agreeing, disagreeing or perhaps even ignoring yourself?

The duality of the awareness of your own awareness is what we mean by the spirit-consciousness. One of the you's is the mind and one of the you's is your spirit-consciousness. Both of them operate as independent agents but they are also both linked together to make you who you are. There is conjecture that the two independent you's linked together form a third entity which is the real you. If this is the case, perhaps each of us is a trinity.

To meet the deepest you in your spirit-consciousness, you do not need to believe in any of this or anything else. If you have not taken the trip to yourself, it something you should try one day. It is an amazing experience. Active participation in the discovery of your spirit-consciousness is the most pure, lucid and awesome phenomenon you can experience as a living being. And the most amazing thing about it is that it requires no drugs, no books, no programs or memberships. It is free to all conscious beings! (See also, *I Think, Therefore I Am*.)

JUNE 14 – THE TREE OF NOT

As previously discussed, the Principles of Not may be used in a reactive way (Cinereo Modo) or in a proactive way (Cinereo Ascensus). In order to visually represent the Principles and to demonstrate their order of precedence and interrelationship with each other, we use the metaphor of a tree, fittingly called "the Tree of Not." As we discuss the Principles we begin with the core of the tree. The core of the tree is where the original seed of the tree sprouted. The seed of the tree represents the nucleus of the individual; the core of your very being. It is your soul or your raw consciousness as distinct from the mind and body that surround it.

The core of the *Tree of Not* is the *first Principle of Not* and it is summed up simply as the word "life." The seed sprouts and begins to grow toward the sky even as roots begin to descend into the earth (which is the universe around your soul) and as the roots descend, the trunk of the tree rises. The trunk of the tree is the Second Principle of Not and can be summed up simply with the word, "fitness."

As the tree continues to grow skyward, the trunk splits into two branches which are equally strong and equally important in holding up the foliage at the top.

The branches are the Third Principle of Not, which can be referred to simply with the word "relationships" and the Fourth Principle of Not which is referred to as "personal code." At the very top, the tree expands fully into the foliage of the last Principle of Not which can be summed up using the word "community." The tree might be imagined to be growing peacefully in a forest or on a grassy hill or you might imagine the tree as growing in the vastness of the universe with stars all around it, above and below.

Today, contemplate the Tree of Not.

June 15 – I Think Therefore I Am

We begin with a thought experiment introduced by Rene Descartes in the 17th century CE. I have modified the experiment for the purpose of our work but the essence remains intact.

Find somewhere comfortable to sit for some contemplation. Now consider some of the things you know to be true. Then ask yourself, "Is it possible I am wrong?"

For instance, how do you know the things you know? You know things because you have experienced things in your life, right? But how did you experience those things? It was through your senses and your thought – or reflection – on the things brought into your mind through your senses. And by "your senses," I am speaking literally about taste, touch, smell, hearing and vision.

But could your senses be wrong? Is it possible your senses have misled you? For instance, when you stick a knife in a glass of water, does the part of the knife under the water change size and move slightly to one side? No, it does not, but your eyes tell you it does. Or when you see someone very far away, they appear to be very small – maybe only an inch or two tall. Are they really small and then they grow larger as they get closer? No. But that is not what your sense of vision tells you. Is it possible to hear something and think it came from one direction when it really originated from a different direction? Yes, this happens when sounds reflects off of something so it sounds like the thing is on the right but it is really on the left.

With these things in mind, we can safely say that our senses may not be trusted. So for the sake of this experiment, as you sit in contemplation, think away your senses. Imagine that you cannot use them. Or if you are having trouble doing that, then just ignore what they are telling you for now because you know that they are suspect.

If your senses have been fooling you all this time, how can you trust anything in your mind? How do you know that you are even sitting there?

The answer is "thought." The fact that you are thinking means that you exist. But Descartes decided that this was still not deep enough. He went a little deeper. To do so, he decided that there was something trying to deceive him.

This part is tricky: What if *you* are not really thinking? What if your thoughts are being planted in your mind by some external entity? It could be a computer, a god, some spirit or an alien perhaps? Maybe it is the Matrix. If your thoughts are being fed to your mind from some external source then they are also suspect. In other words, just like your senses, your thoughts cannot be trusted to be true.

So with that in mind, you will have to think away your thoughts. Any thought that comes into your mind, respond to it with "This thought may be false so I will not regard it as a valid thought. It is not real."

You might think that once you have done that, there is nothing left. But you will find that to be false. There is still something there - something present! There is **that which is thinking away the thoughts!** It is the awareness of being aware. The spirit-consciousness. Or the spirit. Or consciousness. The "soul." If there is absolutely nothing else, there is still that which is doubting the thoughts that you are having.

When Descartes reached this level of understanding he had the epiphany, "*cogito, ergo sum*," (I think, therefore I am.)

If you do what he did, you too will have this epiphany. You will come face to face with your spirit. We should warn you up front that this can be a shocking experience. But it is also a beautiful thing to experience in that it is the experience of pure truth. Nothing is more personal and pure than witnessing, first hand, this absolute knowledge of your true self.

This can act as the first brick in your foundation of belief, for once you have a brick like this you will find that it cannot be broken. Not by you or anyone else. You can pass this brick around to anyone and ask them to try and you will find that they cannot break it. This is absolute knowledge. (See also, *Codice Personalum*.)

In this thought experiment we were able to achieve our objective by assuming there is a deceiver of some kind slipping thoughts into our heads for us to try to think away or doubt. It is probably safe to say that there is no such entity creating thoughts in our minds.

In any event, this exercise not only proves that you exist absolutely, but it also proves that there is a second participant within you. The other participant is the progenitor of the thoughts that the doubter is doubting away. There is that which is having thoughts (your mind) and that which is doubting their validity (the spirit). Or is that the other way around? This is where The Mystery begins and where the Church of Not steps back and admits to being unable to explain this. But none can doubt its validity to those who have experienced it.

We have now started building an unshakeable foundation of belief (we will return to this foundational brick in *Codice Personalum*) while at the same time having proved with absolute certainty that we are alive. In the First Principle of Not, we call this concept the seed of the Tree of Not. (See also, *Vita*.)

June 16 – Cinereo Modo

Cinereo Modo is "the gray way (or path)." The reason the path is described as gray is because we do not believe there is a perfectly black or perfectly white path in life. There are only shades of gray. We call this the gray path to remind us of the inherent innocence of all life and the choice that we have at every moment between good and evil. (See also, *The Gradient Yin-Yang*.)

Often we can go through life making choices which direct us one way or another and we learn and grow from these choices as we move forward on our path. Usually our choices are fairly easy even if they may change our possible futures. However, there come times in our lives when we must make an important decision and we do not know which choice to make. Cinereo Modo is a great tool to pull out when times like these come along.

Cinereo Modo is essentially a reactive approach to utilizing the Principles of Not in your life. To summarize, the Principles are life (or Life), fitness, relationships, personal code and community, in that order. When the time comes to make an important decision and you find yourself somewhat at a loss as to which choice to make, you simply ask some very straightforward questions about your choice relative to each of the five Principles of Not. You start with the first one, then move to the second one, and so forth until you have gone all the way to Community.

In brief, you are essentially comparing your choice to the values of Not. Does one of your choices impact life negatively? How does it impact your overall fitness? Does the choice have a negative or positive impact on relationships? How do the choices line up with your personal code? Does one choice have a better or worse impact on your community?

In the appendix there are some flow charts that can be used to guide you through the process. (See also, *Appendix B – Cinereo Modo.*)

June 17 – Cinereo Ascensus

Cinereo Ascensus is "the gray climb." It describes the figurative climbing of the Tree of Not thereby embodying the Principles of Not into one's daily life. The reason the climb is called "gray" is because we do not believe there is a perfectly black or perfectly white path in life. There are only shades of gray. We call this the gray climb to remind us of the inherent innocence of all life and the choice that we have at every moment between good and evil. (See also, *The Gradient Yin-Yang*.)

There will be times in your life when you reach plateaus, lulls or dead ends on your journey. When this happens, you may feel directionless or unmotivated. Cinereo Ascensus is a great tool to pull out when times like these come along.

In the days that follow, we will walk through the figurative climb as we explore each of the Principles of Not and how we might integrate them into our journey and use them as guides to point the way.

A couple of days ago we visited a thought experiment introduced by Renes Descartes, which gave us the cornerstone we can use in our foundation of belief. *I think, therefore I am.* The discovery of this cornerstone also illuminated the truth of a spirit-consciousness which exists within us. What we ultimately exposed in that daily meditation was the spark of life.

The gray climb is about acknowledging this deepest aspect of ourselves – the very seed of our consciousness and then moving outward from that core depth, out through our mind and our emotion, out through our physical body, then further out as we pass through relationships and our personal code then further out until we release ourselves into our community to acknowledge our interconnectedness with the world around us and our true place in the cosmos. This whole process is the ascent.

Much like a great road trip, the destination is not the objective here. The objective is the decision to make the ascent *toward* the destination and the path we take *toward* the destination. (See also, *The Tree of Not*.)

To begin Cinereo Ascensus, you approach the Tree of Not and regard the entire tree. Having considered the whole tree, you make yourself comfortable at the base of the tree and sit in silent contemplation for a few moments. Sitting there, you can sense the soul of the tree. You can feel the intertwining of the energy of the tree with the energy that is your soul. Together you both sit enjoying the action of blazing your own energies into the universe. You revel in being warm, light, active presence.

Today we consider the gray climb and where we are in our personal ascent.

June 18 – Vita

Throughout Cinereo Ascensus, in order to differentiate between the definitions of the Principles versus the application of the Principles, we refer to them by their Latin names as we discuss their application. To summarize, the following is a list of the Principles and their Latin names, in order of their importance:

1. Life, Vita
2. Fitness, Aciem Exacuitur
3. Relationships, Necessitudo
4. Personal Code, Codice Personalum
5. Community, Civitas

Yesterday you approached the Tree of Not and sat in contemplation at its base in order to consider your imminent ascent.

You now consider these words:

The seed, or core, of the Tree of Not can be compared to the soul of a human being. This is the beginning; the impetus; the progenitor. This is the origin of the wellspring of energy which is ultimately *yourself*. At the center of the core of being we have, "I think. Therefore I am." Authorists call it spirit. Science calls it consciousness. Nobody, either religious or scientific, knows what it really is. Nonetheless, this glimmer, or spark of awareness, is the seed of life. It is the core of your life and being. Everything else that you have been, that you are and that you will become comes from this seed. Here we acknowledge the value of life and how, *for life*, life must be the highest of values. Along with the descending roots, life now runs deep beneath you.

June 19 – Aciem Exacuitur

Throughout Cinereo Ascensus, in order to differentiate between the definitions of the Principles versus the application of the Principles, we refer to them by their Latin names as we discuss their application. To summarize, the following is a list of the Principles and their Latin names, in order of their importance:

1. Life, Vita
2. Fitness, Aciem Exacuitur
3. Relationships, Necessitudo
4. Personal Code, Codice Personalum
5. Community, Civitas

Yesterday you contemplated the core of being, which is your deepest self. This contemplation resulted in the veneration of the highest principle: life (or Vita).

With this in mind, you stand up and regard the trunk of the tree. You are ready to begin the ascent.

The Latin term Authorism uses for fitness is 'aciem exacuitur' which means 'sharpened edge.' If you are not fit in all of the aspects of self, then you have a place to start. Start by becoming more fit. If you are already fit, you can continue to hone yourself – you can keep sharpening the edge so that you remain fit.

As you begin the climb, you wish to be prepared in the event you should encounter strife, antagonists or other barriers to progress. Previously we talked about the necessity for strife. We must have strife in order to learn or to progress. Without strife, we suffer atrophy and stagnation. But this does not mean that we welcome it and it certainly does not mean that we allow strife to dictate the terms of our progress. In order to come out on top and keep a strategic advantage over this unknown opposition, we must maintain a sharpened edge. And because we do not know from which quadrant the opposition may come, we must maintain this sharpened edge throughout our entire self.

What can you do to prepare for a devastating event that shocks an entire nation like "9/11" in 2001? Or an event that shocks the entire planet, like the COVID-19 global pandemic in 2020? It is not really practical or possible to prepare yourself for every possible thing that could go wrong.

But because things can go wrong, some will. The closest we can come to preparing for any eventuality is to be as fit as possible when the time of testing comes. Remaining fit gives us the best chance of winning out or at the very least making it through with as little damage to ourselves as possible.

Just like the pebble in the pool (See also, *The Pebble in the Pool.*), if you make a change to the innermost aspect, that change will ripple out through all the others. If you are spiritually ill, that illness will spread through your mental, emotional, physical and social shells until the whole spirit, mind and body feel ill. If you bring love and light into your spirit shell, that love and light will ripple out through your mental, emotional, physical and social shells until the whole spirit, mind and body feel love and light. The more aspects of the self we can target for fitness, the more fit we will be overall.

We also need to be fit in order to make proper choices (spiritual, mental, emotional, physical and social choices) and further our progress on our spiritual journey.

The more fit we are, the longer we may live and therefore the more we can get from life and the more influence we may exert on Life. Through the second Principle of Not, Fitness, we honor the first Principle of Not: Life.

Today we consider our fitness in all five aspects of our selves.

June 20 – Necessitudo

Throughout Cinereo Ascensus, in order to differentiate between the definitions of the Principles versus the application of the Principles, we refer to them by their Latin names as we discuss their application. To summarize, the following is a list of the Principles and their Latin names, in order of their importance:

1. Life, Vita
2. Fitness, Aciem Exacuitur
3. Relationships, Necessitudo
4. Personal Code, Codice Personalum
5. Community, Civitas

Yesterday you began the actual ascent by climbing the trunk of the Tree of Not. By having integrated fitness into as many aspects of your life as you were able, you honored your life, and all other lives. You payed homage to the universal Life.

By honoring your own life in this way, you make the first and most necessary step into the Third Principle by regarding your *needs* as more important to yourself than your *wants*.

You have taken the first steps in loving yourself.

In the Cinereo Ascensus, you have reached the top of the main trunk and made the climb up to find yourself standing between the two great branches: Necessitudo ("Relationships") and Codice Personalum ("Personal Code").

You are strong and fit and you look out at the amazing view of the universe you have from this vantage point. It *is* amazing. *You* are amazing.

You consider your ascent and wonder if you should take this branch or the other branch. Both appear to be very strong, however the branch called Necessitudo has a foothold that you can use to lift yourself higher. It looks like from there, you will be able to step over to Codice Personalum to continue your climb into the foliage of Civitas. As such, you step up as you begin your ascent of the branch called Necessitudo.

Climbing this branch means asking, "How can I work relationships into my life?"

June 21 – Summer Solstice

Today is the first day of summer! Or at least the celebration of summer! Traditionally, today is the longest day of the year and therefore the shortest night of the year.

Summer puts us in the midst of life! That which was born in the spring has grown and everything outside is thriving. This is a wonderful time to be alive and a perfect expression of warm, light, active presence.

If you can perform the Summer Solstice celebration outside today that would be ideal. Or at least, step outside and feel the sun as it warms the earth, the air and your body, bringing life to this entire planet.

Today's meditation is on this transition point – the halfway point between the spring and the autumn equinoxes. Today we think about the warmth of life and Life.

June 22 – Love Yourself

Looking at the Third Principle, you consider relationships. Your own relationship with yourself is the most important relationship you can have. One cannot love another person unless one first loves themselves.

For some, this may be concerning at first. After all, many people are taught that they are inherently flawed. If I was born broken, corrupt, and evil, how can I love myself?

This comes from the doctrine of Original Sin put forth primarily by Christianity. This doctrine essentially states that all people are born broken or flawed and that only through [insert methods dependent on religion, denomination, sect, etc.] can one atone for the sins they were born with and undo this damage that was placed in their design either before they were or when they were little babies.

The truth of the matter is quite the opposite. Authorism teaches the doctrine of Original Innocence. This doctrine essentially states that all people are born as innocent beings who can choose to take more good or more evil action at any time throughout their lives. (See also *Original Innocence*.)

If you already have some love for yourself, you can start building, enhancing, pruning, etc. external relationships right away. If you do not feel like you have any love for yourself, you should change that immediately. As silly as this may sound, the quickest and easiest way to start is to say out loud, "I love myself." Just that one little action can be a *very* difficult step for many people. If you would rather, you can say, "I love you." Even if you are the only one there to hear it. And even though you know you were the one who said it, hearing it said aloud has a surprisingly profound effect.

It only requires the smallest of sparks to bring forth your internal wellspring of love. Once you allow even the tiniest glimmer of love for yourself, you can begin to love others. Once you accept even the smallest amount of love from yourself, you can begin to accept love from others. Love will begin to flow from you, around you and to you.

If you feel like you do not have even the smallest amount of love for yourself, you should focus on the two most important aspects of relationship: respect and trust.

You can automatically gain some respect for yourself by acknowledging that you were born innocent and that as a human being, no different than mountains, trees or clouds, you have a right to be here. At the same time, extend a small amount of trust in yourself that you can do this. You can find love for yourself. With this little gesture of respect and trust, you have a beginning. The spark of self-love.

Relationships deepen over time. You do not have to reach self-acceptance or complete enlightenment today. This journey is for life and the objective is the journey itself, not the destination. Enjoy the journey.

Humanity is so varied and our paths are so unique that there are no clear instructions that can be used for all people.

That first part was the hardest part of Necessitudo. This does not mean the next part is easy but it is certainly *easier*, and it continues to get easier the more you work on it.

Today, consider and feel the love you have for yourself and know that it was deserved from birth and it is still deserved today. You deserve love. We all do.

June 23 – Love Others

Yesterday we discussed loving ourselves. Today we discuss loving others. It has to be in that order. Before you can love others you must love yourself. The amount is not as important as the placement. Meaning if you can love yourself only the tiniest little bit, that is all you need to start loving others a tiny bit too.

This Necessitudo part of the climb is about fostering relationships anywhere and everywhere you can. The easiest approach to this is to *just be*. This may sound too simple to actually work but it is not as easy as it sounds. People often get in their own way when it comes to relationships with others. It is easy to fall into the trap of trying to *make* a relationship work.

Relationships are not easy and compromise is required but they should not be *too much* work either. If you find yourself working overtime on trying to make a relationship work, it may be time to back off a little and see where it goes without so much guided effort on your part. After all, control is almost illusory. Especially when we're talking about "controlling other people." (See also, *Control*.)

While relationships are extremely important in life, and fostering relationships is an important part of having them, it is more than okay to let some of them go away.

In fact, actively pruning relationships is something you should look into every once in a while. Ask yourself if the relationship is violating the First or Second Principle. (Hopefully it is not violating the First Principle (Life).)

But if it is violating Vita or if it is causing spiritual, mental, emotional, physical or social distress in your life, it may be that this relationship should be pruned.

Your own fitness in all aspects of life must come before your relationships with other lifeforms.

As you continue embracing, changing and pruning relationships, you simultaneously work on building yourself into a stronger more resolute person. This is the natural segue into your personal code.

Now that you have stepped up the branch called Necessitudo, you begin to shift your weight as you look at the foothold a little higher up on the other branch. You are ready to step over to the branch called Codice Personalum.

June 24 – Codice Personalum

Throughout Cinereo Ascensus, in order to differentiate between the definitions of the Principles versus the application of the Principles, we refer to them by their Latin names as we discuss their application. To summarize, the following is a list of the Principles and their Latin names, in order of their importance:

1. Life, Vita
2. Fitness, Aciem Exacuitur
3. Relationships, Necessitudo
4. Personal Code, Codice Personalum
5. Community, Civitas

Over the last few days we approached the Tree of Not, contemplated its existence, considered how to climb it and then began our ascent. Yesterday we shifted our weight over to Codice Personalum in order to climb higher. (See also *Personal Code*.)

In order to build anything that is meant to last, a solid foundation is required. The same is true of your belief system. And in order to build a solid foundation, you need strong building material of the highest quality.

If you have not yet done so, today consider a brief statement that you feel confident about placing in your *foundation of belief*.

Here are some example statements that might appear in one's personal code or perhaps serve as bricks in the foundation of belief:

"To thine own self be true."
"The unexamined life is not worth living."
"No amount of money has purchased a minute more of life."
"Very little is needed to make a happy life."
"Nothing is evil which is according to nature."
"To rebel is justified."

The above list is just an example of what some people might consider bricks of belief. Let's look at the first example.

"To thine own self be true," is somewhat of a maxim for Authorists. As people who believe that authorization for our thoughts and actions comes from within ourselves, being true to ourselves is paramount. To be true to yourself is to be true to life, thus honoring the First Principle. Sharpening the edge by keeping yourself fit is being true to yourself, thus honoring the Second Principle. It honors the Third Principle in that giving yourself respect and trust (loving yourself) opens the way for being true to yourself. Of course, having this maxim as part of your personal code creates a brick that may be used in your foundation of belief and thus your *Personal Code*, which honors the Fourth Principle. The Fifth Principle is honored as well because as someone who is true to themselves, you can stand as a beacon of humanity in your community. You lead by example and you can feel solid in your leadership because the code by which you live runs all the way through your structure and foundation of belief. In this way, you have an unshakeable foundation. This is referred to as *Inconcussa Fundamenta* in Authorism.

The above description of the way one statement can be weaved through all five principles is what is meant by the gray climb. But it is the *action* part in the physical world around you, too. It is actively participating in your own Personal Code by creating it, critiquing it, altering it, testing it and then ultimately by living it.

Authorists believe that one should constantly be checking one's own belief structure and foundation of belief for any breaks, cracks or signs of weakening. More than that, we should try to shake the structure – try to shake the foundation – to see if there is any need for fortification. (See also *Inconcussa Fundamenta*.)

June 25 – Existing Structures of Belief

One might ask, "Why not just use an existing structure of belief? Why should I go through all that trouble of reinventing the wheel when there are so many structures of belief already out there for me to choose from?"

Excellent question. Choosing an existing structure of belief is a great way to start as long as you begin the process of owning that structure right away. In order to truly own such a thing you must become intimately familiar with the bricks that are used in the structure and even more so you must fully understand every aspect of each of the bricks in the foundation. Just because a structure of belief seems to be solid from the outside does not mean it will be for you. The only way to know if it works for you is to test it. You must identify the bricks of belief (the fundamental truths, precepts, core doctrines, etc.) and test them to see if they can be broken. And herein lies the problem in adapting a preexisting structure of belief to be your own.

Most people in the United States identify themselves as Christians, though how deeply they believe is a matter for discussion. But that will have to be a discussion for a different day. (See also, *Conviction of Belief*.) I bring up Christianity because it is a structure of belief that already exists and one that a person could easily grab onto and claim for themselves without even looking at the bricks of belief in the structure or foundation. After all, it has been around for two thousand years. It must be solid, right?

Let's look at Christianity as a structure and a foundation of belief. At the base of the structure is a massive tome of many concatenated books. The tome is called "The Holy Bible" and it has been around for hundreds of years. As a structure of belief, this book all by itself is already extremely complex. One could spend decades studying the bible and still not understand it all. But it gets even more complex because over the centuries there have been countless scholars and theologians who have written massive quantities of additional books which can be used to sort out some of the complexities of the bible. This amounts to massive structures of belief being built on top of an already massive structure of belief. With so many hallways, rooms and angles to choose from having too many choices can sometimes be the same as having none. One can be frozen with indecision. *"Which way should I go?! What if I make the wrong choice?!"*

As a personal code, how can this work for an individual? If one runs into an ethical dilemma, how do they sort out which direction to go through the countless number of rooms and halls in this superstructure? One of the problems with this is that when they cannot find a way, they must seek help from those who claim they know (a religious leader of some kind). This amounts to handing the wheel over to someone else and saying, "You steer." They are essentially saying to this relative stranger, "You are an expert in my structure of belief, so you will have to make this really difficult choice for me. After all, how am I to choose when I don't even understand the foundation of belief beneath this massive superstructure?!"

Most people find that when such a time of testing comes, the religious leader tells them that they are only there as a guide and cannot make the tough choices for them. They will have to choose for themselves. But even if the religious leader was willing to make the choice for me, how can I be sure this person guiding me really understands all the ins and outs of my personal situation? How can this other person be as vested in the outcome as I am? There is also the occasional bad guy mixed into the religious leadership. What if this expert in *my personal code* has nefarious motives and guides me based on *his* desires in the matter, not even considering my best interests?

But even if this other person has truly altruistic motives, they can only understand as much about my personal situation as I am willing or able to convey to them. Only I know what I know, think, feel and desire. This is why my personal code has to be *my* personal code.

As it happens, most people who truly understand their own beliefs did start with some other structure of belief that was handed down to them. But at some time during their lives, something happened that caused them to dig deeper into their beliefs than is required in normal day to day activity. And when the time came, when they really needed it most, their structure of belief collapsed. They had to build a new one.

Each of us has to have our own personal code. And only the self can authorize the self to make one.

JUNE 26 – PREFERRED IGNORANCE

Yesterday we were talking about the danger of using some existing structure or superstructure of belief instead of creating our own. We talked about the danger of allowing someone else to be the expert in our own personal code as opposed to us being the expert in our own personal code.

Yesterday and today's discussion center around dealing with superstructures of belief (see also, *Superstructures of Belief*). We are talking about the dangers of having a massive structure of belief instead of having a simple foundation of belief with a humble structure of belief on top of it that we built ourselves.

There is another danger in adopting someone else's belief structure (especially a superstructure) and it is more subtle and more dangerous than letting someone else be the expert in your personal code. This danger applies to any structure of belief that becomes so large that the person using it cannot trace every single brick all the way through to the foundation.

It can be summed up in the expression, "Ignorance is bliss." While this is true, I cannot help but call out another thing that is important to note about ignorance. Ignorance is the source of all hate. People fear what they do not understand and ignorance is a lack of understanding. Thus, ignorance can breed fear as well as "bliss."

When using a structure of belief so massive that you cannot possibly maintain it by yourself, there is too much at risk should the foundation break. In other words, one will close their minds to other possibilities if they fear that a new idea might jeopardize a brick in their foundation of belief.

Closing one's mind to possibilities of truth is the worst kind of ignorance and is part of the problem of evil. It is evil because it allows for – or even fosters – hate through the initial fear of being wrong. Often people will choose to hate the thing that caused them to question their belief because this seems less terrifying than rebuilding their entire belief system. Intentional ignorance, as it were, is also often more desirable than resisting the collective cognitive imperative of one's environment. So if the majority of people profess belief in a superstructure, individuals are more inclined to adopt that belief structure whether or not it really works for them. Humans are more afraid of being alone than being wrong.

This fear of being wrong is why people are willing to justify killing other people in defense of a belief. No belief is worth dying for. Only life is worth dying for. No belief is worth killing for. Only the defense of other life can justify killing. But the fear of being wrong can be so great as to fill a person with terror at the thought of it. It is almost as if, in just considering the possibility of being wrong, the person briefly considers what it would mean to not just be wrong but to be completely wrong. And in that moment of consideration the person has a glimpse of no structure at all – no belief at all. It is a glance into the void. This might be what a glimpse of Not would feel like. Sheer terror.

Today consider the idea that if you are going to choose an existing structure of belief to call your own, do so with your eyes wide open. Do so with mindful intention. Take the beliefs and understand them. Own them. Scrutinize the foundation and the structure then examine the mortar and then start testing the bricks to see if they can be broken. If they can, either fix them so they cannot be broken or remove them from the structure completely. There is no "one size fits all" when it comes to your own personal code. Truly that is what makes the code personal.

June 27 – What Does it Look Like?

Today we will finish the discussion on the Fourth Principle: Personal Code. Or, since in this case we're talking about Cinereo Ascensus, we should say Codice Personalum.

We have spent the last few days talking about personal code and its importance, but what does it look like?

Well, initially, it looks like words on paper. Or words written in your favorite notes app. Your personal code, just like any scriptures or other doctrines of belief, will start out as written words.

If you have already written some of your personal code, today you should read it over and see if you would like to add or subtract from it.

If you have not already done so, today write out one single statement that you might consider incorporating into your personal code. Get a piece of paper or create a note file titled, "Codice Personalum," and then write out your statement.

Now read it.

How did it make you feel? Is it something you feel good about? Is it something you feel strongly about? Maybe this statement can be a brick in your foundation of belief? It does not fit in the foundation, perhaps somewhere in the structure?

But do not worry if this statement is not "deep" enough to be in your structure of belief. Your personal code may have many aspects that are not deep philosophical concepts. For instance, it might start with something as simple as the statement, "I am kind to people."

Today, consider what your personal code looks like.

June 28 – Civitas

Throughout Cinereo Ascensus, in order to differentiate between the definitions of the Principles versus the application of the Principles, we refer to them by their Latin names as we discuss their application. To summarize, the following is a list of the Principles and their Latin names, in order of their importance:

1. Life, Vita
2. Fitness, Aciem Exacuitur
3. Relationships, Necessitudo
4. Personal Code, Codice Personalum
5. Community, Civitas

Over the last few days we approached the Tree of Not, contemplated its existence, considered how to climb it and then began our ascent. The Tree of Not is the symbolic representation of the Principles of Not. The ascent is the proactive integration of the principles into our daily lives. Today, we have finished climbing the branch called Codice Personalum and we are now ready to pull ourselves up into the foliage of Community. This is the last principle. The fifth Principle of Not is Civitas.

How do we integrate community into our lives?

Let's start by defining "community." When we talk about community we start small by referring to your immediate family (living with you) or your roommates. If you live alone, your immediate community will include your closest neighbors. From there, your community grows to encompass the entire neighborhood, district and town. Then we pan out further to include the city, the state or province, then the region, the country, the continent, the hemisphere and finally the entire planet and surrounding satellites (it would not be fair to exclude people orbiting the Earth or on missions to the moon, etc.).

Can you picture yourself in your community?

What do you see? Whatever it is that you are seeing, this is where you are now relative to your community.

Where do you want to be in five years? Do you have goals already outlined that you are working toward? Have you attained some? Not attained others? Changed directions? Are you unsure what tomorrow looks like, much less five years from now?

One thing you should consider right now if you have not already embodied this knowledge into your life: Five years will pass. At the end of that time, you will still be here. But you could be you as you are now or you could be you with a college degree. Or a black belt. Or with skills as a painter or a dancer. Perhaps a training certificate or a doctorate or with the experience of having roamed the jungles of Brazil, etc. The time is going to pass with or without you. You may as well choose a goal and then accomplish that goal during the next five years. Then even if you are still unsure as to what your next steps are going to be, you will have at least accomplished some great thing that you set out to accomplish.

Five years may be lofty. This works the same with a three or even one year period of time.

Create a plan for yourself. Write down what you want for your life. Look at what you have written. What is the first thing you should do to achieve your goal? Go do that thing. (See also *Manifestation of Chaos*.)

June 29 – Get Involved

In some ways, integrating 'community' into your life is essentially combining all five of the Principles of Not together. Community begins with the people that either live with you or immediately around you. As such, you should immediately think "relationships." Even if you do not know these people in your immediate community, you already have relationships with them.

"Who is that?"
"Oh, that's my neighbor."

Or
"Who is that?"
"That's the person that lives down the hall in 302."

You have interconnections with all of these people in your immediate area and these interconnections spread out into larger networks as you pan out from the immediate area. When we talk about integrating community we mean first and foremost, acknowledging these relationships and nurturing them.

Beyond that, you should involve yourself in your community. Learn about its history and understand the rules and regulations that govern the community. Why are they the way they are? Do they work for you? Do you want to change them or abide by them? Do you want to break them?

One way to meet people (relationships) and get involved in your community is by volunteering for various events, board positions, fund raisers, task forces, committees, neighborhood cleanups, etc. Engaging in these kinds of activities keeps you moving, keeps you mentally sharp (fitness), can foster relationships and allows you to put your finger on the pulse of your community.

If you are interested in politics, volunteering is one way to start getting involved. Becoming involved in politics is a way to stay connected to the various levels of community around you and also a way to exert your positive influence on the greater community.

If volunteering and politics are not good alternatives, there are many organizations that have a more narrow focus that might be interesting and will engage the Principles in the ways already described. These kinds of organizations range from religious, gaming, sports related, exercise related, etc.

Are you already involved in your community?

JUNE 30 – RELIGION

If you are religious (whether it be this one or that one), the fifth Principle of Not is where religion falls. Religion offers all of the things mentioned over the last two days with clubs and volunteer organizations but adds a level of camaraderie that goes deeper than just "we all like chess."

Religion also adds a layer that is missing from most other groups in that it addresses the aspect of spirit.

With most religions, you automatically address the third, fourth and fifth Principles (relationships, personal code and community). Did you notice that I did not say that religion addresses the first Principle? That is because most religions – even if not publicly on their social media sites – still sanction killing other people in the name of their god(s). There are many religions to choose from and if you can find one that resonates with you, this can be a great way to continue your ascent into Tree of Not. (See also *Choosing a Religion* and *Becoming Religious*.)

If you are religious, today ask yourself, "How can I commune with my religion today?" Even if it is silent prayer where you are away from other people such that nobody sees you, the intention of actively being religious while considering your community will have the emanating wave power that comes from, or before, the power of manifestation.

July 1 – Jobs and Career

Work, career and jobs are addressed here at the Community level. What you choose to do for money (which is an aspect of your social self) may echo through all four other aspects of your life. As such, even if it seems insignificant to you, it is very significant.

The amount of impact your work has on your self is further amplified by the fact that you spend so much of your life doing it. Most people work a minimum of forty hours a week. Even people who do not work for money often work anyway in some capacity and this work is essentially in trade for room and board or similar.

While engaged in your daily work, with your five senses you are taking in whatever it is that you are surrounded by when you are at work. How is this affecting your emotional state? Your mental state? Therefore, your spirit, physical, etc.

Is this positively contributing to your Life, Fitness, Relationships, Personal Code or Community principles? If it is not, then there is another question that needs to be asked: Is this work negatively impacting your Life, Fitness, Relationships, Personal Code or Community principles?

Of course this all has to be weighed against your goals and objectives. It may be that some pain now is worth it to attain some other thing you are seeking. Often times in life we have to make the choice of whether to pay now or pay later. And despite how much I would love to say that money is a trivial matter when it comes to the spirit-consciousness and the pursuit of truth (because it is), I cannot actually say that because the state of civilization is now such that no matter who or what you are or do, you will have to use money in order to interact in the world.

July 2 – Putting Good Into the World

If you have been paying attention to your surroundings you may look around at the economy and the mass media and find yourself feeling embarrassed or disgusted to be part of it all.

If you feel this way or have felt this way, you are not alone. Many of us have felt this over the last few decades and the general sense when talking to other people about it is that "it is getting worse."

But I have to ask, how can it be getting worse *all the time*? Is it really getting worse and worse and worse every year, every decade and every century? Or is it just changing into something that the people before us were not anticipating?

Yes there is bad in the world. Money seems to be more important to people than integrity and there is a small percentage of ultra-rich that feed off the majority who are poor. There is still too much bigotry, racism, sexism, ignorance, hate and violence and there appears to be no end in sight to any of it.

But there is a universal truth we have already brushed on that is applicable here. The more energy you focus on something, the stronger that thing will become. In other words, if you sit down and make a list of all the terrible things in your life and all the terrible things in the world and then you devote a few minutes a day to concentrating on those things, you will feel worse every day and the world will get worse every day. (No, I was not trying to describe the daily news, but it might be noteworthy that I did.)

The other side of that same coin is that if you consider all the wonderful things in your life and all of the wonderful things in the world and you think about those things every day, you will feel better and the world will become a better place. And it will not become better just for you. It will get better for everyone else too.

This does not mean that you should ignore the horrors of the world, or hide your head in the sand. It just means that you should be very aware of where you are putting your focus and where you are expending your energy every day.

You can still fight for truth, justice and freedom and you can still fight evil and be a good person. You can make a change to yourself and that change can ripple out through your community and when the ripples reach the other shore and come back, the same change you made will ripple back into you and through you, down through the Principles and through the aspects of yourself until the spark that you ignited is then fueled by the wave of energy that it put forth to begin with.

July 3 – You Have Reached the Top!

Thus ends your ascent of the Tree of Not. You have reached the top. Now what?

Like any challenge you surmount in life, you should appreciate your victory. Take a few moments to look around and revel in your accomplishments. Mentally, you might envision yourself comfortably reclined on sturdy branches amidst the foliage. From here, you can look out at the cosmos and enjoy the mystery and the splendor!

When you are ready, you can make the descent in the same way you made the climb. Each step of the way you explore one of the Principles of Not and how those principles intermix in your life.

Today's meditation is about "taking the compliment." Give yourself credit for your accomplishments, feel good about them and then move on to the next challenge.

July 4 – It's Not a Simulation

There is a tendency for people to frame the current and seemingly relevant creation myth in terms that are derived from modern times and current events.

For instance, the movie, *The Matrix (1999)* introduced, to mainstream thought, the idea that we are all living in a simulation. This was not the first time this idea had been introduced, but it was the first time it was introduced to the masses. As a result many people started proposing the notion that this explanation made the most sense to describe our world in terms of where we came from and what we are doing.

It is tempting to allow ourselves to believe that. Looking around at the technology available to us now we can easily envision the advanced technology of the future that would be necessary to generate such a simulation.

Don't believe it. This is not a simulation. In twenty years (or however long from now) a new more advanced technological wonder will be promulgated and this will inspire a new creation myth to explain the origin of humanity and the whys and what-fors of existence. Perhaps it will somehow be related to quantum mechanics or interdimensional theory or maybe something we can't even really imagine right now. Whatever it will be, don't believe that one either.

When you map the subquanta that we are aware of, then scale up to the atomic particles, the atoms themselves, the molecules, the cells, the things around us, the solar system, the galaxy, the universe and the prospect of a multiverse (or more), it should be a little easier to see why we will likely not be able to wrap all that up in a simple story any time soon.

Look around you. This is real.

July 5 – The Great Tapestry of Life

It becomes clearer over time…

Imagine you are standing in front of a large tapestry. The tapestry is twenty feet high and two hundred feet wide. You are standing around the middle, facing it and your eyes are about eight inches away from it. In your field of vision you can see some animals and some trees. Is that what this tapestry is all about? You step back about two feet. Now you see more trees, a body of water and what looks like it might be the edge of a city. You step back about two more feet and realize that the further you back away from this enormous picture, the more of it you can see. From a distance, you can see how the animals and trees actually form a story when viewed with the water and the city.

Life is like that tapestry. There is a massive story being told that goes far beyond your current vision. When you are five, you can only see a small amount of the tapestry. When you are ten, you have moved back a little bit and can see more. When you are twenty, you have moved back a little bit more and you can see more of the story being told by the tapestry.

The further you step back (the older you get) the more you can see of the Great Tapestry, and therefore, the more you understand about some of the smaller parts you had seen when you were younger. Many questions are answered as you see how various scenes in the tapestry interconnect. Of course, seeing more and more of this Great Tapestry also generates new questions. Questions you hadn't thought to ask before.

What do you think the whole picture looks like?

July 6 – The Linear Spiral

You are standing in an open field west of a white house with a boarded up front door. Look down and you see the ground. Look up and you see the sky.

Look back down. Let's start with the ground.

If you could shrink down small enough in size, the blades of grass would tower over you. What had once been small clumps of dirt would seem like hills and mountains.

Shrink down again to an even smaller size and just small sections of the giant dirt clumps become huge conglomerations of cells. There are mineral cells, plant cells, organic matter cells and various bacteria moving around here. This microscopic world is like nothing you have ever seen but it is vast and teeming with life.

Shrink down again to an even smaller size and what you had seen as cellular life now becomes conglomerations of various molecules. These molecules are massive structures made of atoms from differing elements and they are bound together with unseen forces. The vastness of this molecular-scape is somewhat overwhelming. As far as the eye can see are these massive molecular structures all seeming to move to some unheard orchestra.

Shrink down again to an even smaller size and what you had seen as molecules are now individual atoms. You are somehow just floating in this space and the vastness of the space around you now is inconceivable. There in the distance you see a large object. Something zings by you as you approach the object. What whizzed by you was one of nineteen electrons that are orbiting the large object which you are approaching. As you get closer, you can see that the large object (now appearing to be as big as a ten story building) is a grouping of nineteen protons and twenty neutrons but they are all enormous in size. You realize that this massive structure of subatomic particles is the nucleus of a single potassium atom.

As you approach one of the protons, you shrink down again to an even smaller size. Shrinking in size as you enter this single proton, you see that this single proton is actually a really large construct comprised of smaller particles which seem to be moving around in some interactive dance. You realize that these smaller things that make up the proton are called "quanta."

You continue to shrink in size as you approach one of these quantum particles. The quantum particle you are approaching is an up-quark. You continue to shrink as you get closer to it and it now appears to be massive in size. You realize that you can enter the up-quark.

As you enter the up-quark you see that it is actually comprised of multiple filaments of energy. These filaments of energy are called superstrings and they are all vibrating in such a way that you can kind of see how the up-quark must exist based on the vibrations coming from these energy strings.

In this journey, we are going to stop getting small here before we try to enter a superstring. But before we go on, I do have to point out that the probability that a superstring is comprised of some smaller thing(s) or energies of some kind is exceedingly high. In fact, it is likely that there really is no such thing as "an elementary particle." In other words, there is no such thing as "the smallest thing in the universe."

Let's go back to the open field next to the white house with the boarded up front door. Now that you have looked down into the ground, you turn your attention to the sky. You can see the moon far above, reflecting a crescent of light into your eyes. And there, close to the horizon is the sun.

In order to see the Earth, the moon and the sun all at one time, you have to fly out into space. For the sake of conversation, let's say you can do that. Once you get far enough away to see the Earth, the moon and the sun, you realize that you would like to see our entire solar system from a distance. In order to see the entire solar system in your field of view, including everything within the sun's influence (E.g. the Oort cloud), you have to fly away from the sun for about three light years. From here, the sun looks like a large star among all the other stars. You had to travel for three years at the speed of light to get here and you still have not even come close to another sun. But there are billions of other suns. Hundreds of billions. And that number is only counting the suns that exist in our galaxy. And there are billions of galaxies like ours. Actually, hundreds of billions. So you keep flying – you keep zooming out.

As you get further and further away from our sun, you pass hundreds of billions of other suns and then you finally leave our galaxy. Seeing our galaxy from a distance, you can see that there are hundreds of billions of suns in the Milky Way, all spinning around at varying speeds as the whole massive spiral galaxy rotates and moves through space. Looking around you, you see that unfathomable distances away from you are other galaxies. You decide you want to see what they all look like from a distance, so you continue to fly away from them.

As you get further and further out, you see that thousands of galaxies seem to be clustered together in a galactic cluster. From here you can see that there are other galactic clusters far away. In order to behold all of these clusters, you continue to fly out and away so you can get a bird's eye view of it all.

Once you have flown far enough you behold that these clusters of galaxies actually form larger structures called superclusters. Each supercluster of galactic clusters seems to contain hundreds or thousands of galactic clusters within. As you continue to fly out you see how all of these superclusters form what humanity now calls "the observable universe." Let's stop here. But not because this is the end.

For the same reason we stopped zooming into superstrings, we are going to stop zooming out of the universe. Not because there is nowhere else to go, but because I don't think we could ever stop zooming out. The likelihood of reaching a point where one could "see it all" seems low. Just like there is probably no elementary particle, there is also probably no boundary in which "all is contained."

Existence, as we can comprehend it today, can be imagined as a continuum which exists on something akin to a linear spiral. The linearity is measured from small to large (or large to small depending on which side you wish to start from). And the spiral is the circular nature of the beginning wrapping around to the end which yields a new beginning, etc. From any vantage point along the spiral, the widening or narrowing of the spiral appears to go off to infinity in both the "big" and "little" directions.

You are standing in an open field west of a white house with a boarded up front door. The spiral widens above you into infinity and narrows below you into infinity.

The infinitude of possibilities stretching out in every direction truly blows my mind. Any one small section of what I just described is fascinating, amazing and awesome all by itself. But when taken together it is truly humbling. While it is sometimes frustrating, disturbing and even terrifying, I am nonetheless sincerely grateful to be one of the people who is mystified by the world around him. Perhaps this is greedy, but despite my deep and sincere gratitude, I still wish I could see more.

Today's meditation is to contemplate the linear spiral.

July 7 – The Spark

It is fascinating that consciousness can seem like a tiny spark of sentience almost completely imperceptible in an infinite universe but it can also seem like a boundless energy that permeates all of existence. And it can seem like anything in between. And as a guilty admission, I must admit that I love that neither the religions of the world nor the new religion of modern science can explain it.

That tiny spark of sentience is the spirit-consciousness. It is the awareness of being aware. That spark is what makes us different from a lump of dead flesh. It also makes us more than just an automaton.

The automaton part of us can drive cars and read books and even carry on phone conversations, all with no consciousness whatsoever. But even though the spark animates us, this spark of consciousness is not what makes us smart. It does not even care about that kind of label. In fact, it is not smart. You can sense that when communing with it or in dream states. But - and this is important to note - it is not dumb and it is not ignorant either. How can something be not smart, not dumb and not ignorant?

I don't want to use this word but I truly cannot find a better word to describe it: the spark is "divine" in nature. I want to stress that "divine" is the best word I can find to explain this but I also use the word almost exclusively for the reason that I want to remain within the framework of the current collective conscious imperative of my age. The word I am looking for would be like "divine" but without the baggage of "divinity."

How does your spirit-consciousness seem today? Are you a spark or a universe today? Or something in between?

July 8 – The Glimmer

Today, let us consider the possibilities that accompany a glimmer of consciousness.

Yesterday we considered the spirit-consciousness as the spark of animation that makes us the unique individuals that we are. But it seems "the spark" may actually exist in a greater "pool" of other sparks. The other sparks being those which belong to other people. Because of the pool analogy, "a glimmer" might be a better visual than a "spark," but the net-net is the same in that it seems like a tiny part of something larger. But even that is wrong because "tiny" would seem to diminish it and it cannot be diminished. The other reason a "glimmer" might be more appropriate is that the spirit-consciousness sometimes seems like a reflection of light caught out of the corner of one's eye. A quick flash and then it is gone. Elusive and temporal. And only possible when the water of spirit is present? This is an example of moments where one suddenly becomes completely present – existing only in the here and now. And then becomes aware of the fact that they are existing in the moment and loses the feeling immediately due to the sudden awareness of it. It is as if one experienced a glimmer of truth.

The moments in our lives that we stop autonomous action and become aware of our consciousness are the moments the glimmer makes contact with our minds. Or our minds make contact with the glimmer.

Consider the possibility that the spark/glimmer is actually the 'eternal you' which temporarily makes contact with the temporal you. And the pool from which the glimmer originates(?) is all of us who have ever been, who currently are and who ever will be. Our ego selves (our mind-selves) are not reincarnated per se, but the spark that we belong to – or that temporarily belongs to us – is immortal – timeless – and this aspect of us may be reincarnated. The immortal nature of the glimmer is why we have flashes of past lives, future lives, other's lives, etc. This is also why so much strangeness is introduced to our minds through dreams.

The pool is beyond time and contains all of the glimmers or sparks that ever were, are or will be. And "the pool" is not intelligent in the way we are but it contains all knowledge. Or another way of describing it is to say that it contains no ignorance.

The pool is beyond "intelligence."

To coin a phrase from my wife, April, comparing our *minds* to our *consciousness* is like comparing apples to ducks. They are completely different things. Both are needed to make us who we are but they have different origins and they have different ... purposes. (I wanted to use the word "agendas" but I also don't want to use that word.) The glimmer does not appear to have an agenda. Perhaps, however, it has a purpose?

I cannot discern if that purpose "belongs" to *it* or if it is a greater purpose that the glimmer is only a part of. Perhaps the mind is of this dimension but the glimmer is from a different dimension and the experience of being a conscious being is the experience of this interdimensional connection.

It is magical. It is mystical. It is incredible. It is phenomenal. It is everything that makes life wondrous and spectacular.

July 9 – You are an Energy Being

Many religions, metaphysicians, mystics, magical societies and new age movements talk about how we are "beings of energy." The energy they describe is usually metaphysical in nature and elusive to the tools of science.

However, all metaphysical pondering aside, if you could see yourself right now using different eyes – eyes that could only see energy – you would see that you are a network of electricity buzzing and snapping in an energy cloud that more or less adheres to the shape of your brain and major internal organs. The energy I am describing is the synapse within and between the brain and other internal organs. It is happening all the time throughout your body. In this sense, you are literally an energy being in a fleshy body.

Today, meditate on the fact that regardless of your belief in god(s) or science, or your lack of belief in god(s) or science, none can deny that you are an energy being which exists within a fleshy body.

July 10 – We are All Connected

Yesterday we meditated on the fact that we are energy beings which exist within bodies of flesh and bone.

The energy that exists within us is real, measurable and emanates outside of our physical bodies.

If you could adjust your vision to see only the energy, you would see that you truly are a small star shining in the black of the cosmos. You are a brightly burning, dazzling display of electrical activity zapping and crackling like a floating mass of pure energy. That is you. And me. And each one of us. "The black" we are floating in is actually lit up by the brilliant accompaniment of the billions of other shining stars which are the other people on this planet.

Again, using only your energy vision, from a distance, this planet would appear as a shining star itself. But on top of that, you would also be able to see that the energy sphere that is the earth's energy is *itself* covered in a mass network of tiny little shining electrical networks of energy (us people) all interwoven with each other and the planet.

Pan out further and you would see that the sun itself is the ultimate expression of this shining star in the black. And you would also see that the massive energy sphere that is the sun is interconnected with the smaller energy spheres that are the planets and the sun and the planets are also connected through lines of energy to each of the tiny networks of energy which are the people on this planet. (See also *Everything is Connected*.)

July 11 – Manifestation of Chaos

You cannot just sit there and do nothing. I mean that literally. I mean that as an energy being if you just sit there and be, you are still emanating energy. The synapse does not stop.

The energy that emanates out from you is tied in with the network of all energy everywhere and as mentioned previously, this massive network of energy connects all living things as well as things most people do not really think of as living (like stars and planets, etc.). Even rocks and dirt have filaments of energy running through them (E.g. warm, light, active presence).

It is through this energy interconnect that we can use thought to manifest changes in physical reality.

But what if we do not practice this mindful and intentional manifestation?

Whether we intend to manifest reality or not, our energy ripples out from us trying to change the universe into how we want it to be. And for most of us, how we want the universe to be is an ever-changing picture.

In the morning, I might have a thought about my job and how I want to change some aspect of it. Energy that can be used to change my job situation will thus emanate out from my being into the universe. But within minutes I might have another thought about one of my hobbies or the fact that I don't have any hobbies. Again, energy of change ripples out from my being into the universe in an attempt to make changes. A few minutes later I might consider a relationship that needs to be repaired and ripples of energy spread out into the universe to begin the repair. What I am describing here is manifestation, but it is the manifestation of chaos.

In all of the above examples, only a few ripples of energy for each of these major life changes have flowed out into the universe but in order to affect ordered change in the world around us, mindful and intentional direction of our energy is required, usually over an extended period of time. (Which is why you can't just close your eyes and wish for a pot of gold to appear before you.)

The manifestation of chaos is not necessarily a bad thing. It just is. If you are all over the place with your thoughts and desires, the energy you emanate into the universe will be all over the place.

Will you get tangible results? Maybe. But if you do, you cannot anticipate what those results will look like because the energies that went into the manifestation of those results were all kinds of different energy emanations jumbled together and reflecting back and forth off of each other and you and all the other energy sources all around you.

Chaos is one of the reasons bad things happen to good people and good things happen to bad people. Chaos is "anything goes." We are all well versed in dealing with it, but it is not necessarily the best approach to a directed life.

Today's meditation is to consider the centering-alignment of our personal energy so that we can manifest intentional change around us as opposed to the chaotic and unpredictable change that comes from undirected manifestation.

July 12 – Reigning in the Chaos

Yesterday we talked about the manifestation of chaos. Another term for this might be "accidental manifestation due to lack of mindful intention."

Today let us consider an approach to reigning in the chaos through mindful and intentional manifestation.

For our example, we will start with something small. I would like a new couch in my study but it is going to cost about $1,000 and I'm going to have to figure out what to do with the old couch.

What I would like to make manifest in my reality is the new couch as well as the relocation of the old couch with little or no cost to me.

This can be done with mindful and intentional mediation. Thought. Mind over matter.

First, I write the following sentence on a piece of paper and hang it by the bathroom mirror: "I have a new couch and the old couch found a wonderful new home."

At least twice a day, I read this sentence out loud. At other times during the day, if something reminds me of this desire, I think the sentence "aloud" in my mind: *I have a new couch and the old couch found a wonderful new home.*

It may be days, or maybe even weeks (since I did not really specify a timeframe), but the logistics necessary for me to acquire the new couch and find a good home for the old couch will manifest as result of this mindful practice. It really is just that easy. For instance, it may be that someone with a smaller couch offered to trade me. You never know what the universe is going to come up with to solve your problems.

The big difference between yesterday and today is that in yesterday's paradigm I might think, "I want a new couch," and then move on to some other thought. For instance, I might then think, "I also want a new computer… A new car would be really great. I wonder if I should upgrade my phone?"

This is sending out pulses of desire to the world around you and will generate some kind of response but because these pulses do not stay for very long, there is not enough time for the world to begin to comply with your energetic desires.

Change desire into design. What we are talking about today is creating a design for the universe to follow and then emanating the energy necessary for the universe to comply with this new design.

It is an emanation followed by reinforced flow. Almost like opening a conduit of energy from you into the universe where the energy can be reworked in the act of creation to comply with the design you laid out in advance.

You have to have a plan. Even if it is a tiny plan, you must have a framework which you envision for the manifestation to "adhere to."

What do you want made manifest in your life?

July 13 – Life, the Disease

There is an angle on Not that we have not yet discussed. It is the inversion of how we think. It is basically turning Life upside down and looking at it backwards. (Hopefully.)

It is the idea that Life (and therefore life) is actually a disease which is infecting the purity of Not.

Imagine, if you will, the vast cold, dark, static empty expanse of Not. Imagine that this cold, dark, silent emptiness is absolute perfection. After all, it cannot get colder, darker, more static or emptier than it already is.

And somewhere in this absolute purity, somehow, there appears a blemish. It is an infection. It is a particle of warm, light, active presence. What was once beautiful perfection is now eternally tainted. Then the particle of infection begins to multiply and spread, like a virus, infecting Not with warm, light, active presence everywhere. Over time (or perhaps almost instantly) the infection spreads so far that one cannot even find the purity of Not anywhere. Now all there is, anywhere one looks, is this infected putrescence called Life.

What if we, Life and life, are the disease? That's a horrible thought, isn't it? To imagine that *we* are the disease and that just by virtue of existing, we are destroying something beautiful and perfect?

But is it really that bad? Does the virus which kills life think of itself as an evil killer? Does the horrific cancer that ravages people think of itself as a terrible evil? What if we are like that?

I was horrified by this idea when I first considered it, but over time I began to realize that first of all, I don't believe it to be true, but that second, ultimately it does not matter if it is true or not. Because even if you make the case to me that Life is an infection in Not – that Life (you, me, us) is essentially a cancer that is causing the sickness and death of the only thing that is truly pure – even then, I have to band with my fellow "cancer cells" and exclaim, "We should be the best infectious disease we can be!" Why? Because what we have here, whether it is beautiful Life or what someone else might call infectious disease, is magical, amazing and truly awesome. To *be* is a phenomenal experience. Lucid reality is a transcendental experience. So no matter what it is, it is worth the effort and it is worth fighting for. We should be the best *us* we can be.

No matter what other evidence you present to the contrary, to me Life is warmth, light, active and ever-present! Life is precious, delicious and good. Life is better than Not.

Be what you are, regardless of *"what you are"* actually is. Be warm, light, active presence!

July 14 – Paradigms of Truth

There are countless systems of belief (and/or thought) which assert themselves as having the answers to the most fundamental questions of life. As one searches for the answers, one might find a system of belief, a religion, ideology or philosophy that resonates as "true." What a great feeling it is to find "the truth!" It can be a relief and it can make one feel like they have found a home.

However, over time, immersion into this paradigm of thought (belief or action) may ultimately reveal that while there are elements that resonate as true and "right," there are other elements of this religion, philosophy, etc. that seem wrong. Parts of the religion, philosophy, group, etc. seem to be in error or incongruent, or at least "do not feel right."

As humans, we are all searching for truth, meaning, purpose and ultimately for authorization. We are trying to find ourselves. We are trying to find our path. We are trying to see the big picture.

But the full explanation describing the big picture of "what is going on here" cannot be seen by us. If it could be, what you would see would be equivalent to a grand unified theory of everything. This is not to be confused with the grand unified theory of everything that scientists have sought and continue to seek. That theory, they might find. The grand unified theory of everything we are talking about here would be even more all-encompassing in that it would unify all religions, all sciences, all philosophies, all ideologies and every single possible theory and explanation for the purpose of existence that each individual has ever dreamt into a unified paradigm of thought. We call this the "all-truth" but we do not believe that such a thing actually exists.

But what about all the truth we have seen in some of the religions, philosophies and ideologies that we have so far been exposed to? Why is it that parts of one religion, philosophy or ideology make complete sense feel completely true and right but other parts fail us? We must regard the myriad paradigms that *do* make sense (even if only partially); those that in some way resonate with us deeply. We cannot ignore truth when we find it.

The reason that each of these paradigms that seem to ring so true affect us so deeply is because each one of them is partially correct. You could say that each one of these paradigms that rings true for you is a "splinter of truth." It is as if there were a grand unified paradigm of all-truth and we, as humans, have only just begun to see some tiny splinters of the entire phenomenon. For a more modern analogy, imagine that each of the paradigms you encounter that ring true are a single pixel and that when all the pixels are put together and seen from a distance the image that forms is that of the grand unified all-truth. (See also *Splinters of Truth* and *The All-Truth*.)

Today's meditation is to consider a truth you have added to your personal belief system.

JULY 15 – PURSUING THE TRUTHS

Yesterday we talked about paradigms of thought or belief that one might stumble on in their journey which they find to ring true.

Today we are going to drill down a little further into this idea and call out some examples.

A young man was walking down a sidewalk one afternoon and noticed a beautiful rainbow in the distance. He stopped and stared for a few seconds, marveling at how the colors of red, orange, yellow, green, blue, indigo and violet all transitioned from one to the other in an infinitude of gradients.

A few minutes later, he was looking something up on his phone and a web search brought up "the chakras." As he was reading about the chakras he suddenly made the connection that the chakras, from base to crown are the colors of the rainbow. This epiphany led him to dig further into the chakras and he felt a deep sense of truth in everything he learned.

For this young man, "the chakras" became *a splinter of truth*.

In fact, he was so moved by his discovery that he began researching the origins of the chakras and this led him to the Vedas. As he dug deeper into the Vedas, he was ultimately led to Hinduism. But for this young man, this is where the deep resonance of truth began to feel tainted. He did not like some of the ancient teachings of Hinduism and did not feel a resonance of truth when he studied the religion.

In the above example, the man found a splinter of truth in the ideology of the chakras and most everything that went with that ideology. Does this young man need to convert to Hinduism to accept what he feels is a deeper truth surrounding the chakras? Does he need to learn to read Sanskrit and start an in-depth study of the Vedas?

No, he does not. He can accept the truth he feels surrounding the chakras and integrate that truth into his existing belief system.

The same thing applies to any other truth one might stumble upon.

There are countless splinters of truth we can find spread throughout all of the world religions, the new age movement, paganism, atheism and even humanistic non-religious movements such as Satanism.

Wrapped up with these splinters of truth are bundles of "non-truths." (Note that a "non-truth" here is defined as some belief or practice that an individual does not feel resonates as a personal truth.) One might be drawn to Satanism but repulsed by the idea of worshipping a being such as Satan. (Especially when the Satanists explain that they do not even believe there is such a being). One might be drawn to Islam, Judaism or Christianity, but be repulsed by the idea of a "divine being" that would ask Abraham to murder his son.

Thus Authorism encourages individuals to actively and intentionally create their own belief systems comprised exclusively of the splinters of truth they can find wherever they can find them.

July 16 – Unifying the Paradigms

Yesterday had us consider a paradigm that we felt was so true that it had become a part of our belief system. Today, we consider how to move forward when all we have are these disparate paradigms (E.g. "splinters of truth") to work with.

If there is no way for a us to see the grand unified all-truth, how then do we proceed through this chaos of conflicting paradigms of thought, belief and action? Do we try to find the least offensive religion / paradigm / ideology / philosophy and just make the decision that this one is true? Do we just find the lessor of multiple evils and commit to it?

Finding the least offensive path and committing to it is not a terrible thing to do. One advantage to taking this path is that, for better or for worse, you can stop thinking about it. You no longer have to concern yourself with the perils of the journey to the center of the self. By choosing an existing path, you can change your focus to other things like sports, career or just enjoying your life! When someone asks you what you believe you can just tell them, "I'm a [_____]" (fill in the blank). That will generally make them go away so you can get on with your day.

But for those of us who cannot accept the uneasy feelings of wrongness associated with the existing institutions, there will still be a nagging that comes from deep within. There will be the disturbing after-feel of the unanswered questions or the parts that one feels are just plain wrong coming from the soul, which says, "Something about this just isn't quite right."

In that case, do we instead decide on *nothing* by refusing to choose from undesirable alternatives? By choosing nothing, one cannot reap the rewards that come from the good parts of the things we are rejecting. This can be especially frustrating for the seeker who needs guidance through spiritual or ethical dilemmas.

Here, one is caught between a rock and hard place. I want to join because part of what is being taught feels so right, but I cannot allow myself to join because part of what is being taught just feels so wrong.

What ends up happening is that whether or not people are aware of it, each person creates their own paradigm (a grouping of various splinters of truth they have collected) which encompasses the truths they have gleaned from their religion, science, ideology, philosophy, etc. They may lean heavily on existing paradigms but everyone augments some base paradigm with their own nuanced understandings. Over time, the person refines the splinters of truth into a working system of belief that can guide them in times of need.

Until the work of creating our own belief system is completed, trying to exist within the framework of someone else's can be an unfulfilling and disappointing undertaking. It is also a time of vulnerability. When one first accepts someone else's belief system as their own, they must work within the new alien framework even if it feels spiritually, mentally or emotionally uncomfortable.

How was your belief system constructed? Is it something that formed organically over time? Is it something you put together yourself? Or is it an existing system of belief that was handed down to you? Does it feel completely right and true or are there parts you think should be changed?

July 17 – Inconcussa Fundamenta

Sometimes something (usually external) can come along and shatter one's system of belief. The splinters scatter and one is forced to start all over again rebuilding a new structure of belief – hopefully stronger than the one that shattered.

How do we fortify ourselves such that we can withstand the stress and trauma of finding out that some of our beliefs were completely wrong?

This is where the term inconcussa fundamenta comes into play. Inconcussa fundamenta means "unshakeable foundation." The paradigms we build for ourselves help us find answers to questions of meaning, purpose, and belonging and also provide the external authorization we seek (through internal authorization). As a side note, if one is unable to come to terms with acting on self-authorization, the authorization may be set up in a kind of loopback system where one creates the authorization, then sends it forth to loop back and become the "external authorization" one is seeking. (See also, *Authorization Loopback*.)

For Authorists, our belief system in essence gives us permission to feel how we feel, to think how we think and to believe how we believe without having to make excuses or explain ourselves to someone else. It means validation that we are not an abomination *to* nature but rather very much a part *of* nature. We are meant to be. We belong to the universe and we have a right to be here.

This does not mean that Authorists are given free rein to go about the land wreaking havoc with no consequences. Morality, goodness, the search for truth, personal code and the law of the land still guide our actions.

What it does mean is that we can step forward, proud to be human beings and know that the ultimate authority in what we are has not only given us permission to *be*, but has also given us a mandate to be the human beings we were born to be. You want to be you. And, thou art that.

Our belief system should be built upon an unshakeable foundation. In fact, we call this "our foundation of belief" and once it has been constructed, nothing can destroy it.

We encourage our members to only build a structure of belief after they have established an unshakeable foundation of belief. For the structure that follows one can then construct a personal code to use in moving about life and interacting with others. Authorization for action comes from your personal code, your belief structure and of course from your foundation of belief. (See also *Codice Personalum*.)

July 18 – Proof of Manifestation

Today's meditation is on the proof that manifestation of reality through thought is absolutely real and that it is happening all around us and has been happening since before humanity learned to write.

I am going to foreshadow the conclusion by asking the question, "Is the power of religion real and manifest in this world?"

If you have skimmed over any synopsis of World History, you cannot deny that the power of religion is not only real but has been *the driving force* in shaping human civilization.

Bear with me as we diverge a moment. Do you think the gods, Marduk, Zeus, Ba'al, Odin or Ra are real entities that exist somewhere and have a vested interest in the activities of humans here on Earth?

Most modern readers will respond with something along the lines of, "Of course not. Those are all ancient gods of myth and legend. Everyone knows that those gods are not real!"

Good answer.

What about Jesus, Allah, Krishna, Ahura Mazda or Buddha? Are those real entities that exist somewhere and have a vested interest in the activities of humans here on Earth?

The answer to that question will not come so fast or so definitive. There are people who believe in some of those gods today. Billions of people.

I am not going to try to convince you that any of those gods exist. Nor am I going to try to convince you that any of those gods do not exist. Instead, I am going to draw your attention to that which has been made manifest in our world due to *the power of the belief* in those gods.

The foundation, the structure and the infrastructure of modern human civilization was all built from a religious base. Billions of humans believe in some god or gods.

They believe it so strongly that there are billions of humans who are willing to kill other humans because of the power of their belief. And likewise, there are billions of humans who are willing to die because of the power of their belief.

Any given god of any given religion can be denied, but the power of religion cannot be denied.

Before you argue that it was a god that did it all as opposed to just people believing in a god, I would have to ask you to specify which god it was. Was it Allah? Ahura-Mazda? Jesus? We cannot all agree as to which god it was, can we? But none of us can deny the power of belief.

The power of religion *is* the power of that belief. That which has been made manifest in this world due to the power of religion *is* that which has been made manifest in this world through the power of belief. And belief is thought.

Manifestation of changes in the reality around us are made through thought. The belief in creation causes creation.

July 19 – The Mistake of Atheism

The mistake of atheism is the assertion of a half-truth. The atheist is correct in the assertion that there is not a giant man in space holding the puppet strings who stamps his feet in anger when we are naughty and gives us rewards when we are good. But the atheist is incorrect in their assertion that "god does not exist."

Gods do not exist. But the power of the gods is real.

As we discussed yesterday, through religion, the idea of gods have been a driving form of governance since the dawn of civilization. Is there a giant man in space that is pulling all the strings? No, of course not. That is obvious by looking at the history of mankind and the fact that the faces of the gods change throughout the centuries.

Is there a power called "God?" Yes, absolutely. This is the power of manifesting reality through thought. The more strongly you believe in something, the more real it will become for you.

July 20 – Born Pagan

What if you were born and raised in a Viking community in 1200 CE? The Christians would have called you a pagan. (And they would have wanted to kill you because of it.)

What if you were born and raised in a Christian community in 1200 CE? The pagans would called you a Christian. (And they would have wanted to kill you because of it.)

Are you a Muslim? If so, is it because you were born into Islam? Are you a Christian? If so, is it because you were born into Christianity?

Atheist? Did you convert to atheism or were you born into it and raised that way?

Considering the above questions, how can we seriously consider a single religion or ideology to be "the right one?" Or, stated a different way, how can we say that any one single religion or ideology is wrong?

If you find yourself disgusted with some other religion or ideology, ask yourself how you would think differently if you had been born into it instead whatever you believe now.

We are the product of our upbringing and the path we walked alone after we left the nest. We are here because of the path that we have walked to get here. We can choose which direction we wish to go but changing our direction forward does not change the fact that whatever has happened in our past has led to us to where we are today.

July 21 – The One True God

If you are searching for a god, there is really only one god for humans worth acknowledging. And I say "acknowledging" instead of "worshipping" because like any god worth their salt, this god does not need your worship but gives you abundance and life anyway. It is wise to fear this god, but on the other hand none can incite this god to anger and violence.

This god is an everlasting source of energy, power, abundance and light! This god sends out radiant life-sustaining energy and asks for nothing in return. Nothing known to humankind is more powerful than this god.

You can experience the majestic power of this god every day but you cannot look upon the face of this god. To look upon the face of this god would blind you. You cannot approach this god, either. This god is so powerful that even to come within a few miles of this god would instantly vaporize you.

This god is the source of all life that you have ever known or heard of, all life that is and all life that will ever be here on this planet. Without this god, life as we know it would perish.

This god is the only god that can be proven to exist. It is the first god. This god truly is the Supreme Being. All other gods have been patterned from this one most powerful Supreme Being that we, as mortal humans can barely even conceive.

Our ancestors knew all of this and hoped to gain favor by worshipping this god. What they did not know is that this god is beyond our comprehension. Our worship is not desired and certainly not required.

Of course, I am describing the sun. (See also *Day and Night*.)

July 22 – Original Innocence

The Authorian doctrine of Original Innocence states simply that human beings are born as innocent little babies.

As an innocent little baby, you had no malevolent schemes and you were not predisposed to being evil or creating evil in the world around you.

In fact, for the first few weeks of your life, your spirit-consciousness was operating in a stupor as it attempted to comprehend the new body and world it found itself existing in.

At this stage in your life, you were completely innocent.

As you grew, you began to learn the ways of those around you. Your teachers were everything around you including your parents, guardians, peers and your immediate community. You were also instructed by society as absorbed through print media, signage and the streaming broadcast of the Internet.

I hope this does not shock you too much, but today, you are no longer innocent. Innocence is lost as we move through life making choices that affect the lives of those around us. I am talking about morality.

If you consider an action and anticipate that performing that action might cause harm to someone else but be beneficial to you and then you do it anyway, you have lost some of that innocence (and probably picked up some guilt).

Does this make you evil? Well, of course it does, but only because evil is defined loosely as "acting with intention in a way that you know will cause harm to someone else." But that doesn't mean you are not good.

No child comes into adulthood without having acted selfishly at some point. No child reaches adulthood without having made a choice that brought benefit to themselves with either no regard for the feelings of another person (or animal).

This process is called "growing up" and it is during the process of growing up that we lose our innocence.

Can we get back to that point in our lives when we were completely innocent?

Yes and no.

In the overarching story of who we are we can never become innocent again. We have learned too much about the world.

But in silent moments of now, we can certainly reconnect with that original innocence. During moments of meditation or contemplation such as these we can smile at the purity of that original innocence and imagine the bliss of such being.

But do not pretend to imagine that living in a prolonged state of innocence would be a good thing. It might be fun for you but it would be a disaster for society at large.

The bliss of one being can often be at the detriment of another. (See also *The Detriment of Here and Now*.)

Regardless of how we were born, today we get to choose our actions. We can always choose what we consider to be good over what we consider to be evil. As authors of our own lives we are constantly creating ourselves.

July 23 – The Detriment of Here and Now

Have you ever seen the advice "Be here, now." Or "Live in the moment." Or, "Be present."

Stay present. Stay in the moment. Live for today. Be in the present moment. Etc.

This is great advice for experiencing moments of bliss but not realistic advice for living your life.

Experiencing moments of now is a wonderful thing. And trying to stay in such a moment as long as you can is an experience of bliss. Being in a moment of now is a transcendental state that many seekers attempt to achieve. But we aren't allowed to stay there. And despite the loss of bliss, that is a good thing.

The reason a moment of now contains such bliss is that there is no tomorrow and there is no yesterday in a moment of now. It is a state of pure being. It is a transition from *mind* to *spirit-consciousness*. But this also means, literally, it is a *loss of the mind*.

Imagine your conscious state during a dream.

You are in a jet flying over an ocean. You step into the tiny bathroom on the jet and have to duck under the torch light that someone is holding to light up the cave that opens up before you. As you and your friend (who looks more like your brother (even though you don't have a brother)) carefully move through the cave you hear some trickling water.

Such is the way of dreams. As you experience a weird dream, your spirit-consciousness just rolls with it doesn't it? From one bizarre scene to the next, your conscious state just says, "Oh, I guess this is where we are now," and keeps moving forward. This is because your spirit-consciousness always exists in the moment. Your spirit-consciousness is only here and now. Your spirit-consciousness does not have a yesterday or a tomorrow to worry about.

If you were to achieve a state of being here and now and *only* here and now, there would be no tomorrow and no yesterday. Only today. Only the present moment of *now*. For humans, this would equate to a degree of savagery. With no thought about tomorrow, there would be no need to consider the consequences of any of our actions. Indeed, you would not have the ability to consider the consequences. You could (and would) only do whatever you desired at any given moment.

And with no recall of yesterday, you would have no memory of the past to guide your present actions. Stick your hand in a fire? Sure, why not!? Step off a cliff? Ah, falling through the air is exhilarating!

With no past to guide us and no future for us to plan for, living only in the moment is complete folly.

Perhaps what many of these teachers and guides are trying to say is not to "*only* be in the present," but rather to "be present *while* you remember yesterday, navigate today and plan for tomorrow."

Today, tune into your awareness of your awareness. One of those awarenesses knows about yesterday and tomorrow. The other awareness only knows about now.

July 24 – Presence for Past and Future

Yesterday we talked about how bad for civilization it would be if everyone just stayed present all the time. For the sake of conversation, we were taking the advice of "live in the moment," to the extreme.

While living in the moment all the time is not an option (for several reasons), I nonetheless cannot deny the soundness of the advice to "live in the moment." As also mentioned yesterday, living in a moment of now is experiencing a moment of pure bliss.

The other side of the "live in the moment," coin is living in the past and/or worrying about the future. In fact, the main purpose of the advice to "live for today," is to get a person to stop worrying about the past or the future. Live for today means to just be content with the here and now.

Now you see the predicament: how do we disregard the past, enjoy the present, and not worry about the future while simultaneously remembering the past (to avoid making mistakes in the present) and planning for the future? That's five very different things, all at once.

The solution lies in the interpretation of "live for today." You cannot disregard the past or the future. You must learn from your mistakes (regard for the past) and you must plan for tomorrow (regard for the future). But you can still do both of those things while living for the moment.

Living for today (or living in the moment) can be accomplished by intentionally tuning into the moment periodically throughout your day. Each person will need to find an approach that suits them, but essentially this means checking in occasionally while you are going about your daily life.

For example, while running water in the sink, you might allow yourself to be aware of the moment. See the water. Hear it. Smell. Feel whatever you are feeling. And most important, perhaps, cast your awareness toward your mental activity to get a glimpse into what you are thinking.

Remember that thought, just like action, is often autonomous. The brain and mind engage in thought constantly without being prompted to do so from the spirit-consciousness. What were you thinking? Why were you thinking that? Would you rather be thinking something else?

Maybe you can set an alarm to remind you to do this today. Another approach is to write a message to yourself and post it somewhere where you will occasionally see it. The message can say, "Be present." Or "check into the moment."

Checking in on what you are presently tasting, feeling, smelling, hearing, seeing and thinking is excellent practice in experiencing the here and now. You do not need to worry about living in the here and now for very long. Usually the moment you realize you are in the present is the exact moment you lose it. But experiencing just one moment of presence is definitely worth the price of admission.

July 25 – A Measure of Health : Balance

There is a fantastic quote by Krishnamurti: "It is no measure of health to be well adjusted to a profoundly sick society."

While I cannot deny the wisdom in such words, I still must also highlight the converse.

It is no measure of happiness to *not* be well adjusted to a profoundly sick society. Stated more simply, withdrawal from a profoundly sick society does not necessarily make one happy.

First of all, is our society profoundly sick? Of course this depends upon your perspective. If you look for sickness, you will find it. If you look for well-being you will find it.

For the sake of conversation, however, I will agree that our society is sick. Further, I would argue that our sickness is predicated on the collective conscious agreement to acknowledge an erroneous paradigm. In other words, we are all pretending that we're okay with how things are progressing because nobody is willing to rock the boat. More to the point, I am referring to the need for fabricated scarcity in a world with an abundance of resources. The status quo needs scarcity in order to remain the status quo. But there is plenty for everyone here. Yes, this alone is enough to drive one mad.

But without going down the rabbit hole of macroeconomics, I am going to get back to the point. Rebelling against the status quo and railing against the machine might be the opposite of being well-adjusted to this sick society we live in, but that kind of lifestyle and mentality does not bring peace of mind and contentment.

I am not saying that you should *not* rage against the machine. But I am saying that you should not put all of your eggs in that basket. Remaining completely opposed to everything is not a way to find peace and harmony in your life. In other words, you are going to have to run to the post office and mail in your tax return and pay your utility bill in between your machine-raging episodes.

The point I am trying to make is that finding some kind of balance is the ultimate objective. So while you rebel against this or that particular institution and you support this or that cause as a noble way to unite humanity and advance our civilization, bear in mind that you must also be a part of your community and a part of this society. It is a challenge, isn't it?

Not unlike yesterday's discussion on acknowledging the past but not living there, bringing in moments of presence in your *today*, and planning for the future but not fearing it. Bottom line? Balance.

The same is true in finding your place in this crazy society we live in where well-being and insanity are constantly tugging you in different directions.

Balance.

July 26 – Chaos and Order

Could we point our finger at the universe and accuse it of being chaos? I think we have to answer yes even though beneath every scene of chaos we behold there seems to be an underlying order which "governs it."

A flock of birds seems to create a chaotic pattern in the sky until you realize that the birds are moving based on the Earth's magnetism or thermals or a combination of both. There is underlying order to their apparent chaotic movement.

A hurricane sweeps across the ocean then into the shoreline causing horrific damage. This carnage appears to be complete chaos. But when viewed from above, the hurricane appears to be an image of order with its perfect spiral shape and its clean, open eye in the center.

At the center of a galaxy is a black hole ripping entire suns and their systems of planets into atoms and compressing them into a singularity. This would seem to be chaos incarnate. But the intense gravity sucking in all matter is also the pinnacle of order.

Everywhere around you is the warm, light, active presence of chaos. And underneath it all, at the very base is the most pristine and pure, perfection of order.

In the Philosophy of Not, Not is perfect order. Since Not and Life cannot both be order, this necessarily means that Life is chaos.

July 27 – Nobody Has a Clue

When we talk about "the questions of life, the universe and everything," we are essentially referring to the Linear Spiral. (See also *The Linear Spiral*.) This encompasses the scope of all things from beyond the superstring in smallness to beyond the multiverse in largeness. This is also inclusive of all space, all time and every dimension inside, outside, through or in between those things. The questions I am referring to are the unanswered mysteries of this existence. The questions of life the universe and everything include questions such as, where did it comes from, what is it, is there purpose behind it and where is it all going? (See also *The Mysteries*.)

No religion which has ever existed, no religion which exists today and no religion which will exist has all of the answers to the questions of life, the universe and everything. The Mysteries remain intact. (See also, *The All-Truth*.)

Some people are content to just be and not even ask these questions. These people are probably the lucky the ones.

There are also some people who find comfort in knowing that no science, ideology, philosophy or religion known to humanity has yet to answer the questions of life the universe and everything.

There are some people, however, who will not be content to hear this seeming copout. There are those who will be incensed by such a brash claim that "nobody has a clue."

If you are one of the people that find such a lack of answers as an answer frustrating or disturbing, I can only offer the following for condolence: Think of The Mysteries as a codex of great value which is coveted by all humanity (consciously by those who know about them and subconsciously by those who do not even know there are mysteries). Those who know The Mysteries know something that nobody else knows. Most humans wander around dazed and confused by the lucid insanity that is life (aka. chaos). In fact, if you are paying attention, how could you not be confused?! Most people do not even know that there are mysteries and if they are exposed to one they find themselves baffled and desperate to rationalize an answer. In fact, so much so that they are willing to sign over their wealth and belongings to the spiritual or intellectual leader that promises to give them an answer. And once they have this alleged answer they are so desperate to hold on to it that they are then willing to kill other people who dare to suggest that their answer is not correct. (See also, *Religion as Evil*.)

For those with the will and inclination to exploit the masses, The Mysteries are a codex of great power. They are used as a tool to shape and mold the masses into the machine they require for their own gain. Knowing this is a way to protect yourself from such manipulation and exploitation.

It becomes obvious during the study of history, religion and philosophy that humanity has been asking the same questions since before we could write. It actually may be that humanity has been asking these questions since before we could even speak. (This cannot be known, of course. When did we become *conscious*? Or have we always been "conscious?") Ancient pre-writing buildings and artwork indicate a seeking of answers to some of the questions that comprise The Mysteries. Depending on your understanding of consciousness it might even be argued that these mysteries have plagued us since before we developed consciousness. At any rate, for all intents and purposes these mysteries have always plagued us and they continue to do so.

Instead of finding misery in the fact that these mysteries remain intact after thousands of years of human evolution and advancement of civilization, find comfort in knowing that by collating The Mysteries into your own compendium, you are now privy to the same secret knowledge that spawned the creation of science and has seeded every religion that has ever existed.

The Mysteries are the core codex around which science was created and synthesized. These same mysteries continue to drive science and religion and in fact, through trying to solve these mysteries only more mysteries are created. The Mysteries are the core to everything that drives humanity.

The greatest minds of all time have all pondered these exact same questions and have come up with startling and genius explanations which have driven forward the advance of civilization, yet none of them have yet solved any of The Mysteries.

If you doubt this, I would point you to a section in *The Book of Not*, titled *Cinereo Ascensus*. In that section there is a subsection titled *Choose Your Own Religion* where the reader is asked to go through a list of over one thousand religions and circle the ones that are not true. I would urge you to read that section and pursue that exercise if you are convinced that one or more of The Mysteries has been solved.

The mysteries remain mysteries. Collate your own codex of mysteries and you will hold the information core that is the very reason philosophy, religion and science exist. Solve them if you can, but do not be dismayed if you cannot find the answers. After all, it would seem that the true meaning of life lies in the journey itself, not in the destination. (See also the book titled *The Postulations*.)

July 28 – The Mysteries : Album Mysteria Non

In Authorism, we have a group of questions collectively referred to as "The Mysteries," (collectively referred to as *Album Mysteria Non*). These are some of the mysteries of life that humanity has been trying to answer since before we could write. Creation myths, religions, ideologies and philosophies of all kinds have sprung up throughout the ages in an attempt to solve these mysteries.

We do not believe that any religion, philosophy or ideology that has existed or is existing today can adequately answer these questions. Nonetheless we believe that the seeking of the answers to these questions has been a driving force in advancing human civilization and represents a worthy goal. The evolution of humanity comes from this quest for knowledge and truth.

What is all of this? (Everything around us – The Linear Spiral, from the tiny to the vast – what is this existence? Is it simulation? Is it illusion? Is it lucid reality? What is really going on here?)

Why are we here? (Why are humans here and why is life here?)

What is our purpose? (Is there purpose? If there is, what is the purpose? If there is not, should we create one?)

What is the point of human existence? (Similar to the question on purpose but more focused on the question of why we continue to strive for order when it seems that nature wants chaos).

Where did we come from? (Were we created? Were we seeded here by some alien race? Did we accidentally evolve? Did we come to be by chance?)

Where are we going? (Are we going to create the gods we wished we had to guide us? Are we going to destroy ourselves? Will we become creators who seed another world with life similar to our ancestors?)

Are there gods? Is there a god? Were there gods? Where did the gods come from? Where did they go? If there is a god, why is there any doubt about religion? Why does deity not make clear deity's intentions? Why is there any doubt?

What is consciousness? (Is it contained within the body or can it separate from the body? What is this intrinsic dualism within which is the awareness of our own awareness? Is it evolved? Do other animals have it? Is it the basis for our souls? Is it connected to something greater than ourselves? Is it just an illusion which we make too much out of?)

What is death? (Is there an afterlife? Of those who have died, can they come back? Are they prevented from coming back? Or do they just choose not to? Is there conscious experience after death? What is that like? Does part of us remain?)

Why is there no definitive proof of an afterlife?

What are dreams? (Why do we dream? Who are we when we dream? Can we leave our bodies in dream state? Why can we be aware we are dreaming sometimes but other times not realize this?)

Why are we so different from other animals? (For instance, we form armies and go to war and fight and kill for ideas, causes or for other people. We cook our food. We are the only animals that record our lives (and other things) in written words. Etc. No other animals act like we do.)

Why are we so destructive and self-destructive? (We have a long history of killing each other and making choices that are not good for the collective whole.)

How did the universe come to be? (Is it part of some cyclic loop? Has it always existed? Does it have a beginning and an end?) What is the universe doing? (E.g. what does the end look like? Does the universe serve some larger purpose which we do not yet comprehend?) Where are the other intelligent lifeforms? (E.g.

where are the aliens? When you look at the staggering scope of space, it becomes evident that other life like us must exist. Have they already found us? Will they find us or will we find them? Or are we truly the only life in the universe that thinks this way?)

Can Life ever stop? (Warm, light, active presence is the antithesis of Not. If it were to go away there would only be Not. Is this possible? Or must Life just always exist?)

Can Not exist? (Is it possible that the most perfect forms of coldness, darkness, stasis and emptiness could exist? If so, where? How would we be able to know that it exists? How could we prove it?)

There are more mysteries and there are countless derivatives of the ones we have listed. Some of these mysteries listed here today seem to be the core mysteries that have driven the origins of religion, philosophy and science.

There are many people who might argue that not all of the mysteries listed here are still mysteries. There are those who claim they know the answers. Or some answers. However, we do not believe definitive answers to any of these questions have yet been discovered. And as long as there remains argument, the mystery remains intact.

For example, one of "The Mysteries" of old would have been, "Is the Earth really flat?" With sub-questions such as "Can we reach the edge of the world?" and, "What happens when you reach the edge?"

Today, most of all of us agree that the Earth is not flat. Since we all agree on this answer, Authorism is content to agree that "the flatness of the Earth," is no longer a mystery.

Until there can be no more argument as to the answer, the mystery remains unsolved.

July 29 – Act 'As-If'

What I do not mean by act 'as-if' is to act as if you are something that you aren't. In other words, do not be inauthentic and do not pretend you are something or someone that you aren't.

What I do mean is to act as if you deserve good things in your life and to act as if you deserve success even during the times you do not feel that way.

We all have moments of doubt. There will be times you feel low and times where you might question your resolve. These are the times to "act as-if."

Some people call this "fake it till you make it," but the net result is the same. Another expression that captures the spirit is "keep moving forward." Or "never give up."

That is the spirit of "act as-if." To do whatever you need to do to keep plugging forward to make it through the day. Or the week. Or the month. Or the ordeal or project. Etc.

Also incorporated into this little quote is the basis for manifestation. This "act as-if" phrase is the magical key to manifesting your own reality.

The very method one uses to cause reality to change is *acting as if reality has already changed.* You think it, then you react as if it were real and throughout this mental and spiritual exercise, it becomes real.

Act as if you know that what you seek will come to you. (See also, *Fake it till You Make it.*)

JULY 30 – JUST DO *SOMETHING*

There may come a time in one's life when one is frozen into inaction or just feeling "stuck." Many things can cause this.

Having too many things to choose from can be overwhelming and cause us to choose nothing.

Not being able to work out the many different consequences of our choice can also cause us to freeze.

Fear of making the wrong choice or sometimes even fear of making the right choice can cause us to freeze into inaction.

Inaction can be okay as long as you choose it on purpose. And if you choose it on purpose then it is not inaction. It is "choosing to wait" because you need time to think or process or something along those lines. Inaction due to being overwhelmed or due to fear is not a great state to be in. After all, if you choose not to decide, you still have made a choice.

There is a saying, "a task begun is a task half done." Often times all we need is one little step to get us moving. If you find yourself in a stagnant situation and you cannot see the course to take, or if you feel frozen into inaction due to too many options or too many unknowns, just do *something*.

Take a step. It almost doesn't even matter what that step is as long as it is some kind of *action*. Action will create ripples of movement which will cause reactions. Once the energy is flowing, things tend to start moving almost of their own accord. (See also, *Manifestation of Chaos* and *Proof of Manifestation*.)

July 31 – What is All of This?

Looking around one must at some point ask, what is all of this? How can we not be stunned and awed by the little that we can see and comprehend? There are countless examples of this awe and wonder at various levels of thought. In order to really encompass what I mean by "all of this" in the above question, you should read the entry titled, *The Linear Spiral*. If all of this could be seen from the outside (could it be seen from the outside?) what would it look like?

But there is more. Your own existence is staggeringly unlikely. The calculations vary if you search for an exact number online, but when you calculate the likelihood of the exact right sperm making it to the exact right egg to produce the uniqueness which is you, the chance of that happening appears to be about 1 in 550 trillion. This number is staggering. If you add in the chance of your parents meeting to begin with and add in the chance of the right sperm meeting the right egg for both your mom and your dad such that they could be born, the 1 in 550 trillion becomes a tiny number compared to the new odds.

Before we go crazy with ridiculously unfathomable numbers, let's just suffice it to say that the chances of your uniqueness existing in this universe are infinitesimally small. But you do exist. (If you suspect that don't exist, see the entry titled, *I Think, Therefore I Am.*) And I exist too. Or at least I did when I wrote this.

Just acknowledging our existence is enough to make one stagger in awe. But looking at the vastness of the universe above and the vastness of the quantaverse below is truly a cause for wonder, reverence and astonishment.

These above paragraphs are just a small attempt make sure you truly wonder at the remarkable nature of existence. The fact that nobody knows what all of this is, is frightening, reassuring, disturbing and comforting all at the same time.

August 1 – Why Are we Here?

One of the most enduring and compelling questions of all time is, "Why are we here?"

In this universe of seeming chaos, we seem to be little pinnacles of order. We know we are order because we say we are. (Perhaps the criteria for being order in chaos is choice.) From whence did we come?

Were we created by some being far greater than ourselves for some purpose unbeknownst to us?

Is one of the thousands of religions in the world the only one who got it right and their explanation answers this question?

Were we created by some being far inferior to us so that we could accomplish something they could not?

Were we seeded here by intelligent beings more advanced than us?

Are we mere simulations?

Did we naturally evolve on this planet?

Are we just the result of random chance?

Many religions, philosophies and ideologies have answers to this question but until we can all emphatically agree on a single answer, this question remains a great mystery.

August 2 – Is there Purpose?

This question summarizes two big questions which more or less are asking the same thing:

What is the point of human existence?
What is our purpose?

Is there some greater destiny we are to fulfill? Is there some task are to accomplish as individuals? Is there something we are supposed to be doing individually?

Is there something we are supposed to be doing or accomplishing as a group?

Does humanity have a part to play in some bigger story that we do not yet have a clue about?

If there is purpose, if we do have some objective we should be fulfilling, what is that purpose? What are we supposed to be doing? How do we determine whether or not we have fulfilled our destiny if we do indeed have one?

Many people have many answers to these questions but until we can all agree on a single answer, the questions of purpose and meaning remain unsolved mysteries.

August 3 – Origins and Destinations

Where did we come from and where are we going?

Both religion and science have ideas on where we came from and where we are going but they do not agree with each other. Moreover, within science and religion there are differing and often contradictory ideas of where we came from.

The religious cannot agree on a single origin story. Scientists cannot agree on a single origin theory. As long as there is no definitive and irrefutable explanation of our origin, our origin remains a mystery.

As for where we are going, will we become the gods we thought we had? Will we seed another planet with human life in the future? Will we colonize other planets and become interstellar and then intergalactic travelers?

Where are we heading? What will humanity look like in a thousand years? Is there some goal we are to accomplish?

Like our origin, until we can all agree on a destination or on a story that might explain where we are going, our destination remains a mystery.

AUGUST 4 – WHAT IS CONSCIOUSNESS?

We explain the experience of consciousness simply by saying it is the awareness of our own awareness, but science cannot yet explain the origin or the purpose of consciousness.

Some argue that consciousness is like the light from a flashlight in a dark room which is trying to cast its beam of light on the flashlight itself in order to find the source of the light. In other words, "an effort in futility."

In Authorism we often refer to consciousness as "the spirit-consciousness."

Do we have a soul (or spirit) which animates us? Are we spirits cohabitating with minds which are enmeshed in a physical vehicle? The concept existed prior, but around 2,400 years ago, Plato solidified the idea of a soul as something distinct and additional within the body. Thus, "body and soul." Hundreds of years later this idea was folded into mainstream (not orthodox) Judaism and therefore also found its way into Christianity and Islam.

But different religions have differing ideas of what the soul is. Just like different scientists have differing ideas of what consciousness is.

Authorism does not dictate what consciousness is or whether or not there is a soul, but because spirit and consciousness both seem likely candidates for "that which animates a body," we use the term spirit-consciousness to be all-inclusive.

Meanwhile, what consciousness is, where it comes from and whether or not it has a greater purpose remains an unsolved mystery.

August 5 – What is Death?

In Authorism (and in many other ideologies) death is considered transformation. When one crosses the threshold between life and death one literally transforms from one thing into another thing.

Right now you are conscious and can think about things like yesterday, today and tomorrow, but what will your thinking be like after you cross that threshold?

Is there an afterlife of some kind? If so, why is it that nobody from that afterlife ever comes back with definitive and unarguable proof of the afterlife for the rest of us?

Is the ultimate irony of death the fact that we cannot know death? In other words, do we just completely cease to exist when we cross that threshold thus transforming from a conscious being to an unconscious being? Is death a long dreamless sleep?

Is death the leveling up to the next phase? Is it a recycling of spirit back to this planet again as a different lifeform? To a different planet?

Until someone can bring back irrefutable evidence of an afterlife of some kind, or can in some other way provide irrefutable evidence of what takes place on "the other side," death remains a mystery.

AUGUST 6 – WHAT ARE DREAMS?

Thousands of books have been written on dreams and dreaming. These books range from scientific books on what dreams are and how and why they happen, to books on dream interpretation.

You may not be surprised to learn that of these thousands of works, not all of them agree on what dreams are. (And that is an understatement.)

The bottom line is that we, as humanity, still do not understand what dreams are or why we have them.

Are they altered states of existence? Does our spirit-consciousness dip into another reality? Are dreams the result of some interdimensional consciousness that occurs during sleep? Are they simply the processing of the day's events in a shuffling slideshow for our consciousness? Are they a connection to the spirit world? Your guess is as good as mine.

Dreams and dreaming remain a mystery.

August 7 – Are Humans Animals?

Why are we, as humans, so radically different from the other animals? Did we naturally evolve on Earth or are we transplants from some other place? Why are no animals even close to us in intelligence and evolution of civilization?

If you think we're not that much different from other animals, I would ask you to consider some of the major differences.

Humans are the only animals that cook their food.

Humans are the only animals that wage war. Yes, other animals fight, but no other animals gather together in large forces to face each other in a field of battle. No other animal kills in the sheer quantity that we do based solely on the direction of a seemingly randomly selected leader. No other animal kills because they are told to by another animal.

Humans are (probably) the only animals that will kill or die based solely on an idea.

Human babies take far longer than any other species to reach a point of self-reliance.

Humans are the only animals who have developed reading and writing. We are the only animals that create art and music.

No other animals have demonstrated the level of violence and destructive nature on life and the world in general than humanity has.

This goes without saying, but humans are the only animals that have developed technology to the point of creating vehicles which can carry us deep under water or out into space.

There are two mysteries within this one mystery.

One, how is it that we are so different from all the other animals, and two, why are there no animals even close to us in evolutionary development?

We should punctuate the second aspect of this mystery. To be more specific, if human beings evolved naturally, why is it that no other animal has an evolution that is even remotely like ours?

All of the other animals on this planet have also evolved and some have more ancient lines of evolution that we do. Why have none of them developed language, writing, science, literature and art?

August 8 – Violence and Destruction

Why is humanity so violent? And destructive? And by destructive I mean both self-destructive and destructive to everything around us.

Violence and warfare clearly date back thousands of years before we could even write. Artwork, weapon artifacts and building fortifications of prewriting civilization show that we were engaged in warfare as far back as we can discern.

The methods humans have developed over the centuries to torture other humans demonstrate an embarrassing creativity when it comes to inflicting violence and pain on each other.

Even during times of peace our popular art and entertainment demonstrate a propensity toward violence.

On a mass societal level it would appear that we are self-destructive when it comes to the development of weapons of mass destruction and even on a personal level we are often self-destructive as evinced by addiction and other self-sabotaging behavior that many of us exhibit at one time or another in our lives.

No other lifeforms seem to be as prone to violence and destruction as we are.

Why are we so drawn to violence and destruction?

AUGUST 9 – GIVE PEACE A CHANCE?

Considering our propensity toward violence and destruction, is it possible that we could have peace?

Do any of us really want that?

It would seem that one on one most people would agree that "peace is the answer," but what humanity wants, humanity gets.

In other words, humanity at large determines humanity's goals and achievements. If we wanted peace, we would have peace. Or is peace just not possible? Due to…? (See also, *It is a Violent World*.)

It would seem, based on the current world order, that what we really want (collectively) is scarcity and fear.

Perhaps this is because we, as a race and a great collective consciousness, are in our adolescence (or is it infancy?) and we are afraid of the future and unsure of ourselves? I believe that this is the case and that in the centuries to come we will grow out of this self-destructive inclination and become a mature and loving collective which cherishes ourselves and the world around us.

In the meantime, it is worth taking some time to consider what peace would look like if we were to achieve it. How would we spend our days if the world was at peace? Without the strife to learn from, how would we become better?

August 10 – The Universe

There are three mysteries here wrapped up in this one simple label, "the universe." What is "the universe?" Where did the universe come from? Where is the universe going? (Or restated: what is it in the process of doing?)

We do not even know how big this universe is but there is speculation that it might be one of many. Some theories suggest a multiverse. That is to say, many universes. Considering that our minds cannot comprehend the sheer scale involved in encompassing just our observable universe (much less however big it really is when you add in the parts we have yet to observe), one has to wonder how we can grok the concept of many universes – each being at lease the same vastness as our own.

Where did it come from? There are many theories that describe the origin of this universe, but the *Big Bang Theory* is the most widely accepted among laypeople. Even so, the Big Bang Theory does not really explain where the universe came from. It explains some of the math involved in the movement of matter and energy in the universe but offers zero insight into how it all came to be or what may have existed prior to the explosion. The origin of this universe is an unsolved mystery.

We also do not know what this universe is doing. It seems to be expanding but to what end? Some theories argue that it will keep expanding indefinitely. Some argue that it will stop expanding and contract back in on itself. And there are many other theories which speculate what is going to happen. What the universe is doing and where it is all going remains a mystery to be solved.

August 11 – Aliens

If you run the numbers, the likelihood of there being intelligent life like us "out there" in the universe is extremely high. Some would even argue there can be no doubt that intelligent alien life exists and that it is only a matter of time before we encounter it. Or it encounters us. (If this hasn't happened already.)

The odds of intelligent life existing are extremely high when just calculating the possibilities of alien life in this one single galaxy we live in (The Milky Way). When you factor in the hundreds of billions of other galaxies (and those are only the ones we know about) the probability of intelligent alien life becomes a given.

The question is not "Are we alone?" Instead, the question is, "When will aliens make contact with us?" and/or, "When will we discover evidence of alien life?"

Despite the probability of alien life being a near certitude it is nonetheless a probability, not a certainty. As long as it is not a certainty, the question of whether or not we are alone in the universe remains a mystery.

August 12 – Can Life Stop?

Recall that Life is defined as warm, light, active presence. If there is warmth, light, activity or presence then there is that which we call Life.

A single photon (E.g. light) flying through the cold, black, silence of empty space means there is Life present.

With that definition in mind, can Life stop? Can there be a place with no Life? Isn't there some kind of warmth, light, activity or presence everywhere? Remember, that even if you say there are only two points of light in existence and they are a billion miles apart, the fact that each can see the other means light exists at both points and everywhere in between the two points. And probably everywhere around each point going out to as far as the light has traveled since its inception.

If energy can neither be created nor destroyed, doesn't that mean that Life must always be?

It is because of this – because warm, light, active presence must always be – that we say that Life is immortal.

And because you are made of the same four fundamental building blocks as Life, whether this appeals to you or not, you are also immortal.

Or are you? The question remains open: Can warm, light, active presence be not? Can Life stop?

August 13 – Can Not Exist?

Can Not exist?

Is it possible that the most perfect forms of coldness, darkness, stasis and emptiness could exist? If so, where?

How would we be able to know that Not exists? How could we prove it?

After all, in order to measure Not, we would need to "infect" Not with Life. We would have to introduce warmth, light, activity and presence in order to measure the absolute state of cold, dark, static emptiness which is Not.

As soon as we take the measurement, that which we just tried to measure would no longer be Not. It would be a little warmer, brighter, more active and there would be the presence of a measuring device.

But logically it seems completely obvious that Not could exist if we could remove these constituent building blocks of Life.

Whether or not Not could exist remains a mystery.

August 14 – A Full Solar Eclipse

My friend, David, once posed a simple question to me. He asked me, "Do you think it is coincidental that we only have one moon and one sun? And that our moon is just big enough that at 250,000 miles from the Earth, it perfectly blocks the sun which is sized just right such that at 93,000,000 miles from Earth it may be perfectly blocked in a full solar eclipse?"

What are the odds of a solar system having only one sun? And in such a single-starred system, what are the odds that the only planet that can sustain human life actually has human life develop? And that that one single planet has only one single natural satellite (E.g. only one moon)? And that the only moon of that planet is the exact size and distance it needs to be from the surface of the planet such that it can perfectly block the only sun in a full solar eclipse as seen from the surface? What are the odds that an apelike hominid would look up at such a spectacle with deep awe and wonder?

Like David, instead of making assertions or claims surrounding this coincidence, I am only going to ask the question he asked. Don't you think that is an incredible coincidence?

August 15 – Day and Night

As long as we're talking about the things that might have made our ancestors pause for thought, let's talk about day and night. Day and night are the original good and evil. Before we could even think straight as hominids, day and night set the stage for the concepts of good and evil that have driven the thoughts, ideologies, philosophies and ultimately the religions of humankind throughout our entire existence.

Hundreds of thousands of years ago our ancestors understood the power of the sun and they understood the danger of the night. The sun was warm and provided light for us to see by. In the light of the sun, we could forage for food and we could see other animals lurking around. By the light of the day, we could see dangerous pitfalls, cliffs, quicksand, thorn trees, sharp rocks and so forth. And because we could see them, we could avoid them.

But at night, we could not see anything at all. Or if we could see, we could only partially see. Scary predators could sneak up on us and attack us at night. In the night, it was dangerous to walk around because one could easily fall into a pit or off the edge of a cliff. One could become entangled in thorns or run into a sharp rock face. The night represented danger and foreboding. The night was scary.

Here we have our templates for good and evil and our foundations for deities and religion. The sun became our first god. (See also *The One True God*.) The sun was good. The sun provided for us. The sun protected us. The sun showed us the way.

And the first devil? Night. Night was evil. Thus the devil which represented night was evil. Night attempted to obscure our path. Night provided cover for things that wanted to hurt us. Night made us lose our way and fall into danger.

Thus began the duality that seems to run all the way down to our DNA.

AUGUST 16 – DOUBT AND SELF-DOUBT

Doubt can be really good. But self-doubt is not your friend. How do you distinguish between them?

Descartes said, "Cogito, ergo sum." (*I think therefore I am.*) It was *doubt* which led him to that realization. As he continued to doubt everything he realized that the one thing he could not doubt was that he was *a being which had doubt*. In this way, doubt saved the day. (See also, *I Think Therefore I Am.*)

But we cannot go around thinking like that all the time. You have to draw a line somewhere and say "I will take for granted that this is true." Or "I will take for granted that that is true." It is only by creating these effective bailout values that you can get through the day without sending yourself into an infinite Descartes trip. (See also, *Effective Bailout Value.*)

There is a fine line between doubting the world around you and doubting yourself. Self-doubt can be debilitating and leave one feeling like an emotionally broken imposter.

Yet no self-doubt can lead one to becoming an egomaniacal narcissist.

What is the right amount of doubt about the world and a healthy amount of self-doubt?

The burden of finding the right balance lies on each of us, individually. As the author of what your story will look like, you must decide where you will draw the lines. Just remember to always check in with yourself to see if the lines are where you want them to be. If they're not, move them and try again.

August 17 – Spiritual Hunger

In the meditation titled, *Aspects of the Self*, we introduced the idea that the self can be looked at from different perspectives. In our model we primarily focus on five aspects of the self: spiritual, mental, emotional, physical and social. Most everything that applies to one aspect of the self also applies to the others. Hunger is no exception.

You are probably well aware of the existence of physical hunger. But there is also such a thing as spiritual hunger, mental hunger, emotional hunger and social hunger. Today's meditation is on spiritual hunger.

There are two kinds of spiritual hunger I want to talk about. One is a hunger that is ongoing and never really sated. Many people suffer from this ongoing hunger because they cannot find spiritual nutrition from their current situation.

The ongoing hunger is often felt as a longing for something that one cannot quite put their finger on. It feels somewhat empty. It feels like you are not fulfilled and that something is missing. You can tell something is missing but you can't identify what that something is. The German word for this kind of hunger is "sehnsucht."

Later we will talk about creating a spiritual nutrition plan to satisfy this "long hunger."

The other type of hunger is a more immediate hunger than can be sated by spiritual food. Or, perhaps to keep within the framework of the analogy, a spiritual meal.

Are you feeling spiritually hungry? Spiritually sated?

August 18 – Spiritual Meals

Yesterday we were talking about spiritual hunger and that there are two types. There is a "long hunger" that requires a spiritual nutrition plan to appease and there is a "short hunger" that can be appeased by a spiritual meal. In Authorism, a spiritual meal is the same thing as "spiritual food."

What is spiritual food? Or a spiritual meal? We define a spiritual meal as something that temporarily sates spiritual hunger.

Just standing in the sunlight with your eyes closed and feeling the warmth on your face can be a spiritual meal. Or standing in the moonlight and staring at this wondrous entity which so mystified our ancestors.

Communing with nature. A walk in the wilderness, mountains, dessert, etc. If you can find a lake, pond, river or some other body of water, being near water is good for the spirit.

Meditation. Meditation on a particular topic or just meditation on your breathing is good for the soul. Meditation on a crystal or on a tarot card is a nice embrace of spirituality.

Reading spiritual literature. Read something which has been written with spirituality in mind or perhaps something religious in nature.

Prayer. If you have a favorite deity, say a prayer to this deity. If not, you can say a prayer to the deity you wish existed. Prayer can be good for the soul.

Perform a magic ritual. Open your copy of *Not Rituals & Ceremonies* and choose a ritual to perform. Or pull a random card from your favorite tarot deck and study the card. (Not the same as meditating on a card.)

Conversation can be very nourishing to the spirit. This is true of conversation in any medium but especially true with face to face conversation. The topic of conversation is not as important as the two beings of energy basking in each other's presence.

Just spending time with another soul whether it be human or animal can be extremely nourishing to a spirit. Similar to conversation, mentioned above, it does not matter as much what you are doing but rather that you are enjoying being with the other soul(s).

It is good practice to keep a journal of your spiritual journey. If you can, it might be nice to create a section where you list some of your favorite spiritual meals. After all, why should the physical meals be the only ones which get a menu?

August 19 – Finding Yourself

What does it mean when people say that they are trying to find themselves? If you need to find something that means that something is lost. If you are trying to find yourself that means the self is lost.

Which aspect of self is this referring to?

Obviously it is not the physical self that is lost (although there might be an aspect of that going on as well). It is not the emotional self that is lost (though the emotional self is certainly affected). It is not the mental self that is lost (though the mental self is certainly affected).

In fact, when someone says that are trying to find themselves, it is not any of the outer shells of the person that are lost. Although all of the outer shells of the self are affected when any one aspect of the self is affected.

When we talk about finding ourselves we are talking about a spiritual thing. The spirit-consciousness is the primary aspect of self that the person feels is lost. And when the spirit feels lost, all other aspects of the self feel a little bit lost as well. Thus, one might not feel quite right mentally, emotionally, physically or socially when one feels they are lost spiritually.

Ok, so that is what it means when someone is lost and needs to find themselves. Now, how does one go about finding themselves?

My first response to this is the most succinct and definitive answer I can find: Thou art that.

This is not said to be flippant or to disregard the deep spiritual unease that comes with feeling spiritually lost. It just truly is the most accurate answer to the question of "Who am I?"

So first, take that answer for granted and know that you are not expected to immediately be at ease upon hearing it.

But knowing that thou art "that which you are" should help you understand that there are some common things here that might make you feel better until you do find yourself:

1. Everyone is "that which they are."
2. "That which each of us are" is authorized by ourselves. In other words each person authorizes their own actions. Each person authors their own life.
3. Each and every person is on the exact same journey to find themselves.
4. Some people know they are searching for themselves and some people do not yet know that they are searching.
5. If you feel lost, this is a good sign. It means that you have taken a huge first step in your search. Identifying the problem is the first step to solving the problem.

If "Thou art that," is not a good enough answer yet, then the next step would be to ask yourself what is important to you?

In Authorism we have identified five principles we believe should be the most important things to each human being but we also know that different people, ideologies, philosophies and religions may have their own list of things which they think are "the most important things."

If part of your "lostness" is not being able to identify what you feel is most important, our advice is to take someone else's list (like the Principles of Not, for instance) and determine if you agree with it or disagree with it. It is far easier to critically analyze something that already exists than it is to create something from scratch. (See also *Creation and Destruction*.)

Take what you can from the people, ideologies, philosophies, and religions that you can find and reject the things that feel wrong to you.

In the meantime – and here's the hardest part – you have to just do something. You must make a move. Join the Peace Corps. Or the army. Or go back to school. Change jobs or take a trip. Or none of those things I mentioned. But you need to act. Action creates waves of creation and once something has been created it is – again – far easier to adjust it to what you want.

The most common occurrence for people who are searching for themselves is for the person to find themselves when they are distracted by the pursuit of some other goal.

Not unlike having a solution to a problem suddenly pop into your head while you are engaged in some menial task. The same thing often happens to those on a (or even on *the*) spiritual journey. It is during the journey that the person suddenly realizes that they are no longer lost. Sometimes this occurs as a great epiphany and sometimes this occurs as a gradual understanding about themselves.

(See also, *Splinters of Truth*.)

August 20 – Creation and Destruction

The cycle of creation and destruction is prevalent through creation mythology, religion and even in scientific theories about the universe. While it is excellent material for any epic mythology or great adventure story, it is also extremely significant on a smaller scale in regular day to day life.

The basis for this significance is in the fact that it is far easier to destroy than it is to create.

Besides being an astute observation about the world, this is actually a really useful bit of information. Knowing this can give you an edge in the world and a head start on your own journey.

Why is this information useful?

Because anytime you are in a situation where something needs to be done – where some action needs to take place or some decision needs to be made, you already know something about the outcome. Something must be created and then it must also be "destroyed."

The group will make a decision based on some set of criteria set before them. Where does the criteria come from? It has to be created. How is the decision made? By "destroying" the criteria.

Every interaction between beings is a cycle of creation and destruction. I walk into a room and say, "What a nice day."

I have created an observation.

The person hearing me say that (even if nobody else is there and the person hearing it is just me), then has something they can criticize. The criticism (even if it is constructive criticism) is the "destruction" part of the cycle. They are essentially breaking down the comment in some way.

They might say "No, today is a terrible day." Or they might say, "You're right, it is a nice day." But either way they are reacting to the thing which I created.

They are adding to it, subtracting from it, morphing it, altering it, etc. but they are now manipulating something I had put forth into the world.

The same is true if you create a work of art. Once you have created it, it is now something which exists and can therefore be destroyed whether in real life or in the minds of those who behold it. I say "destroy" but it is not always "destruction" that takes place. Sometimes it is praise or adoration that may result from something you have created. The point I am trying to make though is that the creation part is the hard part. The reaction to the creation is the easy part.

It is easier for the teacher to grade the book report than it is for you to write it. It is easier for your boss to find problems with your project than it is for you to create the project. It is easier for the group to find problems with your plan than it is for you to create the plan for the group. It is easier for the critic to write the review than it is for the artist to create the work.

But here's the beauty of this knowledge. Knowing that this is the case means that you can create something without taking it personally when the group "tears it apart." Just by virtue of creating something you have also created the opportunity for the group to act. Nobody will do anything if there is nothing to scrutinize or to criticize. The surface of the pool remains flat – static – until you throw a pebble into the pool. (See also, *The Pebble in the Pool*.)

Once you put something into the world, you have created waves of action. Or said the other way, your action has created waves of creation. Once you have created there is opportunity for reaction. Maybe they all praise your amazing creation or maybe they tear it apart and say how awful it is. But even in the worst case where they say how awful it is, you still have created the ripples in the pool. You spawned their reaction. You have been a mover. You were the cause that created some effect.

This is a good thing.

So when they ask, "What should we do?" and you give your answer, do not feel bad if they do not like your answer. Instead take comfort in knowing that you created something which could then be added to, subtracted from, or in some way altered.

AUGUST 21 – ALCHEMY 2.0

Alchemy was more complicated than we might think. Ironically, perhaps, alchemy was almost a 'theory of everything' field of study. The alchemist was learned in fields such as mathematics, medicine, philosophy, logic, religion and magic. The irony is that today we (the science of humanity) still seek the theory of everything. This theory of everything will combine disparate equations that describe things such as relativity, gravity, thermodynamics, entropy and even quantum mechanics into a single equation that explains it all. In short, that is what the alchemists of old were trying to do when they sought to unravel the mysteries of the cosmic consciousness (spirit) in conjunction with unraveling the secret building blocks of all things (air, earth, fire and water).

In *The Book of Not*, the idea of *breaking down all of existence to the most fundamental core precepts* is introduced. The discovery of Not was accomplished in phases. First, coldness was ascertained by removal of its counterpart, heat. Shortly thereafter, darkness was ascertained by removal of its counterpart, light. It was more than a decade later that emptiness was ascertained through the removal of its counterpart, presence. Almost immediately after that, stasis was ascertained through the removal of its counterpart, activity. The unveiling of these four precepts exposed the substrate of existence.

In a self-referencing circle, after having reduced the substrate of existence down to the four core precepts of coldness, darkness, stasis and emptiness, an incredible if not somewhat obvious discovery was made. Building the universe back up from Not one must add in the counterpart of each core precept. As such, these counterparts are necessarily the building blocks of everything else. All of existence stems and flows from these four fundamental building blocks: warmth, light, activity and presence.

When all four are combined there is then the possibility of the spark that is consciousness. The spark that is spirit. The glimmer of liquid light that is the soul. The fifth element.

The alchemists of old were on to something when they identified four basic elements on which everything else was based. And they were correct in ascertaining the fifth element of spirit-consciousness. They were correct in the number of elements but they did not see behind the curtain where the fundamental building blocks and the base precepts exist.

This brings us to today. We have deepened and modernized alchemy and thus have upgraded the old occult practice in the form of Alchemy 2.0.

Overlaying the four foundational core precepts with the four fundamental building blocks of all existence and the four classical elements in the associations used by the Hermetic Order of the Golden Dawn we have the following chart:

Precept	emptiness	darkness	coldness	stillness
Building Block	light	warmth	action	presence
Not Principle	fitness	Life	relationships	personal code
Element	air	fire	water	earth
Direction	east	south	west	north
Symbol	wing/sword	wand	cup	pentacle
Season	spring	summer	fall	winter
Color	yellow	red	blue	green

The Philosophy of Not has brought many things of Not into the world. Not Philosophy itself, Authorism, The Book of Not, the

Tree of Not, the Principles of Not, Not Stones, Not Layouts, Not Runes, Not Digital, Not Rituals & Ceremonies, etc.

Alchemy 2.0 is a way to manifest these various Not formations into the world. Through Alchemy 2.0, we can tap back into our ancient roots as seekers of truth and knowledge while at the same time providing practice ritual and ceremony in the modern age with modern relevance.

It may be that the original four elements are no longer relevant to us, but the core precepts and the fundamental building blocks are extremely relevant to all life.

August 22 – The 21-Day Deity

In the realm of physical nutrition there are various nutrition plans that call for adherence to some set of rules for a dedicated amount of time. In other words, you have to go on a diet. Usually the time requested is one, two, three or four weeks. (See also, *Spiritual Nutrition*.)

A diet is not a lifestyle change, but that does not mean a diet has no value. Going on a diet can be a really effective means of teaching you about yourself. After the diet is over you will have learned which parts of the diet worked for you and which parts didn't. After the diet you should be able to explain why that kind of diet will or will not work for you on a more permanent basis as a lifestyle change.

Comparing physical nutrition to spiritual nutrition is a great analogy because we all know what physical nutrition is and we all know that it is something that is important to our physical bodies. Likewise, spiritual nutrition is important to our spiritual bodies. Why are there not more spiritual nutrition plans? Or "spiritual diets?"

Today's meditation offers a spiritual diet for your consideration. It is called, "The 21-Day Deity."

Incidentally, the upside to spiritual dieting is the same as the upside to physical dieting. A diet can teach you what works for you and what does not work for you so that ultimately you can create a positive and effective spiritual lifestyle for yourself.

The way the 21-Day Deity works is as follows:

Adopt a religion, philosophy or ideology for 21 days and see what it does for your life. During the three weeks you adopt this ideology, you maintain an open mind and an active awareness of the things you like about it and the things you do not like about it.

At the end of the 21 days you should have a pretty good feeling for whether or not you want to integrate this spiritual practice into your spiritual lifestyle.

It may be that the spiritual diet was just what you needed to feel spiritually fit. If not, you may need to try a different spiritual diet. Or change the deity in this 21-Day diet. Or perhaps it worked for you but over time the effects started to wane. In that case, you can try the same diet again with a different 21-Day Deity this time.

Over time, you can compile your notes and align on one side all of the good things from the different spiritual diets you have embraced and on the other side, all the bad things from the different spiritual diets you have embraced. Then from the good things and the bad you can create an overall spiritual nutrition plan that works for you.

August 23 – Toxicity in the Mainstream

In the case of physical nutrition, toxicity is present due to massive bodies of misinformation built up over decades of competing research projects with varying agendas, economic forces, market forces, consumer desire (e.g. supply and demand,) etc. All of those things and more contribute to what has resulted in toxic chemicals in the mainstream diet.

Toxicity in mainstream spirituality must certainly be the same. There are things that nourish the spirit and there are things that are toxic to the spirit and it is absolutely true that something that is nourishing to one person may be toxic to another. And then there are countless shades of gray in between pure nutritional value and toxic poison. Everything in between can cause varying degrees of illness and unease – or disease. That is how the mainstream creates spiritual toxicity – spiritual poison.

The solution to spiritual toxicity is to find the spiritual nutrition plan that revitalizes you – that nourishes you. You must create a plan that provides you with spiritual nutrition while at the same time removing spiritual toxins.

As you have surely already discerned: While there is good news in that Authorism can help you, the bad news is that you are the only one that can create your own spiritual nutrition plan. (See also, *Spiritual Nutrition, Spiritual Hunger* and *Spiritual Meals*.)

August 24 – The Church of Not

Religious people who believe in a god or gods have seemingly countless religions to choose from. Within those religions there are countless sects and denominations which ultimately provide countless options to choose from in finding a place to belong.

Atheist people who do not believe in a god or gods also have countless secular organizations to choose from. There are countless organizations, clubs and gatherings for atheists to choose from in finding a place to belong.

But in the middle ground there are those of us who are torn between those two extremes. We do not believe in a god or gods in the way the religious devout do but we are also not devout enough followers of the religion of science to be able to call ourselves atheists. Or perhaps we have an intuitive feeling that there is something deeper. This middle ground is also teeming with organizations and clubs but there are stigmas attached to the labels that come with them. If we are to select one of these middle ground options in order to pursue our spiritual journey, we are accused of blind ignorance by the atheist and we are called godless heathens by the religious devout. Not to mention that we are likely asked to adopt the dogmas set forth by the organization, some or many of which we may not wish to adhere to.

The Church of Not was created for us. The Church of Not is a hub for the congregation of people who want to embrace their intuition and spirituality without being accused of turning a blind eye to scientific reason. Through the Church of Not, one can pursue a spiritual path with the clarity of a rational mind. No leap of faith is required.

In fact, belief in Not is not even required. After all, Not cannot exist.

August 25 – Science & Religion

Religion and Science have long been at odds with each other but in our case they do not need to be. Religion can give comfort to the soul and science can bring assurance to the intellect and we can practice our religion and our science without contradiction or misgiving. In fact, it was through scientific reasoning that Not was discovered.

In the case of most religions, science and religion remain at odds because religion proclaims the existence of a higher power then science comes along and says, "You are wrong. Nothing supernatural can exist." Science says, "Prove your higher power exists." Then religion responds, "Use your science to prove our higher power doesn't exist." They argue and there is an impasse.

The other thing that religion and science are often at odds with is the proclamation by religion that it can answer *all* of our questions. Science tells us that it can help find the answers, which a few hundred years of history show to be absolutely true. But religion claims it already has the answers, which thousands of years of history have shown to be – well, completely wrong. Time and again throughout the centuries the answers religion provided have been proven false and over the last two hundred years the people have started to get suspicious. It is easy to now make the leap in logic that maybe religion does not have the answers after all. But in some cases this includes the religion of science.

The "religion" of science? Yes, there are many who show devout, unyielding adherence to dogmas that have evolved from scientific achievements throughout the last four hundred years. Often, these devotees are unaware of their fanaticism but adhere to these dogmas without question or skepticism.

Blind faith in anything is dangerous and potentially destructive.

August 26 – Good Religion, Good Science

Consider the power of religion by itself. Religion has been with us since before we could write. For thousands of years, we have known religion and despite the ever changing insides, it has remained with us through the hardest of times. Granted, it has imposed some hard times itself, but there are also some wonderful benefits that religion brings to mankind.

Religion offers a template one can use to create a moral compass. Religion offers a place where like minds can come together to form community (something we feel very strongly is important to each person). Religion can provide strength to groups and individuals when times get hard.

Religion, by its very definition, offers a framework for routine that can encourage and promote good health. Religion often offers validity and authorization to action – which is something we will talk more in-depth about later. Of course there is some baggage that comes with religion as well. Countless billions of people have suffered throughout the centuries because of the misuse and abuse of religion.

Now consider the power of science. By comparison, science is brand new. For the sake of conversation, we use the formation of The Scientific Method as our birthday for science. This happened about 400 years ago. Science has barely even woken up in civilization and in these few short centuries it has radically changed the world at lightning speed.

Science has launched humanity into a blitz of rapid change and technological advancement that can barely even be measured. One hundred years (1921) ago we were marveling at the developing telephone, radio, Henry Ford's assembly line, liquid fueled rockets and silent movies.

Here in 2021, we are marveling at things like deep neural networks, bio-quantum computing, 3D printing, advances in artificial intelligence and of course the explosion of this global communication network called the internet. Science has brought miraculous wonders to the world and it has done so rapidly. It has provided great comfort but it has also done so with no heart. Science is cold. Calculating. What science has brought is good, but it is not *all* good. Science has blood on its hands too.

Nevertheless, if you focus especially on the positive, science and religion – when done "right," both have wonderful things to offer the world.

August 27 – Good Religion + Good Science = Not

Most people feel they have to choose a side. Should I follow my heart and devote my life to religious pursuits? Or should I embrace scientific reason and pursue a life devoted to seeking meaning through science?

Of course, in this secular age, with religion rapidly losing its once near omnipotence, one really does not get to even ask such questions. If you want to make enough money to provide for your family and if you want your children to have a better life than you had, you pretty much have to go the route of science (or at the very least, the secular). There is not a lot of money in being a monk or a philosopher these days.

But then again, if you did want to pursue a life devoted to religious adherence and reverent wonder, which religion would you choose? When you break down the larger ones into their various sects and add those to the already long list of other religions there are literally thousands of variations to choose from. (See also, *Choosing a Religion* and *Becoming Religious*.)

Instead of religion and science clashing, imagine the power of combining these two forces into one unified ideology that allows us to pull all of the good things from religion and combine them with all of the wonders and power that science has brought to us.

Considering thousands of years of the advancement of civilization, religion really had to change. Authorism is that change.

August 28 – What it Isn't

In mid-2020, the Sloan Digital Sky Survey published the most comprehensive map of the observable universe ever made. The map was three-dimensional and even though the map itself was comprehensive, the sheer number of galaxies it mapped was truly incomprehensible. (Hundreds of billions, in case you're curious.)

It is estimated that the map covers less than 0.002% of the universe.

Looking down into the quantum and up into the cosmos one can become completely confounded by reality on any given level. It is probable that we cannot even grasp a portion of what is going on here. (See also, The Linear Spiral.) The grasping that we are able to accomplish is only done so at a very human-centric level.

We do not know how far down it goes in size and we do not know how far up it goes in scale. We do not know where we are in the grand scheme of things, we do not know where we are going, we do not know where we came from, we do not know why we are here and we do not really even understand what we are (e.g. What is spirit? What is consciousness?).

Do not get me wrong. I am truly humbled by the incredible brilliance, creativity and ingenuity of human beings and I am awed by what we have achieved. Especially in light of our place in the universe as an ignorant consciousness that has only just barely awoken.

In our attempt to bring some clarity to this incomprehensible chaos that is all of existence (up, down, and in every direction and dimension inside and outside of us) we have created our own answers to the questions we cannot fathom answers for.

In a previous daily meditation titled, Your Avatar, we compare a human life to the life of an avatar in a game. You can imagine a video game or a board game. The avatar is the game piece that represents you. It is the piece that gets moved around the game board.

Humanity's attempt to answer our own questions about life the universe and everything is akin to the avatar suddenly wondering where it came from, what it is supposed to be doing, where it is going in life, what its world is made of, etc. This is all well and good, but can you imagine the answers that the avatar might come up with?

The avatar would have no context with which to answer these incredibly significant questions. All of the knowledge at the avatar's disposal would be the result of its existence in that one game.

Could any of the creation myths or postulations on the meaning of life that the avatar could come up with be even close to explaining the origin of the game or why the animating consciousnesses (the people playing the game) were playing the game? Would the avatar ever be able to dream up the name of the game manufacturer, the purpose the game was produced, trademark and copyright law that protects the publication of the game or manufacturing processes that go into the creation of the game pieces (i.e. the avatar's body)? Much less, could the avatar fathom the player's environment as the player sits in their third floor apartment in a small city somewhere in the American northeast? Could the avatar comprehend or even guess the player's thoughts or feelings as the player distractedly considers the last text from their significant other or how they're going to pay the electricity bill this month?

The avatar can only exist during game play and being able to exist only in the game, the avatar could never find a perspective that would explain what the game was, why it had ever been created or what the purpose of the game was to those who created it or to those who play it. To the avatar, the game (i.e. universe) always existed and will continue to exist after the avatar dies.

It seems likely to me that this is the case for humanity. Humanity is ingenious and I believe we have an incredible destiny to fulfill even if it is a destiny that we created (see also, Humanity's Destiny), but I suspect that as long as we remain in the game, we can never begin to even come close to actually answering these questions we have been plagued with these millennia past. (As an aside, just like the avatar existing only in the game, *we* can never leave "the game" either. The game, for us, is warm, light, active presence and the only thing that is not in the game is Not itself. And we can never be Not.)

Any myth, creation story, religious explanation, philosophy or ideology that lays out an explanation for existence or claims to answer these incredible questions most assuredly has one thing in common. It is incorrect. It can never be correct because it can never achieve the perspective necessary to see the big picture. The same is true for science. The avatar's science can do well to explain the materials the game board is made of, the workings of the avatar itself and it can help define the rules of the game. But the avatar's science cannot penetrate the veil that exists between the players and the game pieces.

You might ask something along the lines of, "How could you possibly have the sheer audacity necessary to make such a definitive claim?"

Only because it is probable that humanity is not the center of all of existence.

All of the religions of the world and the creation myths that go along with them have one thing in common. Next to the creator-god, they all star humanity as the lead character. If humanity is the center of all of existence both micro and macro, then we humans may have the perspective we need to guess the truth. But the more we learn about the world around us, the quantum and the cosmos, the more it seems that we (humanity) are not the main characters in this story.

So for better or for worse, while we may not be able to answer these questions because of lack of context or due to our inability to gain perspective, we can rest assured (even though to many this is not very assuring) that whatever answers we do come up with are not the correct answers to those questions.

We cannot know what it is but we can know what it isn't. And what it isn't is everything we've come up with to try to explain to ourselves what it is.

August 29 – Humanity's Destiny

Throughout the millennia, humanity has shown incredible resilience and tenacity. Despite being arguably the most self-destructive species to ever walk the earth, we are still here. And in order to get through the day, we have to assume we will still be here tomorrow.

The Postulations may offer some ideas about where we came from, what it is we are doing here and where it is we are going, but if you have already read the meditation titled, *What it Isn't*, then you already know that the postulations are all wrong. By virtue of existing, they cannot be accurate.

Nonetheless, I do believe that humanity does have a destiny to fulfill. We do not yet fully understand our destiny because we have not yet finished writing it. Our destiny is being created for us by us.

While we do not yet know what that destiny will entail, I do think we have some glimpses of what it will look like.

Through technology, science and self-discovery, we will likely become the gods we have always wished so passionately existed. We will become the "external authorization" that we seek. We will become the shepherds we wished we had had and that we wish we could have. We will become guides to other intelligent life. We will become a pinnacle of advanced civilization. We will become an example of that which other civilizations may aspire to become. We will make the cosmos better by our existence in it.

AUGUST 30 – SLEEP OR DIE

It is fascinating that humans need to sleep. And not just some sleep, but a lot of sleep. About one third of our lives are dedicated to sleeping.

On the surface one might ask, "Why is this surprising to you? It just is what it is, right?"

Perhaps. It depends on how you look at the "human machine." Mainstream thought more or less approaches humans as biological machines. Perhaps that's all we are, though I do not feel that is true. But if we are biological machines, is sleep a limitation of our biological nature or is it part of a bigger picture that we do not yet understand?

The reason this is somewhat mysterious is because of the way we build our machines. The machines humans build do not require sleep. Computers are left on twenty four hours a day, seven days a week. There are some computers that have been running for decades without being turned off. Refrigerators run all day and night for years. There are many other examples of machines that can run for years without "sleep."

Also, it isn't that we need to take a nap once in a while so we feel rested and content. It's far more important than that.

If we do not get a certain amount of sleep in a given time period, our bodies literally shut down. Sleep is so important that it seems to override what many consider the most powerful of all human instincts: self-preservation.

For instance, one can become so tired when hiking that they literally just curl up and go to sleep in the woods even though they know a predator may come along and eat them. Or perhaps in a more germane example, one can become so tired when driving that one falls asleep at the wheel despite intellectually knowing that sleeping at the wheel is certain death.

I say that it *seems* to override self-preservation but perhaps it doesn't really. Perhaps it is self-preservation that makes us risk death by some other means in order to get some sleep.

Our mind/body must reach a point where it knows that sleep is now more important to sustain our own life than pulling over on the side of the road. It is almost as if our consciousness is saying, "It's ok, I can drive another 15 minutes." And the body responds with, "No. If I do not shutdown right now I will die." Even if death comes a minute later when the person careens off the highway and into a big rock or head-on into oncoming traffic.

It seems that consciousness does not need sleep, but the mind/body does. Or does consciousness also need sleep?

August 31 – Should I Worship Something?

First, let us all agree on a definition of the word. For the sake of conversation, let's say that 'worship' means "adoration, praise, respect and reverence."

There are religions where the primary (or only) creator-god demands that its subjects worship it.

But if you are not part of one of those religions, or you do not believe in such a god, is there something else you should worship?

The answer is yes. Even the secular should worship. But 'should' is the wrong word. It is more like, even the secular *must* worship. In fact, when considering the scope of all of existence, how could one not?

What could demand adoration, respect, praise and reverence from humanity?

Pretty much, everything.

If you consider the idea of superstrings, the quantum world, the atomic world, the molecular world, the microscopic world, the cellular world, the world around you, the solar system, the galaxy, the galactic clusters, the universe, the multiverse and other dimensions, how could you not be filled with wonder, adoration, praise, respect and reverence? (See also, *The Linear Spiral*.)

The sun alone is worthy of worship, as is this planet at any level of scrutiny one brings to bear. But when you add it all together, it is truly humbling.

September 1 – What if You Are Wrong?

The question is usually posed from the religious devout to the one who is not afraid of the religious person's creator-god. In the avatar example, you can imagine one game piece asking this of another. (See also, *Your Avatar*.)

The answer depends on who is right. In some religions, if you fail to choose their god you will suffer eternally for making the wrong choice. In other religions, you will have to do the whole thing (life) over again until you get it right. In some ideologies you will never know whether you were right or wrong because you will not continue to exist after death.

But the question itself exposes a fundamental flaw in the thinking of the person who asks it. The question is about the eternal consequences of a choice made here in this mortal realm.

It is a fear-based question and implies a fear-based life.

"What if you are wrong," is the same question as "what if you fall," which is asked of the person going out on the limb to get the fruit. You have to go out on the limb if you want to get the fruit. If you fall, you may hurt yourself or even die. Or you climb back up and try again. "What if you fall?" is asked to justify the decision to not try.

It is the same as asking, "what if it doesn't work out," when there is an opportunity before you. If you let the question stop you from trying to seize the opportunity then you have missed an opportunity that you could have had. You cannot seize the opportunity if you don't reach out and try to seize it. If you fail, you fail. But you have to try or you will stagnate.

Some people are afraid of making a mistake and will choose the path of least resistance and the path of least risk. There are others who will risk everything on the throw of the dice. As with all else in life, one must find a balance between these things which one is comfortable with in order to move forward when choices come along. Especially when *difficult* choices come along.

There are several possible answers to the, "what if you are wrong," question. I will highlight the top three:

1. It depends on who is right. If a religion I did not choose is right and I am wrong, then I will be subject to the whim of that creator-god and must endure whatever consequences that god sees fit as reward or punishment.

2. What if I am wrong and everyone else is also wrong? Then it was good that I did the best I could and tried to make the world a better place.

3. The first two responses assume that I can somehow be aware of my choice after this life ends and I transition to the next life. We cannot rule out the possibility that we do not get to know whether or not we made "the right choice" here because there is no hereafter. In that case, my answer is similar to Number 2. It was good that I did the best I could.

I do not want to make decisions based on fear of failing, so instead I make decisions based on hope of succeeding and in the meantime, I choose a path through life where I do the best I can at making the world a better place.

SEPTEMBER 2 – NOTHING MATTERS

If you have read the meditation titled, *What it Isn't*, you may ask the question, "If nothing we can imagine can explain this, then why should we even participate?!" What difference does it make? Why bother? If we can never know, what is the point in continuing to try? Doesn't that mean it is all just an effort in futility? Why shouldn't we just quit?

This kind of thinking can be summed up in the nihilistic philosophies that nothing matters and there is no point to human existence.

But just because we cannot know what the big picture looks like does not mean there is not one. Just because we cannot know the answers to the questions of life, the universe and everything does not mean there are no answers.

The counterargument to, "In that case, nothing matters," is that we can't know that either. You can claim there is no point to existence and that nothing matters but you can't *know* that nothing matters.

And to counter the argument, "Nothing exists," we have two responses: "I think, therefore I am." And "Thou art that." Besides, we know that human existence is important because of what we are ultimately doing. That is to say, becoming the gods that we'd always wished we'd had.

I exist (I have proven this to myself in meditation) so in all likelihood you exist also.

So instead of choosing "nothing matters" as your mantra, enjoy this warm, light, active presence as long as you can. No matter what comes next, it will come soon enough and unless you are absolutely certain about what it is, it would be wise to learn some more about *this* (gestures all around us) before you move on!

September 3 – It is a Violent World

In *Album Mysteria Non*, we point out the mystery of humanity's violent tendencies and self-destructive nature. (See also, *The Mysteries : Album Mysteria Non* and *Violence and Destruction*.) Today's meditation is not focused on the violence of humanity but rather on the violence of the world.

But perhaps the violence of the world is the reason for humanity's violent tendencies? Did it imprint itself onto us? After all, we do learn by example and with the world around us as our only example as to *how to be*, it does stand to reason that we would mirror that violence. We had to learn it from somewhere.

But postulations aside for now, what do I mean by "the world is violent?"

Of course there are obvious scenes of violence all around us. The most obvious are natural disasters. Tornados, hurricanes, volcanoes, earthquakes, violent storms, tidal waves, floods, avalanches, cave-ins, forest fires, sink holes, etc. Every manner of natural disaster is a display of the violence inherent in nature.

There is also inherent violence in the interaction of all of the other animals on this planet. There are animals that are generally peaceful, but they must coexist with violent predators. The way insects treat one another is truly terrifying and horrifically violent.

We don't really see this up close (it would instantly and violently vaporize us if we tried) but the sun is the epitome of violence. It is an inconceivably large inferno that is fusing 600 million tons of hydrogen into 596 million tons of helium every second. It is akin to four million ton fusion bombs detonating every single second.

On a smaller scale (a bit of an understatement), deep down inside, the striking of a match is also a violent and explosive chemical inferno. Or turning on a faucet to fill up a glass of water. Watch as the deluge explodes out of the faucet and smashes into the bottom of the glass, splashing in all directions.

But there are also examples of violence in what otherwise might seem like mundane, everyday activities.

Eating is an act of violence. You must break down the food you eat first by tearing and smashing it with your teeth. Consider biting into an apple - your teeth tearing through the skin and then the flesh of the apple in order to rip a piece out of it to further smash into pulp so that it may be consumed.

Can you imagine opening a nutshell to get to the nut without cracking or smashing the shell?

Like chaos and order, it would seem that violence and tranquility are interlaced throughout nature. In any given scene of peace and tranquility, there are (sometimes hidden) layers of violent action.

There is also tranquility and calm interspersed throughout nature, but truly violence is everywhere, all the time.

We can talk about the violence of humankind, but perhaps it is a wonder that we are not more violent than we are. Perhaps we should be applauded for the amount of peace and tranquility we continually impose on a world that seems to resist it.

SEPTEMBER 4 – DICTATE TO THE WORLD

Part of Authorism is understanding yourself and dictating to the world how you will be in the world. You are the author of that. You tell the world what you will be, what you will do, how you will do it and when.

If you do not dictate these things to the world, these things will be dictated for you. Or to you. By the world.

Authorism starts as a fundamental philosophy about authoring your own life and about being the creator – the author – of your own existence.

But as this philosophy bubbles up from the wellspring of our own spirit-consciousness it goes further out of the depths and into the shallows of everyday existence.

This is where things like streaming media, smartphone technology, social media, email and interaction with our peers takes place.

These external things should not author you. In other words, these things are tools, or resources for you.

If your phone rings, must you answer it? Must you set your phone to notify you any time there is a change in status? Must you receive text notifications, social media notifications or email notifications? And if you get a notification should you drop everything immediately to focus on it? What if you were thinking about something important to you? Does the notification rip you out of your thoughts and back into the world?

After all, when you need a hammer or a screwdriver, you go and get one. You do not allow your hand tools to continually ping you to see if you are in need of them.

Maybe you need that sometimes. But when you utilize notifications or respond to them it should be because you choose that in your life, not because you operate as an automaton who is controlled by the world around you.

Generally speaking, this applies to more subtle aspects of life as well. For instance, watching a movie or going to a party. Just because you have committed to sitting down to watch a movie does not mean you have to. You are free to change your mind at any time. If you decide your life would be better spent doing something else, you should do something else. You are the author. Not the conditions set forth by external parameters.

SEPTEMBER 5 – LIVING WITH INTENTION

It is truly a strange thing that humans can operate with no intention. One can do nearly anything without being mindful or having intention behind their actions.

Just like living "in the moment" all the time is unrealistic, so is living with intention. However, also just like living in the moment, it is extremely beneficial to bring intention into your actions anytime you can.

You might ask, "If I can open a door and walk through or drive through a parking lot without intention, what difference does it make if I do it *with intention* or not?"

It is true. You can do those things and many more while you are thinking about something completely different. This is acting without intention. You can do that and you can even get away with it most of the time. But, truly, this is how accidents happen.

Before we look more closely at an example, there is another layer of mindfulness we should address. It is that when you act with intention you should also intend with intention.

This means that you should mindfully consider where your intention should reside.

Let's look at the example above about driving through a parking lot to help explain this.

Let's say for this example that you are driving through the parking lot to get to the other side. You do not need to park in any of the spots between you and the other side so there is little need to put your intention toward looking at those parking spots (whether they be empty or full).

In fact, most people would focus their intention on the other side of the parking lot because that is the next place that a decision will need to be made. Once you reach the edge of the parking lot you will have to slow down or even stop and look both ways before you pull out of the parking lot.

The mistake here is that with your intention on the end goal, you may drive faster than is safe through the lot on your way to the end goal. With your intention set on the other side of the lot, you are less likely to notice someone suddenly stepping out in front of you or another vehicle suddenly pulling out in front of you.

It is fine to have your intention on the edge of the lot but you must also drive mindfully on the way there. Instead of "the other side of the lot" being your next step, you should have your intention on your immediate surroundings as you are passing through them. You can then mindfully observe the empty and the full spots and see if there is activity that may pose a danger while still flickering your intention to the edge of the lot.

Besides being aware of danger and opportunity, life can be very magical when you live with intention. Filling a glass of water from a sink is an amazing display of fluid dynamics and flow. Watching a fire is a dazzling display of the energy of creation. Opening a door is an exercise in balance and anticipation…

And so it goes, on and on. There is a Zen poem that describes this well:

> "Magical Power,
> Marvelous Action!
> Chopping Wood,
> Carrying Water."

SEPTEMBER 6 – FAKE IT TILL YOU MAKE IT

Some people are repulsed by this cliché because they think it means that you should pretend to be something or someone that you aren't. They think it is telling you to be an imposter.

That is not what I mean when I say it. What I mean by it is rather complicated though and will take a moment to explain.

I am going to use an example from real life. I was overweight and felt bloated and thick. I wanted to feel fit and trim.

I looked online for solutions and there were so many different opinions on how to become more fit that I had no idea where to begin.

Moreover – and this is the subtle part of this whole thing that makes it so difficult to explain – I thought I needed to be an expert in order to move forward.

This is a side effect of there being thousands of expert views online. Bear with me a moment. When you see hundreds of different viewpoints, each one coming at you as if they are an expert on the subject matter they preach (whether they are or are not actual experts on the material they sermonize), it leaves you with a mistaken assumption that in order for you to participate in the same field they are preaching about that you also must become an expert. It is a subconscious assessment we make that says something like, "There are so many conflicting viewpoints on this matter that in order for me to make an educated decision I will have to learn about all of it."

In the case of physical fitness, this means that you must become an expert in nutrition, dieting, biology, physiology and exercise science.

But this is completely wrong. You do not need to be an expert in fitness to become fit.

There is a similar broken paradigm around going to college. Many people feel they are not smart enough to go to college. But you do not need to be smart to go to college. It is the other way around. College is what teaches you how to become smart. You do not need to be flexible in order to do yoga. It is through the practice of yoga that you become flexible.

In order to become physically fit, I chose a random diet and started doing what they told me to do. I followed the directions of this diet program for five months and became fit and trim. I decided to "fake it till I made it."

I learned a lot about food, nutrition, exercise and my own physiology in the process. When I had achieved my goal, I could have sermonized "How to become fit and trim," and someone searching for that knowledge might have found my online channel and thought, "Wow, this guy sounds like an expert on this." This is part of the fallacy of so many online experts. What these people are experts on is themselves. They have found something that works and therefore they can explain how this thing really worked for them. The challenge for us in deciphering all of this is that they are right but they are right for them. Not necessarily for everyone else.

When I first selected a diet to work with, I "faked it till I made it." The "fake it" part was the commitment to the program even though I did not understand the program or if it was really going to help me.

Another way of referring to this "fake it till you make it" idea is to "act as-if." (See also, *Act 'As-If'* and *Reflection and Manifestation*.)

SEPTEMBER 7 – PRAY TO WHAT?

Should I pray to a god or to my spirit-consciousness? Should I pray to the Universal Consciousness? Should I pray to the Supreme Being? To the Universe?

The answer is that you should pray to that which you believe will be most likely to answer your prayer.

Wait – doesn't that seem like a sellout? Isn't that kind of scheming and dishonest?

It isn't. Here's why. If you believe that a god will answer your prayer why would you not continue to pray to that god? Of course you should. Even if the power to affect change is coming from within you and not some external god, it is not going to hurt you to keep using that authorization loopback.

If you believe the power to affect change begins from within yourself, you should pray to that wellspring of energy and life that is your spirit-consciousness.

If you believe that the Universe will provide if only you ask, then you should pray to the Universe.

Go with what works for you. If it stops working for you, change it into something that does work for you. If you don't know what works for you, try one and then another until you find something that works.

Here's the rub, though. You have to be the one that decides what works for you. And you can only know what works for you by continually asking yourself, "Is this working for me?" (See also, *The 21-Day Diety*.)

SEPTEMBER 8 – CREATION HASN'T STOPPED

As authors of our own existence we are constantly creating ourselves. Who we were before is not necessarily who we are now. Nor is who we are now going to be the same as who we will become at some future time.

We are constantly learning, changing and growing. Much like the Linear Spiral (see also, *The Linear Spiral*), we sometimes feel we are going in circles, but it only looks like circles when viewed from above. If you change your perspective you can see that you are not going in circles, but rather you are going in spirals. You are moving forward in a linear fashion even as you travel in a "circle."

Creation hasn't stopped, and in fact, as the energy of creation continuously emanates from you, into the world around you, creation cannot stop.

September 9 – Conviction of Belief

Believers come in all shapes and sizes. And so do their beliefs. When I talk about belief, I am talking about belief in something greater than ourselves. I am talking about the answers to the questions of life, the universe and everything. The answers to the questions in Album Mysteria Non. (See also, *The Mysteries : Album Mysteria Non.*)

There are two types of belief: perceived-belief and actual-belief. Perceived-belief is the amount of belief one perceives they have. As we know well from the world around us, what we perceive is not always what is real. Perception, by its very definition, is almost completely subjective.

Actual-belief is the person's true belief. The person may think they are willing to die for a belief but if pressed may discover they are not willing to die for it. Or they may not realize they feel so strongly about a belief until pressed and then discover that unbeknownst to them, they *are* willing to die for their belief.

What we are measuring is the belief in the answers to the great mysteries of existence. There is a massive and varying range of possible answers to these mysteries, most of which are seated in some form of religion. To summarize a million books on philosophy, ideology and religion in half a sentence, we have postulations ranging from "everything is random and all of existence just happened accidentally," to "all of this is part of a larger design and there is deeper meaning and a greater purpose to this existence."

Most people think they believe strongly in something when in fact they do not. Using the structure analogy, most people think they have a pretty solid structure of belief, however, if pressed, most people's structures will crumble under pressure. This is one of the reasons people would rather talk about the weather or sports instead of their beliefs.

The upside for the majority is that they are almost never pressed. Most people are able to go through life enjoying the game on TV, voting for whoever their peers say to vote for, eating whatever the ads say to eat and liking whatever happens to be trending. This is called, "going with the flow," and it works for the vast majority.

There is however some danger in "going with the flow." The danger is that the person touting their belief really thinks they believe strongly in [_____] (fill in the blank) whether they actually believe it or not. The reason this is dangerous is because the higher the perceived-belief, the more willing that person is to fight for their belief.

As discussed in *Superstructures of Belief*, there is also danger in that the person fighting for their belief becomes more and more vested the more they fight and they become less and less willing to analyze their beliefs or ask critical questions that might cause them to doubt their structure or foundation of belief. The danger is to others and to themselves. In this way they paint themselves into a corner and if pressed it turns into "fight or flight" with them. Actual belief no longer even matters at this point.

Having no beliefs is not a great approach either. If you believe in nothing, you can be led down paths you probably don't want to go. People who believe in nothing can be talked into doing things they shouldn't do or would normally never otherwise do. Ultimately, people who believe in nothing will not be working toward the greater goal of advancing human civilization and making the world a better place.

On the other hand, having extreme belief (blind faith) is also not good. If you are willing to die for a belief then you are likely also willing to kill for a belief. In the weighted importance of the Principles of Not, Life is the highest principle whereas belief is not covered by the Principles until the fourth Principle: Personal Code. (See also, *Your Personal Code*.) In other words, even if you are willing to die but not kill, this is still not the right thinking. Life is worth more than an idea.

If you haven't really done a deep dive into your perceived versus your actual conviction of belief, today is a good day to explore this aspect of yourself.

SEPTEMBER 10 – YOU ARE DEEPER THAN BELIEF

Your foundation and subsequent structure of belief are important but they are not what you are made of. You are separate from your beliefs even though the beliefs in question do belong to you.

You are a deeper person than you think. Or rather, that which you are is deeper than your thoughts. That which makes you you, is deeper than your beliefs.

This goes counter to what you have probably been led to believe but your beliefs do not define you. Your beliefs are *used* by you to make decisions about how to be, but your beliefs do not make you who you are.

If your beliefs did define you then you could never recover from having your beliefs shattered. But deep down inside, people who have had their beliefs shattered fundamentally remain the same people they were before their beliefs were shattered.

I know this because I have met people who had their beliefs shattered and not only were they still alive but they had better, richer and more fulfilling lives after having lived through their crisis of belief.

I also know from personal experience that when my beliefs were shattered nearly thirty years ago, I was afraid that I might become someone else when I had to build a whole new foundation and structure of belief. I was afraid that whoever I would become when I adopted this new structure of belief would be someone I did not recognize or even like.

But throughout the whole ordeal I was still who I was. I did not become someone else. I changed, most certainly, but my deep, down core self stayed the same. I was still me. I existed before my beliefs were shattered, during the shattering and afterward as I built a new structure from the ground up.

You did exist before your foundation or structure of belief was built. You exist now. You will continue to exist even if your beliefs are shattered. You use your beliefs to help guide you through life, but you are not your beliefs. You are deeper than that. You are the wellspring of warm, light, active presence that is your spirit-consciousness and you exist whether you believe it or not, and you exist with or without beliefs.

SEPTEMBER 11 – DON'T BE AFRAID

Some people, when questioned about their beliefs, will respond with agitation or even aggression. Some will even be willing to use physical force to stop you.

Why such a violent reaction? It's not as if you assaulted them! Or is it?

There is an inherent terror in considering your beliefs to be wrong. There is a very real – though unwarranted – fear of ceasing to exist. (See also *Existing Structures of Belief*, *Preferred Ignorance* and *You Are Deeper than Belief*.)

This fear is completely understandable. After all, not only are we led to believe that our beliefs are what define us, but we also rarely questions those beliefs, much less search for something that might be even deeper than belief.

If I believe that my beliefs define me and I am considering changing my beliefs, it is perfectly natural for me to fear that I might become someone that I do not want to be. Or at the very least that I might become someone I am not. In other words, I may become someone else who I don't know and may not even like!

This brings into focus two of the things we fear the most: fear of ceasing to exist (if my beliefs change, I might no longer be) and fear of the unknown (if my beliefs change, I might become some *unknown* entity).

More than an expectation to change the world, it is these fears that drive people to "fight for their beliefs." The fear is real but the source of the fear is not fully understood by the person feeling it. As such, they will act as if you have attacked them because your questions carried with them the equivalence of an assault of such force and magnitude that their very existence feels threatened.

The kind of person I am describing is dangerous to themselves and to others. The danger to themselves is that they are acting out of fear, not intention. They may make some irrational choices which they could live to regret.

The danger to others exists because this person who is terrified of redressing their own foundation of belief will often go out of their way in an attempt to find external authorization and validation of their structure of belief.

Even if their conviction of belief is low (see also, *Conviction of Belief*) they will evangelize their belief in an effort to validate themselves. They will rally against anyone or anything that suggests to them that they should reconsider their beliefs.

Inside, the person enters 'fight or flight' mode and becomes willing to die for their belief (even if they don't truly believe whatever it is they're fighting for). The reason they are willing to die is not because they believe so strongly in the belief in question, but rather because they believe they will die (E.g. cease to exist) if they stand down.

What these people need to understand is that they will continue to exist even if they discover their beliefs were wrong. It is terrifying to lose your structure of belief and even more so to lose your foundation of belief, but even so, because we are deeper than our beliefs, we do not cease to exist when our beliefs change.

SEPTEMBER 12 – RELIGIOUS DELUSIONS?

If there really are no actual gods in space (or wherever), how can so many people have it wrong?

This is a tricky one to answer. They're not wrong. And they are. It is a paradox, but much like Not, gods are not real and they are real. (See also, *Introduction to Not* and *Not*.)

There is postulation that before the advent of writing, we had internal guidance on what to do and how to act. This authorization came directly from our minds, we considered it to be divine and we did not question it. When writing started to become prevalent, writing started to provide guidance for the masses in addition to our gods. However, writing could be interpreted. Writing could be argued about. Writing could be doubted. Soon thereafter, the unquestioning allegiance to higher powers started to wane and humanity began to doubt the existence of our gods.

Does this mean that 80% of the world is delusional?

By no means. The gods were never actual entities that walked around and did things in the world, but they were nevertheless very real to all of us thousands of years ago. They are still very real to some people. To other people they are only mostly real. To others, they are half real. To yet another set of the population, the gods are just kind of real. Then there are those who don't believe in them at all.

So are they real or not?

They are very real to people who believe in them.

Consider Not.

Not cannot exist.

But through reason and logic we can demonstrate the existence of Not. It is real and it is not real.

Gods can hurt their believers because their believers believe their gods can hurt them.

But gods that we do not believe in cannot hurt us. Ahura Mazda, Zeus, Allah, Jesus and all the others all have this in common. If you do not believe that these are supreme beings that exist somewhere, they can have no power in your life.

The theistic religious are not deluded. They just believe in things that the secular do not believe in.

September 13 – Belief in Fate

Is there such thing as fate? Do you believe in destiny?

On the one hand we cannot answer this question without knowing whether or not we were created or just happened to become.

Without knowing what the bigger picture looks like we can't necessarily know whether or not there is fate or destiny.

But on the other hand, we've already seen experiments in quantum physics like the double slit experiment where it seems particles (or waves) change their behavior based on observation and can even go back in time to change their behavior in order to satisfy the observer.

Also, considering all of life being looked at as a big picture there is evidence that everything is interconnected with everything else, so in this regard perhaps fate or destiny is real.

There is another answer that indicates that fate is real: belief. As discussed in several other places in this work and others, strong enough belief in something can cause that thing to manifest into reality and in that regard fate can be real if one believes in their fate and manifests that fate into reality.

SEPTEMBER 14 – ARE THERE SUCH THINGS AS ACCIDENTS?

Do you believe in accidents?

Looking back on events that seemed like accidents, it is often easy to draw lines between causes and events, connecting the dots into a cohesive picture that makes it easy to believe "the accident" actually happened for a reason.

"If I hadn't lost my keys that morning and been delayed in leaving the house, I would have been in the twenty-car pileup that killed 15 motorists."

Was it *an accident* that I lost my keys?

Whether or not accidents happen depends completely on your perspective. It depends on how you look at the world and your life.

However, with everything completely interconnected it is hard to imagine that an accident could occur.

SEPTEMBER 15 – EVERYTHING HAPPENS FOR A REASON

Or, conversely, nothing happens by mistake. Today's meditation is similar to yesterday's meditation where we considered whether or not accidents can happen. If we say that everything happens for a reason, we are saying there are no accidents.

Do you think everything happens for a reason?

It does appear that everything happens for a reason, but that does not necessarily mean what it might seem to mean.

The reason everything happens for a reason is because after the thing has happened and the effects and consequences have been experienced and we have grown or changed from the thing that happened, we can then draw the lines of reason – the lines of cause and effect – and from that vantage point we can see that some seemingly random thing was not random and that because of that thing some great achievement for us became possible.

It is said that someone who can read cannot look upon words without reading them. Just by glancing at a written word that you know, your mind reads the word whether you want it to or not.

It may be the same with consciousness and time. It may be that looking back on any event (looking back in time), the spirit-consciousness creates reason whether or not there was reason there before the event took place.

At any rate, if this is a choice that we can make, then life does seem better when everything happens for a reason.

September 16 – Free Will

Yesterday we mentioned choice. Do we really have a choice? Or is this all a matter of perspective?

Some might argue that even those of us that live in a free country are not free. We are all prisoners trapped within a blue spheroid orbiting a medium sized yellow star in an outer arm of a spiral galaxy hurdling through space at speeds we cannot comprehend.

Yesterday we considered whether or not everything happens for a reason. It might be nice to think that everything happens for a reason but would that then obviate the possibility for free will?

Can you imagine a system in which we can choose freely yet all things are interconnected in such a way that causes and events are all tied together in order to yield some preordained outcome?

Why not?

We have awoken as seeming agents of order in a swirl of what appears to be chaos. Anything goes.

One thing is certain. There is certainly the appearance (or illusion) of free will. Whether or not we can really freely choose, the net result is the same.

As long as we think we have free will, what difference does it make whether or not we really do?

SEPTEMBER 17 – HOW CAN I BE GOOD?

By asking this question and exhibiting concern over the answer, you have already demonstrated that you are good.

Being good means caring about how you are affecting the world around you.

Look at what you are putting into the world. Do you think you are putting more good than bad into the world? If so, you are being a good person.

If you think you're putting more bad into the world than good you should take a look at how to stop that.

If that were the case, how would you go about changing?

Start by asking other people how they put more good than bad in the world. Starting those kinds of conversations and then really listening to the answers can be very enlightening. (See also, *Cinereo Modo.*)

SEPTEMBER 18 – YOUR SPIRIT CAN DO NO WRONG

You, as a physical being are capable of wrongdoing. But you, as an energy being, are not.

I mean the spirit-consciousness which is your inner self.

Your spirit-consciousness cannot do wrong. It is the epitome of warm, light, active presence and being warm, light, active presence is the objective. Thus, just by emanating warm, light, active presence, you are achieving the objective and "doing right." (See also, *Original Innocence*.)

SEPTEMBER 19 – KNOWING RIGHT FROM WRONG

Without the gods to tell us right from wrong, how can we tell good from evil?

When we are faced with a decision about whether or not something (let's say an idea) is good or evil, we begin to break the idea down and compare it to different sets of rules we have in place that will help us decide the final outcome. These layers of rules equate to methodologies we have learned throughout our lives for determining right from wrong. The first one that we use is the furthest one from our spirit-consciousness. In other words, the first questions we ask are the shallowest questions as they are furthest from our deepest inner-self.

The shallowest most outer layer is essentially the beliefs of the community at large. That is to say, the laws of the land. If the law says this thing we are contemplating is illegal then it is often wrong as well. Of course this is not always the case. Right action can be illegal just as wrong action can be legal. Thus it may be that the legality of a decision is not enough of a test to determine whether or not it is right or wrong.

The next layer down we have our greater structure of belief. Our structure of belief can be compared to building with doorways, rooms and hallways. We use these various rooms and hallways to determine which way to go when faced with difficult decisions. Our beliefs guide us in coming up with an answer.

In the event our structure of belief cannot provide guidance, there is another layer, deeper still, which is our foundation of belief. Our foundation of belief is comprised of truths that we value. These truths can be used as ethical guideposts on our journey throughout life.

By the time you have reached your foundation of belief, you should be able to determine if the idea you are considering is right or wrong.

There is a feeling you get when you know something to be wrong. That part is easy.

The hard part is when something seems right but is wrong. This is where your personal code must be relied upon to pull you through.

SEPTEMBER 20 – HOW CAN DEATH BE LIFE?

Light a candle.

Blow out the candle.

Watch the wick glowing orange as the smoke streams up.

Imagine that the orange glow is a life.

The glow is the animation of the life. The glow is the blazing spirit of this life. How it burns in celebration of life and being!

Watch as it fades away and then is completely gone.

Imagine that what you just witnessed is the death of that life.

Where there was orange, glowing heat, there is now cold, gray ash.

Now for the important part.

Keep staring at the cold gray ash and realize that the ashes are not death. Keep looking. The fact that you see something there means there *is something there*. And what is it? It is not just cold, gray, dead ash.

If you zoom in deep enough, you will see a world alive with molecules and atoms. You will see subatomic particles zooming and zinging in all directions.

It is Life! It is warm, light, active presence!

This is why even death is still considered Life.

September 21 – Love your Past

The path that you have walked is the path that led you to where you are today. That is to say, you are the sum of all the decisions you have made and all of the experiences you have had.

Do you like where you are? Because the path you take from here is the path you will have walked to get where you will be sometime in the future. In other words, your five year older self will look back to today and see that "Five years ago, I was there."

There are many lessons in this. Foremost is gratitude. Could you be in a better place today? Perhaps. But it could also certainly be worse.

If you love yourself now, then you should be grateful to your past self for taking the steps necessary to achieve this level of self-acceptance.

If you have some work to do on self-acceptance and self-love, take a step forward today so that your future self can look back with gratitude and thanks for the work you did today.

September 22 – Autumnal Equinox

It is autumn!

Today we mark the beginning of autumn and the halfway point between the summer and winter.

Traditionally we consider day and night to be of equal length on the equinox, although we also note that after today the days will continue to get shorter as the nights begin to lengthen.

If you can perform the ritual celebration of the autumnal equinox today, you should.

If you cannot, then perhaps you can still honor this day by finding some sign of fall outside and bringing it in to set upon your altar. If so, you should also light a candle in honor of autumn.

In autumn, we reflect on the beauty and the thriving life of the summer which has just passed and we look forward to the winter that is to come. We consider "the harvest" which will sustain us through the winter.

For today's meditation, consider what you will need to weather the winter that lies ahead. Will it be determination? Indomitable spirit? Self-control? What character strength will you need to embrace for this?

September 23 – Faith

Faith is good.

When we talk about faith, we are talking about a belief in something that cannot be proven. Many of the theistic religious devout have faith that their deity exists. They have faith in their gods. By far, this is the most common understanding of the word, "faith."

But there is also faith in science. Most everyone has faith that science will one day explain the mysteries that remain unsolved. We cannot prove that science will answer these questions, but we have faith that it will.

Truly, at our cores, none of us knows what is going on here. Various people think various things but any postulation about what is happening here (the meaning of life) is posited solely on faith. And in order to carry on, we must have faith that this existence has meaning. Even if the meaning is only personal and transitory.

SEPTEMBER 24 – BLIND FAITH

Blind faith is not good. But yesterday we said that faith is good.

What is the difference?

The difference is very significant. Blind faith is having faith in something regardless of any evidence provided by the senses, mind or spirit-consciousness.

Let's discuss two extremes:

It is perfectly reasonable that if I were raised to believe there were no such thing as gods that I move forward in my life not believing in gods.

What is not reasonable is that I should have blind faith that there are no gods. This means that even if I were to have a revelation from a god or an experience where I felt the touch of a god that I refused to acknowledge it even though it was very real to me. Ignoring evidence that contradicts my faith and moving forward irrationally is a result of blind faith.

Contrariwise, it is perfectly reasonable that if I were raised to believe in gods that I move forward in my life having faith in the gods.

But it is unreasonable that I should have blind faith in the gods. This means that even if I were to have a revelation (forgive the term) or an experience where I suddenly felt deep inside that there were no gods that I refuse to acknowledge those feelings even though they are very real to me. Ignoring evidence that contradicts my faith and moving forward irrationally is a result of blind faith.

Action tied to blind faith can be very dangerous. This is the basis for terrorism and often murder.

SEPTEMBER 25 – DETACH FROM OUTCOME

Anxiety is the result of fear and expectation. Whether or you are expecting something good or bad to happen, as the expectation becomes stronger so does the anxiety that goes with it. Or, if the outcome of the upcoming event cannot be anticipated, fear can result. The fear is a heady mix of fear of the unknown combined with fear of the worst possible outcome.

It is normal to be somewhat anxious about some event; a little bit of anxiousness is to be expected. However, in most circumstances we have virtually no control over the outcome of future events.

The energy you expend on attempting to discern an outcome is misaligned energy. In fact, that is part of the problem. This undirected energy becomes energy that feeds the anxiety.

The best approach is to "detach from outcome." Easy to say but sometimes hard to do. The way to pull this off, is to know that you cannot know the outcome and therefore simultaneously prepare for multiple outcomes. Imagine the worst case scenario and then see your way through it. Yes it could be bad, but even the worst experiences become past events that we learn from in due time. Know that in the end, you will get through it and be wiser for the experience. Once you have imagined a way through the worst of it, let go of it, knowing that you'll persevere and then imagine the best case scenario. This is usually less daunting, but this possible future you should also let go of. Once you have imagined the possibilities and understand that you'll still be you when all is said and done, detach from outcome. Let the river flow and see what the universe brings forth.

The further you can detach from outcome, the more balanced, centered, and in control of your inner self you can be.

September 26 – Love

Today's meditation is on love.

In the NR&C there is a ritual called the Ritual of Emanation which is used to emanate love energy into the world.

But how do we do this? How do we feel love for people we don't know, or even more difficult, for people we know. Especially for people we think are not good people.

Oddly, once you understand the complete and utter vulnerability of a person, love comes naturally. And people who are mean or nasty are often the most vulnerable.

A couple points of clarification here: one, you do not have to love a person's actions to love a person. It is very difficult to parse out action from being sometimes, but they are not the same thing. Two, loving the person does not mean allowing the person's actions to harm you. Never allow a person to harm you in any of the aspects of the self. But you can still love.

At any rate, for today's meditation it is not necessary to hyper focus your love on an individual. Today, focus on emanating love energy in waves that ripple out into the universe washing over everything and everyone outside of you. Make the love unconditional and limitless. You have that power. If you have never done it before, trust that you can do it. Try it right now and you will see how simple it really is. (I know: just because it is simple does not mean it is easy.)

Close your eyes, envision your glowing white energy center, feel the love pouring forth from there and let is flow outward.

SEPTEMBER 27 – LIFE AFTER DEATH

Is there life after death?

Yes, there is.

For many reasons we can say with relative ease of certainty that there is life after death. The first and most prominent reason is because life is part of Life and Life is warm, light, active presence. Even in death, we are warm, light, active presence. (See also, *Death is Life* and *Life is Death*.)

Similarly, energy may neither be created nor destroyed and we are all energy.

Finally, consciousness seems to be something that transcends physicality. At the risk of getting too far into postulations, it seems that consciousness is likely something that not only transcends physicality but is likely something that transcends time as well.

And now, at the risk of sounding too far out, this literally means that consciousness transcends time and space.

Considering the meditations titled *What It Isn't* and *The Linear Spiral*, is it so much of a stretch to imagine that consciousness is an aspect of something that is beyond the third or fourth dimensions?

SEPTEMBER 28 – ABSOLUTE AUTHORITY

One of the problems of most religions is the assertion of absolute authority. Most religions in general (and all theistic religions) have no choice but to assert that they have the only true religion and that they worship the only true god(s). Being one of the believers in the only true religion and the only true god(s) gives one absolute authority on the purpose and meaning of life.

It is kind of a trap that they have set for themselves. Or perhaps it is fairer to say it is a trap they have inherited. If they claim their god is true (and especially if they claim their god is the only god), and that they themselves have the only true path which was ordained by the only true god(s), they have painted themselves into a corner. At this point they have to profess that they alone have absolute knowledge and absolute authority.

What is wrong with having absolute authority?

Well, for one, power corrupts and absolute power corrupts absolutely. Having absolute authority brings with it absolute power. This is bad for everyone. It is bad for the followers because they may be exploited by the leadership. It is bad for the leadership because they may be tempted to believe that they really do have absolute knowledge and absolute authority when it comes to understanding the world around them.

The other problem with people thinking and acting like they have absolute authority is that other people might believe them. If someone believes them, they may follow them and if they really believe that the religion and therefore the religious leaders of that religion have absolute knowledge or absolute authority to represent the creator-god(s), they may be willing to do anything the religion or the religious leaders tell them to do. Even if it violates principles that should be held above all others such as the respect for the sanctity of life.

This absolute belief and the subsequent walking around as if one has absolute knowledge and authority is the result of blind faith. It also continues to foster blind faith in the believer. Similar to the way the religion is trapped into maintaining that they alone have absolute authority, so is the believer trapped into that mode of thinking. The believer must preach that they alone have the only true knowledge on this planet and that everyone else is wrong and that everyone else must either join them or suffer whatever consequences their creator-god(s) deems fit for people that do not believe in it/them.

Ironically, the burden this places on the believer is the same burden that falls upon those who do not believe in any kind of higher power. (See also, *Your Higher Power*.)

If you think you have absolute authority when it comes to the purpose or meaning of life, it gives you an overinflated sense of self which can manifest in egotism and other undesirable behavior. In other words, you can become arrogant, overconfident, self-serving and just generally unpleasant to be around.

Second, if you think you have absolute authority in these matters, whether you know it or not, you automatically take on the responsibility for all of the world's problems. When things go wrong, you feel like you (or your deity) should have or could have done something to prevent it. Over time, when things happen in the world that are incongruent with the teachings of your deity, this weight can be overbearing and lead to intense mental, emotional, and spiritual anxiety.

Nobody knows what is really going on here. (See also, *What It Isn't*.) So regardless of what you believe, you should always hold on to a glimmer of doubt. There is only one absolute: there are no absolutes. Oh wait. There are two. One is that *there are none* and the other is *Not*.

September 29 – The Need to Believe

As humans, we all want to believe in something. Most of us want this desperately. But what can we believe in? Is there somewhere we can put our faith where we will not be let down?

We can believe in science until the answers stop and the mysteries continue to confound us. We can believe in gods until we really need one and it isn't there. We can believe in religion until our religion asks us to believe in things or do things we are not comfortable with. We can believe in humanity until we see the ugly side of human nature and want to turn away. We can believe in ourselves until we realize that we need to believe in something greater than ourselves.

This desire to believe in something is extremely dangerous for us and can lead us astray. The Nazi Party is a good example of what a burning desire to believe can yield. Other good examples are Waco and The People's Temple. There are more examples: holy warriors, jihadists, crusaders and suicide bombers.

We must find something we can believe in that cannot let us down. Something that is true and pure that will not lead us astray. Something that can withstand the scrutiny of science and stand its ground against any religion. Something that is greater than ourselves but that doesn't belittle us. Something that cannot be used to make us hurt others or ourselves.

Not is all of those things.

We can believe in Not.

SEPTEMBER 30 – THE WORLD IS GETTING BETTER

How can I say that? There's war, gross inequality, famine, terrorism, hunger, massive forest fires, pogroms, jihads, economic crisis, mass poverty, killer storms, global pandemics, all manner of terrible sex crimes and overall complete imbalance.

One could go on listing all the things wrong with the world. There are far more than that small list above.

But thinking that the "world is going to hell in a handbasket" is normal. Thinking that the world has gotten worse and continues to get worse with every passing decade is a generational norm.

But let me ask you this: Can the world really be getting worse and worse with every passing year? Did it start in the Garden of Eden and then begin to decline every day from there until now? And as it continues to slide into the miasma, what does tomorrow look like? Or the next day? How far down into the muck can it go? Is there a bottom to how awful it can become?

This idea that the world is getting worse every year is a fallacy. It is something people say because they see change around them and they fear it. They feel the changes happening around them and it makes them uncomfortable.

The truth is, the world is getting better.

We are becoming smarter and more connected to each other. We are learning more and more about ourselves, the quantum, the macro and world around us. We are able to synthesize more vitamins and proteins in order to sustain us thus minimizing the need to take life.

We are learning more about our own bodies, our nutritional needs, the science and art of exercise and our spirituality. This is increasing longevity and maintaining our fitness. With the Internet, we also have instant access to an astounding plethora of information thus enriching us intellectually and culturally. Despite ourselves, globally we are becoming more civil.

We need each other – the whole world – all of us – and we can now reach each other. We communicate far better than ever before. The entire globe is connected in a way that has no precedent. Technology is introducing new problems for us to overcome but it is also allowing us to connect in ways never before possible. Being connected to each other resonates with Relationships and Community – two of the Principles of Not.

As we expand our awareness of our world and universe we also expand our awareness of ourselves.

There will always be calamity and horror in the world. But we are becoming more civilized as we learn more about ourselves and the world around us. And this is making a better world for us to thrive in.

The world is getting better every day!

OCTOBER 1 – NOBODY CAN RUIN YOUR DAY

Today's meditation is on this idea that nobody can ruin your day. The intent of this expression is to drive home the point that if you have a bad day it is because you chose to have a bad day. It is not someone else's fault, it is your fault. You are not a victim of circumstance but rather the active creator (or author) of your day.

As with most truth, there is paradox here.

It is true that we choose how we will react to any given situation. When someone repulsive or evil is nasty toward you, you choose to be upset or to be happy after you get away from that person.

But it is not as easy as it sounds. Perhaps if you are a saint or you have reached transcendence you can remain happy after being thoroughly immersed with negative energy, but most of us are not transcendent saints.

It is good to remember that "nobody can ruin your day," but do not be too hard on yourself if someone does come along and ruin your day from time to time.

OCTOBER 2 – THE VALUE OF CHURCH

In western culture there is an unspoken nobility that comes along with going to church. Or at least with "being a churchgoer." For people who do not subscribe to a religion, this can be a dreaded but common question to hear when meeting new people: "What church do you go to?"

When discussing religion with another person, the theistic believer will often feel elevated above anyone that does not attend a church. As an individual, one may not be able to establish equal rank in the discussion and in this case, one's argument will fall on deaf ears just by virtue of the fact that it comes from "a heathen that does not even attend church."

Being a member of the Church of Not automatically "elevates" you into equal footing with any other churchgoer.

It is nice to have the power of the Church behind you. As a member of the Church, you have the full canon of scripture to back up your belief as well as the religious body of the church, the religion itself and all the membership and clergy.

With this power, you may stand toe to toe with a churchgoer from any other religion and hold your ground when it comes to belief, principle and conviction.

There comes along the occasional person who will argue their point of view in such a way as if they know with certainty that their truth is the all-truth.

When this type of person comes along, it is nice to have the power of the Church behind you to fend off such an attack.

OCTOBER 3 – THE SUFFERING OF DEATH IS ONLY FOR THE LIVING

When someone we know passes, it is not the person that passes that suffers, but rather those of us left behind.

The person who enters the great transformation is now free from the limitations and constraints that we suffer.

They are transformed into whatever comes next and as such we suffer their loss even when we know they may be in a better place.

Meanwhile, we mourn because of this. We miss the warmth and love we used to feel from them; that live energy connection we had with them. We remember the joy they brought into the world. We consider how they made the world better just by being. But most of all we mourn the loss of what they had yet to bring into this world.

October 4 – Science

Today's meditation is on science and more specifically the question of the value of science to humanity.

Although science and the ideas of science date back hundreds of years (perhaps more than two thousand years – to Aristotle), the scientific method as more clearly defined is only around 400 years old. At any rate, if you graph the curve of technological breakthroughs due to the development of science you will see a geometric curve.

There is no doubt that science has changed civilization for the better. Through science we have advanced technology to "boundaries" that are difficult to even comprehend. I put quotes around the word, "boundaries," because there really are no boundaries. Our boundaries are only brief stopping points which temporarily cause us to pause. We must be grateful for these because the rapid pace at which we are advancing certainly needs to be examined from time to time to ensure we are not going down the wrong path.

Would we be better off without all of this amazing technology? Some people think so. There is an aspect of no-tech that is certainly appealing. The idea of being more one with nature is a tempting dream.

The reality of being one with nature, however, is the reality of being one with chaos. While many would have you believe that the universe is chaos and that life is order, it often seems quite the opposite.

Whether you consider nature to be an agent of chaos or that of order, one thing is undeniable. Nature is terribly beautiful but also cruel, harsh, dangerous and unforgiving. Technology allows us to live side by side with nature in relative comfort. We can enjoy environmental control while the cruel danger rages on outside.

One of the questions we should often ask is, "To what end?"

Where is this all going?

While this is a great mystery and is more thoroughly treated in *The Postulations*, there is one obvious answer that we should contemplate today.

As alluded to in the entry, Future Humans, humanity has barely changed in the last hundred thousand years. One hundred thousand years ago we were banging on rocks with sticks and grunting at each other. It is only our access to technology that separates us from our early ancestors.

If you took a group of babies and put them in an area of nature where there was no technology and no human parentage to teach them language, writing, civics and the scientific method, I daresay that they would grow up to be hominids that went around banging on rocks with sticks and grunting at each other.

However, in time, through the integration of technological advancement with our own genetics and biology, we will evolve into a new humanoid. This new humanoid will be born with technological advancement already in place. It is a leap in technology we may not see for many decades but it does seem inevitable and it will allow us to continue to advance ourselves and our civilization in ways that we can only write about in science fiction today. (See also, *Modern Humans*.)

OCTOBER 5 – PHILOSOPHY

Speaking of advancing civilization…

Strictly speaking, philosophy is not a science but it is not an art either. Nor is it religion. But it is tied into all of those things.

Philosophy is the study of the nature of existence. Philosophy allows us to ask questions about the world around us and allows us to examine conjecture which surrounds the answers.

When neither science nor religion can help us, philosophy often can. Through philosophical discourse we can address the great mysteries (See also, *The Mysteries : Album Mysteria Non.*)

Arguably, philosophy has done more to advance human civilization than any other field of study.

There is another meaning of the word philosophy that applies to us today. It is about the Fourth Principle, Codice Personalum. Your personal code is also the basis for your philosophy.

OCTOBER 6 – BEING PART OF THE PACK

Humans are pack animals when it comes to hunting and survival. Another way to express this idea is to say that we are social creatures. We need each other. We are "tribal."

In the not so distant past we needed each other in order to bring down large game animals for food. Times have changed radically since then, but we still need each other.

However the cooperation we need from each other now is more along the lines of validation and acceptance than the need for someone to flank the beast while the spear throwers prepare for the kill.

We look to each other for guidance on being. Technological advancement in food production and housing has solved most of our primal needs. Of course, we need each other in order to make our technology function – we need each other to make our cities work. But with our primal needs satisfied, many of us have to come up with a plan on how to be, what to do and how to act.

Sometimes it is nice to be alone, but this is almost always only in the context of "getting away from other people." In other words, it is only nice to be alone because we have other people to get away from. If we were isolated from other people indefinitely, for most everyone, being alone would be a dreadful prospect.

Truly, most of us would rather be the Omega Wolf than be alone. This means that we would rather play any role in a social structure than not be a part of it. We need our tribe.

October 7 – Belonging

Yesterday we meditated on our need to be with other people. The idea that humans need each other for more than just help in building a house or hunting big game but for validation and acceptance as well.

We need to feel like we belong. This is a powerful idea and a powerful compulsion within us. It is ironic that social media makes us feel so disconnected from each other. Through the Internet we are connected, but just a connection alone does not bring a feeling of belonging.

Many of us spend much of our lives looking for "our people." Wanting to feel like we belong is not a bad thing. It just means that we are human. But feeling that longing to belong is also a dangerous thing.

There are unscrupulous predatory humans out there who prey on this need for belonging.

One of the first steps in defending ourselves from being exploited due to our own need for belonging is to understand at the deepest level that we do belong here. We belong here and we also belong to each other. All of us do. Not just as humans, but as beings of energy and light. As beings of warm, light, active presence we belong to the warmth, the light, the action and the presence of Life.

Perhaps in knowing that we belong to Life already, we can relax a little bit and take our time in finding "our people."

October 8 – If You Are Lucky, You'll Hit the Bottom

Hitting the bottom is a terrible feeling. It is a forlorn feeling. It is despair, despondence and misery. It is a feeling such as, "all is lost."

But like the phoenix, sometimes one must fall all the way to the bottom before they can rise again.

When we've hit the bottom, we have lost most everything. But this includes some of the things that caused us to hit bottom in the first place. While we may lose our way and even our hope, the upside of "hitting bottom" is that we also lose the predispositions and various beliefs that led us to the pit we have fallen in.

There is another upside to having hit the bottom. From the bottom, there is only one direction we can go. That is to say, we can only go up from there.

And when we do rise again after having hit the bottom, we often rise stronger and smarter – E.g. *more fit* – than we were before.

We have to bottom out before we can recover. When we recover we grow. When we grow, we become better people. Better people make a better civilization.

There are some other expressions that are based on this same principle. For instance, "It has to get worse before it gets better."

This is a reflection of the cycle of destruction and creation that we see in myth and legend dating back to before humanity could even write, when stories were handed down from one generation to the next through spoken words or songs.

Before the perfect utopia can be bestowed upon mankind, there must be a destructive apocalypse. Or perhaps less epic, before we can remodel a house, we have to gut the old house.

There is one other jewel that hitting the bottom provides is. Regardless of what we have lost or gained in the process of hitting the bottom and rising back up again, one thing remains with us the entire time.

Self.

This is the inner self – the deeper self. The spirit-consciousness. This is the self that witnessed the approach, the fall, the rise and the new flight! Your self is continuous and true despite what may go on around it.

Even your final transformation here on Earth will not extinguish your spirit-consciousness, but rather the warm, light, active presence will just change into something else.

OCTOBER 9 – INDOMITABLE SPIRIT

This is another way of saying, "stick-to-itiveness." Your spirit is a roaring fire that cannot be extinguished. (See also, *Death is Life* and *Life is Death*.)

If you take a few moments to consider this, you will see the truth in it and therefore the value in that knowledge.

The value in knowing that your spirit is unquenchable is that no matter how bad it gets out there in the real world, the fire that is your spirit – the warm, light, active presence that is your spirit-consciousness – will continue to burn brightly deep within you.

It can get very dark outside. It can become very scary. Terrifying even. And there may be times you feel you are not going to make it. There may be times where you feel like your only recourse is to quit. You may feel beaten and defeated.

But as long as you can still feel beaten and defeated, you are neither. As long as you can still feel anything at all – even the blinding sun or the cold fear of night – this means that your spirit still burns with warm, light, active presence!

As hard as it might be, take one foot and place it before the other. Take the next step. Then the next. Keep moving forward. This is the embodiment of indomitable spirit.

October 10 – You Have to Have a Plan

Where are you going with your life? What are you working toward? Are you just drifting from weekend to weekend or from year to year?

What do you want?

Add five years to your age and ask yourself, "What does my life look like at [___]?" (insert your age + 5)

There are two things to do right now. One, make a plan. Even if it is just a temporary plan. For instance, you may think, "I don't know what I want to do." In that case, choose something – anything. I want to be a game reviewer. I want to be a carpet salesperson. I want to work in a factory. I want to be a computer programmer. Or if you already have a profession you are okay with, maybe it is something like learning a new instrument. I want to learn how to paint. I want to learn how to make spreadsheets and use a word processor. Pick something.

That thing you picked is "your plan."

What is the first step in achieving your plan? Write down this first step. Now go do it. (See also, *Reigning in the Chaos*.)

OCTOBER 11 – THE MIND/BODY CONNECTION

Today's meditation is on *the mind*. Where is your mind? Is it in your brain? Is it in your body? Is your mind an ethereal concept that doesn't even really exist? Can it be quantified? Is your mind the same thing as your consciousness? Is this, then, also the same thing as spirit?

Before we try to answer the question of where or what the mind is, we have to ask another: Does it matter? Isn't it a moot point when it comes to using the mind?

But for the sake of conversation, we should put forth a working definition. The mind is the combination of thought and consciousness. Thought is the awareness generated by the body and consciousness is the awareness of that thought-awareness. Consciousness is undefined. We usually call it "spirit-consciousness" in order to mentally tie those two concepts together.

The mind is what the spirit-consciousness is aware of when the mind is having thoughts. The mind (probably?) ceases to exist when the physical body perishes. The spirit-consciousness is another story.

OCTOBER 12 – DEPTHS OF THOUGHT

In the Towns and Prairies
In the towns and prairies people talk about sports and the weather. You cannot even see the ocean from here.

The Beach
On the beach people talk about things that pertain to governance and survival. Here is where things like politics, nutrition and fitness are discussed.

The Shallows
As you head into the ocean you start by entering the shallows. The shallows are about ankle-deep. This is where you will find religion. For most people, religion (or science as a religion) answers the questions of life before the person even asks the questions. Having been born and raised within a framework where one already knows the answers before the questions are even asked, one may go through their entire life never asking questions that run deeper than "the shallows."

Knee-Deep
Out here where the water is about knee-high are some of the initial questions about life, the universe and everything. Where did this all come from? Why am I here? What is the purpose of life? It is here that one might first question their belief system.

Waist-Deep
At this level we have the full gamut of *The Mysteries*. (See also, *The Mysteries: Album Mysteria Non*.) Considering these questions of life requires some deep thought and in attempting to answer these questions one naturally stumbles upon new questions which may also require deep thought or even deeper thought. This is where you will find people who live "examined lives." This means people who continually look within to see if what they are doing is matching what they believe in.

Neck-Deep
The contemplation or discussion from the waist-deep waters often brings people into these neck-deep waters. Here the ideas

are deeper and often bring us face to face with our most core beliefs and ideologies. Being this far out can be really scary but also can be exhilarating.

Underwater

This is where one sees beyond the structure or foundation of their own beliefs. This is where one encounters their deepest self and the most fundamental aspects of spirit-consciousness. At this level one understands that their true selves are separate from their beliefs. Here we see that everything that is not the spirit-consciousness is essentially illusory.

In the Black

This is Not.

October 13 – Victim Mentality

Is the sun burning the face of Mercury on purpose?

Is Mercury a victim?

What about you?

Is the universe happening *to* you?

Or is this all happening around you? (Or maybe this is all happening *for* you?)

Every moment of our lives we are free to recreate the moment.

We all have old recordings we replay when something happens but we are free to change these automated responses at any time. We usually do not even know we are playing old pre-recorded responses. That's the "automated" part of the process. But when something happens that kicks off one of these automated responses, we all have a split-second where if we are paying attention, we can stop the automation and insert a live response.

Do not play the victim. Even when you are being victimized. Think of the interaction differently. Change your response and turn the outcome into something that works to your advantage.

You are not a victim. Even when you are.

October 14 – Belief

Can a belief be more important than a life? Can belief hold more value than life?

The Authorist would say no.

The reason is very straightforward.

Belief cannot exist without life.

Imagine a barren planet completely devoid of life. Is there belief there? If you say yes, then the only explanation for there being belief there is because you have placed it there. And *you* are life!

Belief cannot exist without an entity doing the believing. Some form of life must believe the belief or the belief will not be.

How can a belief hold more value than life when, without life the belief cannot be?

It is for this reason that Authorism asserts that no belief can be more important than life.

OCTOBER 15 – PERFECTION

What is perfection? Perfection is the highest level achievable.

When we are talking about human activities, theoretically and generally speaking, perfection cannot be achieved.

This is all rather subjective but nonetheless, in any given field or discipline what was thought to be the highest level of achievement can usually be topped by a higher level achievement at some later time. For instance, what was thought to be the perfect photograph may be topped by a photograph that is even better. The perfect vehicle may be topped by a vehicle that is even better.

If we can agree that absolute perfection cannot be achieved, then I would like to pose the question: Should we strive for perfection?

Is it tempting to say that since we know perfection cannot be achieved, we should not even bother trying?

Perhaps.

But we should strive for perfection anyway. But like all things, we should take this approach in moderation. We should strive for perfection but we really must settle for less or we may drive ourselves crazy.

Nonetheless, striving for perfection allows us to set a higher bar for success and pushes us to achieve greatness. If we are constantly pushing ourselves past what we thought our limits were, we will become better people, better communities and a better civilization. (See also, *Not, Perfect?*)

OCTOBER 16 – TOLERANCE IS EASY

Or at least, it should be easy. All you have to do is realize that were you born and raised under different circumstances you could very easily be something or someone that you might be intolerant of today.

There are many reasons to avoid feeling hate. The fact that you could be a racist bigot if you had been raised to believe in those ideals is one of many reasons not to hate racist bigots. And while you should not hate racism or bigotry either, that does not mean that you should love them. You should not give them any energy at all. Only then will they wither and die. Ironically, perhaps, we should not tolerate intolerance. But even intolerance of intolerance should not turn into hate. Marcus Aurelius said, "See that you never feel toward the inhumane what they feel toward humanity."

Do not let hatred of any kind twist your soul into convolutions that bring you suffering. Hatred brings suffering to whomever does the hating and to all of those around them.

Avoiding a racist bigot is certainly advisable. But hating one is a waste of your energy and feeds the disease instead of eradicating it. You will do nothing to make the world a better place by practicing hate.

Instead, understand that education is what makes us who we are. When we are children we learn from watching others and when we get older we learn from asking questions about the world. Try to teach others as you continue to learn.

And in the meantime, be tolerant of those who were raised to believe different things than you were. Never tolerate being harmed by them, but tolerate the fact that they exist. It is not their fault. They have just not yet been shown the way.

OCTOBER 17 – THE COMFORT OF FAMILIARITY

There is a certain comfort we derive from that which is familiar. This is a pleasant idea when it comes to slipping on old leather boots which you have had for years or when visiting a building that you have intimate familiarity with.

But this can be a terrible detriment to us also.

For those who suffer from addiction or abusive environments the miserable world one exists in can become the norm. When misery becomes normal for us, then misery is what becomes familiar. Safety, clarity, health and fitness become alien feelings and misery, despair and hopelessness become familiar. They can become so familiar that one becomes more comfortable in the miserable environment than in a healthy environment.

What I have described here are two extremes. There is a middle ground we should discuss as well. The middle ground is where complacency can happen. This is where the familiar becomes easy and then easy becomes comfortable. Once one goes along taking the easy path over and over again, a difficult path will seem alien and uncomfortable.

Do not let that happen to you. You can safeguard against the dangers of the comfort of familiarity by examining your life on a fairly regular basis. Ask yourself if you are too comfortable in any given situation. Your love life, your job or career, your hobbies, your health or your spirituality.

OCTOBER 18 – GO TO THE WOODS

Can you go to the woods today? Or the mountains? Or the dessert? Can you find a slice of nature to surround yourself with? If you can, today's meditation is more along the lines of homework.

Raw nature has the bewildering ability to recharge and invigorate us. Superman used our sun to recharge. This will work for us too. If you cannot find some nature to surround yourself with today, can you at least stand outside? Feel the sun or the wind or the rain on your face.

Finally, if for some reason you are unable to do any of the above mentioned "assignments," take a minute to close your eyes and imagine that you are in the woods or that you are being recharged by the sun. It is nothing like the real thing but it is still better than nothing when it comes to providing nutrition for your spirit-consciousness.

OCTOBER 19 – THE EMPATH

Why should we empathize with others?

Don't we have enough going on without us having to burden ourselves with other people's problems?

Shouldn't they just suffer through like everyone else does?

There is a very good reason to empathize with another's plight.

It is through empathy that we can fight ignorance. When we empathize with another we place ourselves in their shoes.

We then realize that we are the same as them and they are the same as us.

It is only through chance and circumstance that we are not them and that they are not us.

October 20 – The Tightrope

It is possible that somewhere in interstellar space, the galaxy or the universe at large there exists life with an incredibly large window of conditions that allow for it to survive.

But here in our solar system, according to what we understand about that which makes us "life," the window is extremely narrow.

The air we breathe must be a perfect mix of primarily nitrogen and oxygen. The temperature in which we can survive will depend on what tools we utilize to help us but either way it is a tiny slice of temperature ranges.

The frequency and composition of what we need to put in our bodies to live also exists in a narrow window. That is to say, food and water and how often we need to digest it. We can go about three days without water or seven days without food before we perish. In the grand scheme of things this is a very narrow window of time.

For that matter, apparently we need sleep to survive as well. And we need a lot of it daily!

We are incredibly strong, but we are also incredibly vulnerable. There are countless scenarios where we can easily be injured or killed from slight mishaps (bumps to the head, twists of the neck, etc.)

Of course, we only survive on the surface of this relatively tiny speck of earth which is flying through space at 67,000 MPH (108,000 KPH). Hopefully we don't hit anything big.

It would seem that we walk a tightrope through the chaos and only on this tightrope are we able to survive. We survive in a very narrow window of conditions.

The technology our ancestors have developed for us in clothing, building and environmental control has widened our window considerably but the window is still frighteningly narrow.

Today's meditation is not intended to hyper focus on how remarkably surprising it is that we survive from one minute to the next. Instead, the thought for today is to consider how fortunate it is for us that we survive from one minute to the next.

Truly, every minute that we feel the warmth, see the light, actively breathe the air and are present to consciously behold our own awareness is a minute we should be incredibly grateful for.

October 21 – Dichotomy

This tightrope we walk (or narrow window in which we live) exists in many other areas of our life as well.

The dark and light, good and evil, male and female, X chromosome and Y chromosome, plus and minus world around us gives us two opposing poles in which we frame all of existence.

The tightrope we walk extends between these two poles and we must constantly make adjustments as we walk in order to not fall completely to one side or the other.

In Authorian Philosophy we try to maintain a positive attitude, look for the good in the world and only think about bringing love and joy into the world, but the world is not a positive-only, loving and joyous only, light and cheery only place.

There is darkness all around us and sometimes we need to feel that darkness in order to appreciate the light. We can embrace the darkness but just as we should not delude ourselves that everything is rainbows and puppy dogs, we should not give ourselves all the way over to the dark side either.

We need to keep our balance as we walk the tight ropes between opposing poles.

I wonder if things would be easier if there were a third pole.

OCTOBER 22 – THE THIRD POLE

Today's meditation verges on a Postulation in that today we consider the addition of a third pole. (See also, *Dichotomy*.)

Yesterday I suggested that it might be easier if there were a third pole. If you are not fully tracking on what I mean by that, consider this beginning of a list of dualities that frame our thoughts:

1. Night and day
2. Good and evil
3. Right and wrong
4. Left and right
5. Up and down
6. In and out
7. Over and under
8. Darkness and light
9. Coldness and warmth
10. Activity and stillness
11. Presence and emptiness
12. Female and male
13. Plus and minus
14. Forward and back
15. Zero and one
16. Heaven and Hell

One could go on building such a list. In the last few days we considered the analogy of life being like walking a tightrope between some of these dualities of thought and being.

But what if there were a third "thing" in the mix? What if instead of dichotomy we had trichotomy?

Would this make our fundamental framework of thought more complicated? If so, would that be a good thing?

In the tightrope analogy, I was confusing the analogy somewhat when I mentioned the addition of a third pole. Instead of imagining the two poles on either side, in order to make the analogy work, we would need to imagine the tightrope being attached between two poles. And in this case, we are not walking the tightrope between two sides we might fall into, but between one pole and the other. The suggestion of a third pole would necessarily connect another tightrope from some new point to where we are on our tightrope. This turns our tightrope into the beginnings of a net instead of just a single line we must walk.

Wouldn't standing on a net be easier than standing on a single line?

OCTOBER 23 – FEEL THE AWE

If you were able to participate in the meditations from the last few days – and especially if you were able to meditate earlier in the year on the Linear Spiral (see also, *The Linear Spiral*) you may already feel the awe that accompanies your own awareness of a single moment of now. And in this case, I am not talking about your awareness of your awareness, but rather just your raw awareness of lucid reality.

Today's meditation is on the awe that we should feel when we pause and reflect on what it is we are doing.

Behold the sheer wonder of seeing light streaming into your eyes or the remarkable miracle that is your physiology turning the light into meaningful information you can then manipulate with pure thought.

At any moment in time, you can behold with all of your senses the warm, light, active presence of an incomprehensibly mind-blowing quantity of molecules and atoms which are all interconnected through the fundamental building blocks of Life. And the knowledge that this web of interconnectedness is, at least for all intents and purposes in our limited mapping of the universe so far, infinite. You are the Linear Spiral walking the Tightrope and in each moment of now you have the ability to witness the reality of all of this.

Again, this must be taken in balance. While one might be able to stay in a constant state of awe as the universe continues to explode around us in every seeming direction at the speed of light, it is ill advised as it might be difficult to focus on anything less mundane such as breathing and eating. And we must keep doing that in order to experience the awe that is Life and life.

Hmm... This seems like a circle. Perhaps a spiral?

OCTOBER 24 – THE BREATH OF AIR

Today's meditation is on taking a breath. Considering that this book offers a meditation for each day of the year, we should probably spend at least one day meditating on breath.

But this is a not a "breathing meditation." Instead, the thought for today is the contemplation of a single breath. It may take a few of these single breaths in order to feel the one we are trying to find.

The breath that we are looking for is "the perfect breath." This is not unlike the perfect golf stroke, the perfect jump or the perfect throw of a dart. It is something you feel inside and out when it happens.

The perfect breath is not just the perfect physiological process whereby you exchange air within your lungs. It is also not necessarily a *deep* breath, but it can be.

This "perfect breath" carries with it gratitude for air and the ability to breathe the air. You may also experience a moment of joy during this breath (this is just the joy of being – the joy of breathing). You feel every moment of this breath on the breathing in, the moments "at the top of the breath" before you begin the exhale and you feel the exhale also.

It feels good.

October 25 – Communication is the Key

There is an old expression that says, "Communication is the key to every relationship."

While trust is probably another element to consider, the expression is still not wrong. Communication *is* the key to every relationship. And the word, "every" needs to be in there for the expression to carry the weight of truth.

We often think immediately of love relationships when we hear this expression but love relationships are just one of many that we have with the people we encounter in the world. The relationship that exists between a clerk and a customer is dependent on communication as is the relationship between an employee and a boss.

Through communication we express what we want and what we are willing to give. This process of communicating what we want and what we will give defines the boundaries of the relationship and these boundaries must be defined in order for the relationship to be understood and for that matter in order for the relationship to develop and grow.

We should not assume that those we are in relationships with already know how much we care about them or how much we want from them or how much we are willing to give them. We should make sure we communicate these things to them.

Words are tricky and can be used to harm people or build them up. Words can be misinterpreted and misunderstood. We should endeavor to communicate as often as possible especially in relationships we wish to foster.

Today's meditation is on communication.

October 26 – Trust

We have already discussed that communication is the key to any relationship. What else is needed in a strong relationship?

Trust.

Any relationship that is destined to grow needs communication and trust. You must trust your partner and they must trust you.

One thing interesting about trust is that just because you trust someone else does not mean that they will naturally trust you. Love is similar. When you give your love freely to someone else, you should not expect that they will in turn give you their love just by virtue of having received some from you.

So if trusting someone else does not cause them to trust you back, how do you get someone else's trust?

There is really only one way to get someone else's trust. You must be trustworthy to that person. This is just as simple as it sounds. Being trustworthy means being worthy of trust.

How does one become worthy of trust? In order to be worthy of trust, you must not break trust. And, as it turns out, you really can't break trust with anyone. If one person sees you break trust with another even though you keep your trust with the first person, the trust will be broken with both people.

When you demonstrate that you are worthy of being trusted, other people will naturally trust you. This is a visceral thing that happens on a subconscious level.

October 27 – The Highest of Authorities

If Authorism were a theistic religion, our highest authority would be our god. If we were a polytheistic religion, the highest of authorities would likely be the most powerful god of the pantheon. This is all very "alpha" in nature, isn't it?

In the United States, the highest of authorities is the Supreme Court.

In England, the highest of authorities is Parliament.

In the world? Well, as of now there is none.

However, if one were to assert the existence of a creator-god, one could argue that their creator-god was a higher authority than any found on Earth. In fact, this has happened many, many times throughout the history of human civilization. The results are never good.

In Authorism, the author is you, but the legal authorities outside of Authorism still have power over you. In other words, local, regional, federal and international laws still apply. You may author your life, but that does not give you leeway to break the laws.

Authorist Church leaders are not authorities over members but rather authorities on the topic of Authorism. They may be consulted regarding questions about the religion but they may not exert authority over any member. In Authorism, there is no higher authority than the law, whether that be municipal, regional, state, federal or international law.

October 28 – Intellect

A keen, sharp intellect has never been more important to life. Over the last 50 years we have seen the completion of the move from the industrial age to the information age and over the last 20 years we have seen our full immersion into the information age.

In the industrial age, brawn was more valuable than brain.

In the information age, brain is more valuable than brawn.

We will transition from the information age to ... Well, we don't know quite yet.

When we do transition into the next age, we cannot be sure that our intellect will still be our greatest asset, but in all likelihood intellect will remain a very important strength to hone.

Intellect is the driving force behind philosophy and science and as such is the core artifact behind the advancement of human civilization.

Today, do something to keep your intellect sharpened.

OCTOBER 29 – BULLIES AND THE MARTIAL ARTS

Yesterday we talked about the importance of "brains over brawn." But what does this mean for brawn? Does this mean brawn is no longer important?

No, brawn remains very important. Just because intellect is more valuable and being intelligent may get you further in today's world than being physically strong, this does not mean you should ignore your physicality. The brawn aspect of physicality may take the form of just being strong, but there will always be someone stronger than you. For most of us, the best course of action is to enhance our strength through the creative use of strength in combat. This means training in the martial arts.

The bully is real and bullies will always be with us. We can outsmart a bully but there will come a time when even the outsmarted bully becomes physical and no amount of being smart will be able to match the bully's brawn. It is then that you will need your strength and your knowledge of the martial arts.

You should hone your intellect but you should also hone your physicality so that you are in the best shape. Not only to thrive as Life and life but to defend yourself when – quite literally and physically – push comes to shove.

If you know nothing of the martial arts, you should familiarize yourself with the concept. If you are familiar with the concept, you should look into studying one. If you have already studied one, perhaps it is time to study another.

For the martial artist, the art of martial movement becomes a way of life. It wraps around the inner core, fusing with one's Personal Code, wrapping around the structure and indeed sending roots into the foundation of belief in such a way as to strengthen the entire structure.

OCTOBER 30 – PRESSURE AND STRESS

Today's meditation is to consider the impact pressure and stress may be having on you.

Internal and external pressure placed on you by yourself and others result in the generic term "stress."

Stress is the root cause of more illness than any other single factor. Stress can cause us to lose our minds. Truly, stress can kill.

We must control our stress levels. And only you can control your own stress level. In order to even begin to control the amount of stress you are under, you must first be able to identify it.

Many people will say they are living with less stress than they are actually living with. In other words, most people are more stressed out than they think.

How is this possible? It is because stress is insidious. It can creep up on you.

The examined life is the most stress-proof life. Not because those who examine their lives do not experience stress but because those are constantly examining themselves discover stress before it can become so great that it becomes a problem. Once you realize you are experiencing stress you can begin to take steps to eliminate it from your life.

Today, if you are experiencing any stress, for just a minute, completely release it. Then consider its source and take one step – only one step is necessary – toward eliminating this stress from your life.

October 31 – Halloween

What an amazing opportunity this is in the West. Today, you can be anything you want to be.

Today it is socially acceptable for you to dress up as someone or something else.

You can be scary, sexy, strong, weak, ugly, pretty, etc. You can go out into society and be seen and not be seen all at the same time.

What fun you can have today!

Of course what's truly amazing is that you can be anything you want to be on any day.

November 1 – Sanctuary

Is everything in the outside world a reflection of what is in your mind or is everything in the outside world reflected in your mind?

In either case, regardless of what is in the outside world, what is in your mind is under your control.

Yesterday we were talking about pressure and stress and I said you should take one minute to completely release all of your stress. How do we do this?

One way to do this is to go to a sanctuary. If you have a real life sanctuary you can go to, that would be great. Go ahead and go there.

What I mean by a sanctuary is a place where nobody can hurt you. Nobody can find you there or bother you there. In your sanctuary, you are completely safe as long as you stay there.

If you do not have a real life sanctuary, you can make one in your mind. You may have to close your eyes for this. It is almost akin to lucid dreaming. Or directed meditation.

First, create one. Maybe it is a small garden with a stone bench. Or an underground cave. It could be a palace on a mountain in another time or even on another planet. It could be the center of a star. Maybe it is floating on a lake or a space ship deep in space. There are no limits whatsoever as to what, when or where your sanctuary is.

Once you create it, you can go there and just be. Spend a minute there just enjoying the safety and seclusion from anything that can bother you.

November 2 – Achievement

Are you familiar with crab fishing? Apparently, when fishing for crabs, if you fill a bucket full of water and place a crab in it, the crab will swim to the top, climb out and escape. But if you place two or more crabs in the bucket, each time a crab swims to the top to escape, the other crabs will pull it back down so that no crabs will ever escape. It's an incredible phenomenon really and as an analogy to human behavior the parallel is disturbingly accurate.

People, as a whole, tend toward mediocrity. It is not because we, as people, are mediocre per se, but rather it is because we tend to become complacent and we are uncomfortable with change. When you break away from the group in pursuit of some other goal – especially a lofty goal – the others will try to pull you back down.

Your peers, friends and family who try to pull you back down are usually not even aware of the fact that they are doing it. It is a kneejerk reaction. They can't help themselves.

You must not let them stop you. Keep your sights set on the horizon and keep driving toward your goal. They will try to plant the seeds of doubt but one thing to remember is that even if you fail, you cannot completely fail. This is because with failure comes knowledge. If you go for it and it doesn't work out, you will have learned much more than you would have learned had you done nothing.

You can take that knowledge and try again or you can use the knowledge to backstop your next endeavor. Never give up. Never stop reaching.

November 3 – Your Salvation

Are you looking for some kind of salvation? Some kind of redemption? Deliverance or liberation, perhaps?

If you are an Authorist, you are already saved! You were born saved. Well, not really. Not really, because you were born innocent to begin with and did not need salvation.

But even so, you do not need to be an Authorist to author your own life. We, as Authorists, believe that everyone is the author of their own life whether they know it or not and whether they admit it or not.

And when you are writing the script, you are the one that decides if and when you should have your salvation or redemption.

It is not something that is bestowed upon you but rather it is a choice that you make.

NOVEMBER 4 – THE FRAMEWORK (OF THOUGHT)

It is interesting that "modern times" change from age to age. It was once understood that in "modern times" our science had established that all things were made from four elements: earth, wind, fire and water.

Later, in "modern times," we understood there to be a fifth element: aether (or spirit).

Later still, in "modern times," we understood that all things were made of these tiny elementary building blocks called cells. There was nothing smaller.

"Modern times" is a moving window in which life exists. In the center of modern times is "now." Before *modern times*, was "in the past," and after *modern times* lies "the future."

With modern times (no matter where this window is – whether it be backward or forward in time) come certain paradigms of thought. These paradigms build the framework in which we think – most of us without ever even knowing that there could be different paradigms or that having different paradigms might construct a different framework.

If you could shed your current paradigms of belief and temporarily step outside your current framework of thought and step inside another one, the world would look very different to you. It is noteworthy that the world would not have changed. Only you would have changed.

This shifting around of frameworks is easier than it sounds and some of us dally with it frequently in our day to day lives. When we study history, we learn about certain paradigms of belief that our ancestors operated under and therefore we can imagine a framework of thought which governed their understanding of the world around them. Likewise, when we read science fiction we contemplate new paradigms of thought that the author may postulate our progeny will use to build their frameworks of thought.

There was a time when no human could doubt belief in the gods. The fact that gods were responsible for everything was just known. It was part of the framework of thought we all operated in without even knowing that we were in a framework. Before the advent of writing, it would seem we lived in an age where everyone in "modern times" knew there were many gods and everyone knew that the sun, the moon, the stars, the weather and everything else was governed by the will of the gods.

When one looked around at the world, one saw evidence of this in every single thing. A budding flower, a rainstorm, the sun rising or a full solar eclipse were all understood and fully explained by "the gods."

Today, "modern times," has built for us a framework in which everything is framed in terms of science. We know that cells are not the smallest things but rather atoms are. But we also know that atoms are built of even smaller things called quanta. In fact, we are seeing new paradigms of thought becoming stronger and better defined through the advances in the fields of quantum physics and quantum mechanics.

When these new paradigms appear (E.g. scientific discoveries) they fill us with awe and wonder and without us even noticing they begin to shift their way beneath the structures of our thoughts thus fortifying a new foundation for our entire framework of thought.

Today's meditation is to consider that understanding our paradigms of thought and therefore our framework of thought is something worth considering since it is through this framework that we see the world.

Do you want the world to look different? Then change the way you look at the world. Remember, the world does not change when we change the way we look at the world. We are the ones who change.

But it may be that that distinction is not even relevant.

November 5 – The Nucleus

Yesterday we were talking about paradigms of thought. One of the paradigms of thought in these modern times is the idea of consciousness being like a well or a body of water. When we talk about consciousness or spirituality we often talk about it in these terms. We say that *deep* inside we feel this way or that way. We say that some idea that is further away from our innermost feelings is *shallow*.

Using this paradigm, what does it look like within ourselves as we go deeper?

If we start as far away from our true inner self as possible we should start with our material possessions. Our houses, cars, toys and other belongings may reflect aspects of ourselves but in real-life they are only material items that are almost completely disconnected from our true selves.

Dropping down a level, on our surface we have our face and the clothes we wear. This external image of ourselves is as shallow as it gets. What my face looks like and what I wear is as similar to who I really am deep down inside as apples are similar to ducks.

As we go deeper than just how we appear to others, we have our mental self. This next level down in depth is where our *mind* is. We are going deeper into thought. What are our thoughts like? These surface thoughts are generated from the physical self. These are called *surface thoughts* because they come from sensory input. Are these things we think really *us* or are they just thoughts that we have? If they are just thoughts that we have, then the deeper self that is truly us is the "we" that are having these thoughts.

Dropping down another level we have the emotional aspect of self. This where feelings and beliefs intermingle. It is from this deep well of feeling and belief that some of our deeper thoughts arise. As these deeper thoughts rise, they intermingle with the surface thoughts that have been generated from the senses. The mind is where all these thoughts swirl around. This swirl of thoughts is what we may try to quiet during meditation.

This is still not the "we" that is having the thoughts. We have dropped deep within ourselves but we have not reached the nucleus yet.

What is deeper than feelings and emotions? Instincts? Instincts are physiological tie-ins of thought with body. Instinct is "buried deep" but it is not "us." Instinct is not what we truly are.

We need to drop down one more level.

Below the mind, feelings, emotions, and our fundamental structure and foundation of beliefs is the actual core. The nucleus. This nucleus is a singularity. It is infinitesimally small but it is infinite. This is a single point in space but it is glowing.

It is a point of warm, light, active presence. It is the spirit-consciousness.

November 6 – Fear

As with all things that we experience in this existence, our experience begins from within and moves outward from there. Fear begins deep within the self.

There is a core fear that we all share as human beings. It is our deepest fear and it is ultimately responsible for all other fears. It is the fear of the unknown.

In terms of Authorism, you could say that fear of the unknown is essentially the foundation of belief for fear itself in all other forms.

You will find that through your spiritual journey, as you deepen your knowledge of yourself, more and more of your outer fears will fade away. One by one, things that you once feared will lose their hold over you.

To put this in perspective, let us say that the nucleus of the self that we described yesterday is your true self and that wrapped around this nucleus are layers and layers of everything else about you.

With this model in mind, we can say that the very first fear we find when we start looking at the layers that surround the nucleus is the fear of the unknown.

It is almost as if the nucleic point of warm, light, active presence, looking toward the layers of self does not know where it is and this makes it nervous. I want to draw a distinction between "looking toward the layers of self" versus looking anywhere else because I do not believe that our nucleic self is normally afraid of anything. It is only when we begin adding the layers of self that we begin to encounter fears.

November 7 – Perspective

In Authorism we talk a lot about "manifestation" because the whole idea behind manifesting your own reality is exactly what writing your own narrative is all about.

When you are the author of your own life, you manifest what you want in your life. There's a weird twist to that too, which is that if you do not actively author your own life but let someone else write the story, you can still manifest what you want in your life. However, in that case what you want is being written by someone else and therefore what you really want is not understood.

The reason this meditation on perspective starts out with talk about manifestation is that *perspective* is the thing allows for manifestation.

Your perspective is like a filter through which you see the world. (See also, *The Framework (of Thought)*.) If, in your perspective, you are a victim, then you will continue to be victimized. If you have the perspective that you are a winner, you will win a lot.

Perspective is a weird thing because it will exist for you regardless of whether or not you take an active part in creating it. It always frames the world for you but you can change it suddenly and radically any time you want. It is completely subject to your will.

November 8 – Fine Lines

Have you heard the expression, "There is a fine line between [one thing] and [another thing]?"

For instance, "There's a fine line between love and hate." (See also, *The Opposite of Love*.) Or, "There's a fine line between right and wrong."

This expression calls attention to the fact that you can transition from one thing to the other thing suddenly and without even realizing that the transition has occurred.

For instance, in the above example of a fine line between right and wrong one may be doing something right (like fighting in a war to defend lives) and in so doing, end up doing something wrong (E.g. killing people).

As you move about life, you begin to see these fine lines everywhere. There are countless areas of life where a fine line separates one side from the other.

When framed in the perspective of the gradient yin-yang this makes a lot of sense. (See also, *The Gradient Yin-Yang*.) The shades of gray that exist between the polar concepts of good and evil also exist between other polar concepts. And as you traverse the shades of gray from one side to the other, somewhere in the middle is where you'll find that fine line. It is the examined life that can discern the crossing.

November 9 – Futility

It may be sometimes tempting to look at the chaotic splatter which is the world around us and think this is all just one giant effort in futility.

You might see this in smaller examples throughout your day that are a little less extreme such as, "Why wrap this present when wrapping paper is wasteful and they are just going to tear the wrapping paper off?"

Or, "Why should I take the time and effort to wash my car when it is just going to get dirty again?"

This kind of nihilistic thinking could be extended: why build a house when it will eventually just fall down and fade away? Why have children when all people end up just dying in the end?

Do not fall into this nihilistic-thinking trap!

Life is incredible! Seize it! Be! Do!

Nothing you do is futile because everything you do is connected in a long chain of events that goes back to primordial times and tells an incredible story. You are very much a part of that story, and the story does not end even after we move on.

NOVEMBER 10 – THE UNIVERSAL YOU

The meditation titled, *The Linear Spiral*, gives us an idea of how uncomprehendingly vast even the smallest of things in our day to day world really is.

Any one item contains an absurdly large number of atoms. And with each atom being comprised of mostly empty space, if one could shrink down small enough to visit the surface of an atom, one would see that the atom itself is comprised of (literally) an unknown quantity of smaller things. Subatomic particles? Superstrings? Out science is still trying to figure that out. But in the meantime, suffice it to say that any one object, if looked at deeply, is an unbelievingly complex and vast system that no person can fully know.

But what about a person?

Any single part of a human being can be looked at in the same way. All of that vastness of scope can be applied to just part of a person. A person's ear, for example.

But if we pan out and look at the whole human being our mind is blown again by the awesome scope of wonder that is a single person. On top of the relatively mundane aspect of sheer scope, there are layers and layers of additional wonder. Most noteworthy is the way the parts of a person all interconnect to make the whole person.

We must also consider the spirit-consciousness of that person and how the spirit-consciousness is fused and interwoven throughout the flesh and through the varying arrangements of physiological function such as the respiratory, circulatory or nervous systems.

And finally, of course, the person's thoughts feeling and emotions. In short, everything that makes a person a person.

When we stop to consider everything that makes a person uniquely that person, we can see how each person is like unto an entire universe. Every human being is an entire Linear Spiral.

In this way, we can look upon any other person with respect and awe.

NOVEMBER 11 – BEING MEAN

Are you a mean person?

Are you a nice person?

There are occasionally people on either end of this spectrum, but considering Authorian philosophy, you will not be surprised to hear that the meanness or niceness of a person is not a fixed value but rather a variable that moves along the shades of gray between these two extremes. (See also, *The Gradient Yin-Yang*.)

While there are really mean people in the world and there are really nice people, most of us fall somewhere further away from these poles. Fortunately for all of us, most of us are in the shades of gray closer to the nice side. Or is this merely a matter of perspective? (See also, *Perspective*.)

But knowing we are all mostly nice also means that we all have the capacity to be mean.

Try to be nice but forgive yourself for being mean sometimes.

November 12 – A Day is a Life

How important is a single day? Does one day really make a difference? Each day on Earth can be compared to an entire lifetime.

Birth/Renewal [Waking up]
Waking up in the morning is like being born into the world. For some, this process may be easier than others. At any rate, this is a brand new day and anything is possible today! How exciting and exhilarating to be alive and have the chance to seize another day!

Childhood [Morning and breakfast]
The sun is only just beginning to warm the world. Childhood may be compared to the thoughts and feelings about the day one might have as one begins to look around themselves and take in what the new day is bringing. This where breakfast occurs and the rituals of the average morning take place such as morning chores, a commute to work, breakfast, etc.

Teen years [Midmorning]
In midmorning, as one gets well into their daily chores or work one begins to better understand what this day is going to look like overall. You are moving away from childhood and will begin to see glimmers of your future as an adult in your community. This is a time to remind yourself that it is good to be alive. This is a time of wonder and this day may still bring surprises you had not anticipated. The sun is still rising and anything is possible!

Adulthood [High noon, lunchtime]
At high noon the sun has reached its zenith. Much may have happened already today but the day is not over and there is much more to come.

Midlife [Afternoon and evening, dinnertime]
The sun is beginning to move toward the horizon. The afternoon has turned into evening and the lion's share of today's chores have now been accomplished. You can relax a little bit and reflect on some of the day's events while still imagining what the evening

may hold. There is still the possibility of a surprise this evening but for the most part you have a pretty good idea of how the evening will progress. You may reflect on this day and feel disappointed or you might feel content. You may decide you want to change how the rest of this day will unfold or may choose to just go with the flow.

Old age [Night]
The sun has set. It is now nighttime and this means it is time to start closing the shutters and locking the doors for the night. Things should be put in their proper places and you can prepare for bedtime knowing that it was a good day. And whether or not it actually was a good day, you can drift off to sleep content in knowing that tomorrow is a new day where anything is possible!

The Transformation of Death [Sleeping and dreaming]
It is night and it is dark outside. As you sink into a deep sleep your spirit-consciousness is released from its daily labor and is free to fly or sing or flow with the rest of the sparks or glimmers of life or the collective consciousness, etc. (Insert your version of what happens when we dream). This officially ends your day and begins the transformation into tomorrow (or is that, "the next life?")

Considering that each day can be compared to an entire lifetime, perhaps today can make a difference. Perhaps today *is* an important day.

November 13 – Control

Or perhaps we should say, "The illusion of control."

The greatest source of angst and frustration in the lives of most people is the frustration surrounding the inability to control other people and certain outcomes.

Control over our environment is almost completely illusory.

Wait a minute? How can control over our reality be an illusion when we can literally alter our reality through thought? Recall that paradox is prevalent in truth. Herein is a truism and another paradox.

We can alter our reality through thought but we cannot control the outcome. We can influence others through thought and manifestation but we cannot control what other people do.

We can even influence the weather through thought but we cannot control the weather.

Watching other people become frustrated and angry you can often see that the source of their anger is the fact that they are desperately trying to control a situation or people in a situation and they are filled with angst and frustration at their inability to control the people involved.

In truth we have virtually no control over the outside world. When we imagine a new reality for ourselves, we can manifest this through thought, but we cannot control how it is done. There is an important distinction there.

For instance, I might put into the universe the thought that, "I will learn how to play the keyboard." Now, I must not try to control how the universe achieves this for me.

In other words, an opportunity to go on a hike might come up and I decide to go because it would be nice to get out of the city.

On the hike, I might run into someone who teaches keyboard and lives near where I live, back in the city. This is the universe providing what I am trying to manifest into my life.

I had no control over the invitation to go hiking. I had no control over the person that I met who was also (coincidentally) hiking the same trail at the same time. These were things the universe provided for me. I had control over my decision to accept the invitation. And I had control over my interaction with the keyboard teacher.

You see, the common theme in control is that you can control what you do and what decisions you make, but you have virtually no control over others.

Put your desires into the universe but do not try to control how the universe manifests them in your life.

November 14 – Reconciliation

Today's meditation is on relationships, resentment and reconciliation.

Resentment can cause deep sickness inside of us and this sickness can grow and grow over time filling our souls and lives with disease.

Just like perspective, resentment is a choice. (See also, *Perspective*.)

Sometimes we can feel resentment over things which are entirely out of our control. (See also, *Control*.) For this resentment, the best choice is to just stop feeling it. To do that you must change your perspective.

Another major source of resentment can be people or events that have taken place *with* people. For this kind of resentment you can also just change your perspective but another approach that is most recommended for Authorists is to reconcile with the person in which the resentment is attached.

The reason this is a better approach than just changing your perspective is that reconciliation with people who have harmed us or who we have harmed brings us closer to repairing or fostering relationships and Relationships is the Third Principle of Not.

If you have a pending reconciliation, today is the day to reconcile your differences.

November 15 – The Universe is Unfolding as it Should

Consider these feelings and reactions: regret, remorse, resentment, hatred, anger, bitterness, guilt, shame, grief, sorrow, disappointment, unease, displeasure, discontent, frustration, dissatisfaction, sadness, dejection and depression.

What do these things have in common?

These are all reactions to a universe that is unfolding exactly as it is supposed to.

Or do you think the universe is not expanding correctly? Do you suppose the universe needs to be fixed? If so, if you have not already started, you should begin that process today.

But if the universe and all of existence past, present and future, is exploding into that which it is meant to be exploding and expanding into, why should you have such feelings and reactions?

Instead, know that all of existence is meant to be and that you, me and everyone we know are meant to be. This is an axiom. If we were not meant to be, we would not be.

November 16 – The Past

Yesterday we said that existence is as it is supposed to be and therefore that the universe is unfolding as it is supposed to be unfolding. The stars which are exploding are supposed to be exploding. The black holes which are sucking in incomprehensible amounts of energy and matter are supposed to be doing that. Our sun, a massive fusion reactor, is supposed to be burning intensely and therefore warming the planets which – by the way – are supposed to be caught in its orbit.

Everything external to us – the solar system, the other stars, the galaxy, the universe and all of existence is as it should be.

Since everything out there is connected to everything "down here," we can infer that everything here (on Earth) is also as it should be.

This includes the past.

Do not linger on the past or allow yourself to feel bad about it. Learn from it, yes, but do not feel bad as there is no value in choosing to feel bad right now.

Feel good right now.

Everything that happened in the past needed to happen in order for us to have the present. Everything in your life that has happened has led you to this moment.

NOVEMBER 17 – THE PRESENT

Over the last two days we have talked about the universe as it is unfolding into [the void? Into Not?]. We talked about the galaxies which are spinning and we said that these galaxies are supposed to be spinning. We said that our sun – a massive ball of burning gasses – is supposed to be burning and that the planet we live on is supposed to be orbiting our sun.

Due to the speed of light being constant, everything we see in the sky is past history. Even our own sun we cannot see in the here and now. When we see our sun, what we see is the sun as it existed eight minutes ago. The nearest star to us we see only as it existed four years ago. We can almost see the moon in real-time but even what we see on the moon was what the moon looked like 1.33 second ago.

If we agree that everything in the sky is the way it is supposed to be, then we are agreeing that the past is the way it is supposed to be. And if the past for everything else in existence is as it should be, then isn't our own past as it should be? If nothing else, it must be for people who look at us from their own skies.

We can understand, then, that everything past and present is exactly as it should be. Feeling discontent about this is not useful. But if you are still unhappy, then there is some action you can take. It does not involve the past or present as these are things we cannot really control. It involves the future.

Now is the time for you to make the changes you think are needed to correct the expansion of all of existence.

November 18 – The Future

The future will be "the now" when we get there.

In other words, now is "the future" to your past self.

This may seem banal, but it means that we could have changed "the now" by making different choices in our past, and that we can change the future by making different choices now.

The unfolding of decisions and events which took place in the past inevitably led to the present moment. It may seem odd that we cannot really change the present but truly, we cannot. The present moment exists, right now, as the consequence of the past.

But, paradoxically perhaps, here in the present, is the only place we can actually operate. Since we cannot yet go back and change the past and we cannot alter the future in real-time, all we can really do is make decisions and take actions in "the now," and these decisions and actions can, in turn, create different futures for us depending on what we do (or depending on what we have done when it comes to "later.")

What do you want your future to look like when you get there? Start shaping it today.

November 19 – Liberation

This entry is about liberating yourself (or being liberated) from the societal and communal chains that bind us without our knowledge or permission.

These chains are modalities of thought and various paradigms of belief. The chains that bind us are practically invisible but they can be seen if one looks closely enough.

Two examples of these chains are the way that media and culture convince us that we should complain about our life-partners. "My wife does not give me the freedom to be who I really want to be." Or, "My husband doesn't do anything to help out and I am forced to carry all the weight in this marriage."

Other examples of chains that bind us are these things we hold as true without ever questioning them: When my phone rings, I need to answer it. When I receive a text, I need to read it right away and respond to it. I should setup apps and devices such that they notify me when things change. If someone knocks on the door or rings the doorbell, I need to go see who it is. I need to be on social media. I need to stay informed and so I should tune into the news often.

There are countless others of these kinds of little one-liners that we adopt as guiding rules for our day to day being.

If we do not identify these things, we can be chained by them. After so many chains are attached we become prisoners of methods of thought that we did not even know we were thinking.

By examining your life, you can ensure you are not being chained. Ask yourself if you enjoy what you are doing. Ask yourself if you are achieving your goals. Ask yourself if you are choosing to act or if you are just acting out of habit.

November 20 – Infinity

Can we, as human beings even comprehend this concept?

Everything we have ever known in our own lives and in the history and real-time observation of the world around us indicates that there is a beginning and an end. Doesn't everything have a beginning? And doesn't everything have an end?

How then, could we even have come up with this concept of "infinity?"

On the other hand perhaps infinity is an axiom.

After all, how could all of this (all of existence) ever have begun in the first place? Wouldn't that beginning have to have been the result of some cause? Wouldn't something have had to make the beginning happen? When we try to comprehend how this all could have begun and we keep stepping back in time in order to place "the first cause" further back in time we find ourselves thinking that infinity must exist.

In fact, quite the opposite of not being able to understand the idea of infinity, instead we find we cannot understand the idea of infinity not existing. (E.g. the idea of no infinity.)

This works the same way for the end. We can imagine all manner of endings to our own lives, to our planet's existence, our sun's existence and the end of the universe itself. But we cannot imagine a final and absolute end to all warm, light, active presence. We cannot imagine, Not.

NOVEMBER 21 – FINDING EVIDENCE

Often when we have a given perspective we seek evidence to support the validity of our perspective. This is most evident in web searching and the books people read but it is also evident in regular conversation. (See also, *Perspective*.)

In web searching you find that people will search specifically for websites, articles or blogs which support what they already believe. In books, people will read the books which they believe will back up their existing views. And in the books, you will find the person has underlined or highlighted the sections which back up their beliefs.

In regular conversations, you might hear someone complain about a certain aspect of their lives but when you offer them solutions for their problems, remarkably, they have reasons why each one of your solutions will somehow not work for them. If you are paying attention, it does not take you long to figure out that this person is not asking for a solution. What they are really seeking is evidence to support their perspective. They think they are seeing the world correctly and they want evidence to back that theory up. They want validation that they are seeing the world correctly.

There is nothing wrong with this behavior. We all do it. But what is fascinating is that we do this regardless of our perspective. If I feel like I am a loser, I will search for evidence that proves that I am a loser. If I feel that I am a victim, I will search for evidence that proves I am being victimized. If I have the perspective that I am successful, I will find the evidence that substantiates that viewpoint.

In each case I am building a virtuous cycle (or a vicious cycle, depending on the direction and outcome) where the evidence I collect backs up my already existing perspective. As I find more evidence I feel more strongly that I have the right perspective. I believe I am seeing things more and more clearly. For better or for worse, as I gather more and more evidence to support my views, it becomes more and more difficult for anyone to convince me that I have the wrong perspective.

Today's meditation is to consider what kind of evidence you find yourself looking for. Just observe this for a while and ask yourself, "What is the perspective I am trying to validate?"

NOVEMBER 22 – BEING HEARD

Is it important that your voice is heard?

Is it important to you? Is it important to others?

What would happen if your voice were not heard?

What is it you are trying to say? If your voice is not being heard, what is the message that you are trying to convey? What is this unheard message?

Our voices are important. Words are important. It would seem that language and perhaps more specifically, writing, is what separates us from the other animals. (See also, *Are Humans Animals?*)

If your message is not getting through, keep trying.

November 23 – The Garden

You are a like a flower that is born under the world and grows in this beautiful little garden. You look around you and you see all the other beautiful flowers. You see the beautiful sky and you feel the beautiful earth and you taste the beautiful air and the sunshine and you ask, "What is this? Why am I beautiful? Why is everything so beautiful? Why is everything so wondrous and amazing?"

The larger flowers tell you "It is because of the gardener."

"The gardener?" You ask. "What is the gardener?"

"The gardener brings us music and joy. The gardener prunes us and guides us so we can be our most beautiful. The gardener ensures that the earth is rich and that we have the sunshine and the water we need."

"Does the gardener have a name?" You ask.

"We call the gardener, Dan." The other flowers reply.

"I love Dan." Says the little flower.

"We love Dan, too." Say the big flowers.

But wait. There could have been a different end to that story. It might have gone like this:

"Does the gardener have a name?" You ask.

"We call the gardener, Allah." The other flowers reply.

"I love Allah." Says the little flower.

"We love Allah, too." Say the big flowers.

Or it could have ended like this:

"Does the gardener have a name?" You ask.

"We call the gardener, the Universe." The other flowers reply.

"I love the Universe." Says the little flower.

"We love the Universe, too." Say the big flowers.

* * *

You see, you could have been told by the larger flowers that the creator of all things was Jesus, Krishna or Ahura-Mazda or that there was no creator at all and that it all just randomly happened. We believe what we are told until we learn to ask the deeper questions. And we get our ideas about the world from those who were here before us.

November 24 – Hate

How can you truly experience hate? How can you feel this for life when you, yourself are life?

Is it because you hate yourself?

There is a school of thought that says that when you hate someone it is because you see in them something you do not like about yourself.

Considering that one must love one's self before one can love another, it is all too probable that one must hate one's self before one can hate another.

The reason today's meditation started with the questions of how one can even feel this is because if you consider the path that someone else has walked, it seems improbable that you could hate that person. (See also, *Tolerance*.)

Ignorance is the source of hate. Education is the fix for ignorance.

If you can experience hate, you would do well to trace the roots of this feeling within yourself and find a way to heal yourself.

NOVEMBER 25 – PASSION/DISPASSION

Are we to give in to our passion's or should we strive to be dispassionate so that our passions do not rule us?

If we allow our passions to rule us we might better feel the intensity of life but the candle that burns twice as bright burns half as long.

Should we strive to master our passions such that we completely control our feelings and emotions and thus become dispassionate? But if we become dispassionate, where is our sense of wonder and amazement when we behold the awesome spectacle of lucid reality?

Neither of these extreme approaches are appealing. (See also, *Fine Lines* and *How Do I Be?*)

Moderation and balance are required for a healthy, happy walk through life. We should allow for passion in our lives but overall we should also remain calm enough that we can temper our actions with wisdom and intellect.

NOVEMBER 26 – RIGHT AND WRONG

Right and wrong in Authorism are fairly simple to define.

"Right," is action that is moral and aligns with your personal code.

But what is moral? Moral action is action devoid of the intent to harm yourself or other life. (See also, *What is Moral?*)

Aligning action with your personal code means that you should act in such a way as to demonstrate your personal code in the world. On the other hand, you should not perform actions that your personal code forbids.

For example, let's say you have the following sentence as part of your personal code: "I am honest."

Because this is part of your personal code, you should endeavor to be honest. Right action will be action that aligns with your intention to be an honest person. Wrong action would be lying or in some other way being dishonest.

NOVEMBER 27 – POINTS OF PRESENT

While each and every being is certainly considered to be a point of presence in the philosophy of Not, each and every being is also a point of *present*.

"A point of present" just means *presence*. Presence, as you know, is the fourth of the four fundamental building blocks of Life.

So what is a point of present? To explain this, we are going to have to talk about time.

In the meditation titled, *Time Cannot Pass*, we made the argument that humanity does not know how to measure the passage of time.

There is something else that is interesting about time and in fact adds to the argument that we do not know how to accurately measure time. It is the fact that each of us exists at a point in time known as "the present," but that we cannot share the present moment with anyone else. Perhaps this fact about our relationship to time also helps support the notion that each of us is an entire universe unto ourselves. (See also, *The Universal You*.)

How is it that we cannot share the present moment with any other being? According to our greatest and most current science and mathematics, nothing can travel faster than the speed of light and the only thing that can travel as fast as light is light itself.

But even light takes time to travel. Therefore, something that emits light that is farther away from us may take longer for us to see than something that emits light that is nearer. In other words, we will see the light from a nearby sun before we see the light from a faraway sun.

Let's get more specific. Our own sun is eight light minutes away from us. This means that when a stream of photons blasts out of our sun and starts flying through space toward our planet, it takes about eight minutes for those photons to travel from the sun to your eyeballs. To punctuate this point, if you were walking around enjoying a sunny afternoon and the sun just suddenly vanished from existence, you would not even notice it until about eight minutes later. Then the sunny day would turn black as night.

So what does all this have to do with time?

When you look into the night sky and see stars, you are seeing light that has traveled hundreds, thousands and in some cases even millions of years to get to your eyes. Let's take, for example, a star that is 5,000 light years away. Photons blasted out of that star 5,000 years ago (around the time human beings started learning how to write). Year after year, these photons flew through space, passing many other stars and planets and vast expanses of empty space until after flying through space for 5,000 years, they smashed into your eyeballs. This, by itself is utterly amazing.

But the point I am making is that the star you see twinkling there in the sky is 5,000 year old light from that star. You are not seeing that star in real-time. None of the stars you see are actual present with you. They are *all* in the past. The one that is most present is eight minutes past. The next most present star we can see is four years ago (Alpha Centauri).

Everything we see in the sky is in the past. Even our own moon is about 1.3 seconds ago. That moon you see is only the light of the moon, not the actual moon. The actual moon exists over a second ago.

Nothing you see is in your present moment. In our present moment, we cannot see anyone or anything in their present moment. The only thing we can see are flickerings from the past. Likewise with them. Nobody out there can see us as we really are right now. In their present moment, they cannot see us in our present moment. They can only see our past.

As we get closer and closer to something the time dilation that occurs becomes smaller and smaller until when we are standing right next to each other the difference in how long it takes for the light to reach us is so trivial as to not even be worthy of our thoughts.

Even the moon, at just over a light second away from us, is close enough that a second means virtually nothing to us.

But there is a dilation of time there. These things we see really are in our past. Everything we see is, to some degree, in our past.

What this means is that nothing we see is in our present moment. There will always be a delay between beings experiencing each other. Thus, we are the only thing in our present time. In practicality, we can certainly share the present moment with everyone around us. But technically, each one of us is the only point of existence that is in our own present moment.

November 28 – Enveloped in Energy

We think of things as existing in three dimensions because that is how we were taught to interpret our senses.

It is fascinating to consider the fact that what is really happening when we sense something is not necessarily what is really happening in the world we are sensing.

Yesterday we were talking about looking up at a star whose starlight takes 5,000 years to reach our eyes.

We see the star way up in the sky as if it is "way up there." But what we are "seeing" is the light beams from the star as the photons make impact on our retinas.

In truth, one could argue that we are not seeing the star at all. We do not *see* beyond the surface of our retina. Photons hit the retinas of our eyes and only then do we physiologically and mentally process the impact. In our minds, we turn this into a story which says "there is a star far away." But the light is not far away. It is literally streaming into our retinas.

We interpret that the star is far away from us and that between us and the star is empty space, but there is not empty space between the star and our eyes. There are solid light beams (or flickering light beams in the case where the star is flickering) connecting the star directly to your eyes. As long as we can see the thing, there are solid beams of light maintaining this connection.

The same is true for anything we see.

Let's take another example of a reddish-yellow apple sitting on a desk. We see the apple "over there" and we think that in between us and the apple is empty space.

But the same thing that was true with the star is true with the apple. We are not "seeing an apple over there," but rather light beams reflecting off of the apple are streaming into our eyeballs.

These are solid beams of red and yellow light that do not desist. The pattern they make on the retinas of our eyes we have learned to interpret as "an apple which is some distance from us."

If someone were watching you watching the apple from the side, they would not see the beams of light as solid. We cannot see light from that angle. But if the beams of light were solid looking all the way around, they would see what would appear to be a reddish-yellow smear connecting the apple to your eyes.

If you could see (from the outside) all of the beams of light which are streaming into your eyes at this very moment, you might feel a bit claustrophobic. You are literally enveloped in energy right now and with your senses, you detect all of the energy that is touching you.

Our spirit-consciousness (or our mind?) has learned to interpret this sense data in such a way as to imagine that there is emptiness between us and the things we are sensing, but quite literally, there cannot be. If there were true emptiness between you and the apple, you would not see the apple. The light from the apple must maintain this solid and constant connection with you for you to be able to see it.

The same is true with smell, touch, taste and hearing.

Today's meditation has us contemplate being enveloped by energy and reminds us that true emptiness as a core precept cannot exist within Life (and nor would we want it to!)

November 29 – Ardentis Animae

This translates to "blazing spirit."

This is a direct reference to "the fire within."

The fire within is that which animates us. When someone dies, this fire leaves them and what is left behind is a corpse.

What the fire is, where the fire goes and all of the other questions that make up The Mysteries are addressed elsewhere (See also, *The Mysteries : Album Mysteria Non* and *The Postulations*.)

In today's meditation we contemplate the fire within.

The Chinese call this ball of energy "dantien." If you were to consider yourself as something deeper than just flesh, this burning fire would be it.

Imagine a small ball of energy – like a tiny sun – about the size of a baseball or a softball. This ball of energy burns with white-hot fire. Westerners generally think of the fire within as their mind and usually picture it located in their heads. Easterners generally think of the fire within their abdomen about an inch below the sternum.

Wherever it might reside it animates your mind and your flesh.

It is the source for the wellspring of love that flows out of you. It is the source of the energy that keeps your mind alive. It is the source of your awareness. It is the spirit-consciousness.

NOVEMBER 30 – TRANQUILLITAS ANIMAE

This translates to "inner calm."

While ardentis animae (blazing spirit) is our inner core and the energy that animates us, the idea of "inner calm" is a way of temperance so that your blazing spirit does not catch the world on fire. (See also, *Anti-Not*.)

The fire within you is real. It is "a thing."

The inner calm within you is not a thing but rather "a way."

Think of your inner calm as a way to shape the fire within. You can form your inner fire into a ball, or a flame, or any other shape you desire. You can also change its color.

Being a powerful source of energy means you have a certain responsibility to control that energy. You can walk about the world blasting things, or you can remain calm and direct your inner flame to burn evenly.

In the outer world (the world of flesh and blood), this inner calm can be seen as self-control. It is what allows you remain calm and relaxed in the face of adversity.

Today, consider your blazing spirit, then understand that your fire within is yours to control. It is yours to control because it is you. Change yourself into a blue energy ball. Or purple or yellow. Or let the energy flare out to encompass your entire being. But know that you are the one that determines how this fire shall burn.

December 1 – How Deep Should I go?

The average person only wants to talk about the weather, the latest sports game, which political party is worse or some kind of complaining about their job or family life.

If you steer the conversation into deeper waters you will find the person becoming repulsed and they will often go away in short order.

Why is it that most people do not want to discuss matters of depth? There is actually a reason that makes sense. This comes back to personal code plus structure and foundation of belief. (See also, *Don't be Afraid*.)

I wish there was another way of saying this that doesn't sound so harsh, but unfortunately the average person is just not very deep. It isn't that people aren't capable of being deep, it's just that they have never had a reason to go deep within themselves. Most people have not thought deeply on their own beliefs, much less have they entertained the idea that others might have radically different structures or foundations of belief than they themselves have.

As soon as you start moving into deeper waters, the other person detects this and becomes afraid. The fear is real and primal. Subconsciously they know they are being led into areas of thought that are alien to them and viscerally they know two things: One, they do not know how to navigate those depths (E.g. Fear of the unknown). Two, they are afraid of what they may find if they go there (E.g. Fear of the unknown). (See also, *Fear*.)

Knowing this about people can help you when you do want to go into deeper waters. If you're going to take them in, do it very slowly! (See also, *Depths of Thought*.)

DECEMBER 2 – EVERYONE IS ORANGE

In 1987, an action/science fiction movie called *Predator* came out. In the movie, the bad guy was an alien with advanced technology and he was going around the jungle killing humans.

The reasons I reference this movie really has nothing to do with the plot but everything to do with the antagonist ("the Predator") and how the antagonist saw the world.

The Predator did not see like we do, in what is called, "the visible spectrum" of light. The Predator saw the world in the infrared spectrum. This means that the Predator saw the warm, light, active presence of a person, not just the surface of a person. There is a really interesting side effect to having this kind of vision when it comes to how people see each other.

In the visible spectrum, we can see differences in each other's skin color. To the Predator, everyone was more or less orange. Everyone! If the person was generating heat, they appeared orange.

If you were to point to a crowd and say, "Those white people are not the same color as those black people," the Predator would not understand what you meant. The Predator would say, "Those are all people."

I wonder how race relations would be on this planet if we could all switch to infrared vision.

December 3 – Divinity

The most succinct definition of divinity is 'that which is godly.'

Even though Not epitomizes perfection, it cannot be divine. In short, this is because Not is not godly. (See also, *Introduction to Not* and *Not*.)

However, an argument could be made that Life is godly and therefore Life can be divine.

But even so, divinity does not come from Life itself. Divinity comes from within each of us. Your divinity is the "godliness" that is within you.

We are not gods, however the idea and power of gods is sourced within us. There is no god on Mars because there are no people on Mars (yet). The existence of a god requires a person to authorize that god's existence.

Human beings have the power to create the divine.

Therefore, when you hear other spiritual practices discuss the divinity within each of us, you can know the truth in those words.

December 4 – Our Most Valued Commodity

Time is the one commodity that each one of us possesses in equal amount. Queens, kings, homeless people, CEOs, fry cooks, presidents and city clerks all have 24 hours each day which they must decide how to use.

To life (at least to our temporal experience here in this flesh and blood body), there is nothing more valuable than time. The reason for this is that our lives are measured in time. We are born, we age, and then we die.

Our experience of the passage of time is an incredible wonder. There are times in which seconds can seem to drag on for hours and we wish for time to speed up. Other times, seconds pass all too quickly and we wish time would slow down.

Regardless of how we experience time, the seconds keep flowing toward our ultimate transformation which comes at the end of our time.

Western culture makes it so easy for us to trade our time for virtually nothing by encouraging behaviors such as scrolling through social media posts or mindlessly watching hours of streaming media from the internet. The content itself helps defocus us from the reality of what we are doing. We are trading the elixir of life for … for what?

Today's meditation is on the value of time, the fact that we all have the same amount of it to use each day and finally to ask yourself, "what should I do with the 24 hours I have to use for this day?"

December 5 – The Collective Conscious Imperative

First let us get on the same page with what "collective consciousness" is.

Perhaps one of the reasons consciousness is so difficult for science to dissect is because it can exist independent of a single entity. There is a phenomenon known as "group consciousness" also known as "collective consciousness."

A group consciousness is born of a group of independent consciousnesses. The group consciousness becomes most apparent when there is some kind of division between members of a group or between a group and a "group leader" of some kind. For example, between a classroom and a teacher.

In the case of a classroom and teacher, the individuals that make up the classroom form a new consciousness that is "the classroom group consciousness" and there is an interplay that takes place between the teacher's consciousness and the group consciousness. This is a subtle thing that may even be mostly subconscious but nonetheless this is a very real thing. Sometimes a teacher will encounter a class that they just "bristle" with. Or vice versa.

Any group of people can create a group consciousness. Or maybe it is the case that any group of people automatically creates one. What that group consciousness does or how detectable it is to anyone else may just vary based on need.

Today's meditation is not to dive into the study of group consciousness but it was necessary for us all to agree on a definition before we discuss the collective conscious imperative.

The collective conscious imperative refers to the collective consciousness of the country and region in which you are raised. Our own consciousness is affected in large part by the collective conscious.

The imperative is the unspoken command issued by the collective conscious. In this case, "the collective" is everyone, but in truth there are many collectives that when grouped together form the entire whole. In other words, there are collective conscious imperatives that arise from your high school, your work group, your church, your friends, etc.

The imperative tells you what to believe, what to wear, what to buy, what to eat, how to look, how to act, what to think, how to be and even who to be. The imperative is not a demand that you be a certain way but rather a subtle unspoken suggestion that you comply.

If you rebel against these suggestions you will feel somewhat out of step with the collective and the collective will feel that you are somewhat out of step with it.

This "out of stepness" can give you an uneasy feeling if you don't know what it is. As with most things, however, once you identify the fact that you are out of step with the collective, you can usually relax knowing that you are choosing to be out of step.

If you *are* choosing to be out of step, that is. In other words, if you know you are choosing to go against the norm then you should feel good about being out of step and your unease can be conciliated. If you did not know you were out of step then you can either get back in step with the collective or consciously decide to remain out of step. Either way, you should feel better once you have identified what was causing the unease you were feeling.

Today's meditation is to consider, are you aligned with the collective conscious imperative? Regardless of your answer, this next question is equally important: Do you want to be?

December 6 – Righteous Indignation

Hopefully this is either a very rare feeling you have or you have never experienced this feeling.

If you feel righteous indignation often, you are likely looking at the world using a skewed perspective.

Who are we to look around us and dictate that the universe is not unfolding as it should?

If, however, you do find yourself making such a judgement that the universe is not as it should be for this reason or for that reason, instead of basking in the glow of righteous indignation, ask yourself what can be done to help the situation. How can this be corrected? Then start fixing it.

DECEMBER 7 – HEAVEN OR HELL?

Luckily neither of these places actually exist.

How can I be sure? Listen to the way they are described:

What is heaven like? You get to live there forever, you will never experience pain again, you will never experience suffering of any kind again, you will never experience death and you will never experience anything bad or even uncomfortable. On top of all that you will feel happy. *All* the time. Since there is nothing to compare it to it is difficult to imagine how one could feel happy for all eternity.

Does this sound a bit extreme to you? If you really think this through, would you really want this? Of course, the alternative is a bit worse. The alternative is quite the opposite.

Hell is eternal pain, anguish and suffering. There you will feel nothing good. Ever. Only suffering. Every moment of every day of every week of every month of every year of every decade of every century of every millennium of every age for all eternity. Even though suffering would quickly become the norm for you and you would no longer really know suffering from pleasure (since there could be no pleasure) we have to assume that Hell's keepers somehow know how to make suffering not become the norm.

Like Not and Anti-Not, these places may be described but neither could exist. By definition, pain and pleasure both require the other for us to experience them. You cannot have an eternity of pain without having some pleasure to compare it to. Likewise with pleasure. You cannot have an eternity of pleasure without having some intermittent pain for comparison.

December 8 – The Allure of Evil

The "dark side," is a catch-all for everything evil. The dark side is where we find evil spirits and demons, necromancy, wicked witches, ghosts, devils and various other malefic monsters.

We human beings are beings of love and light. Yes, we all have a dark side within us, but more often than not we are good people and we want the world to be a place of love and happiness. As beings of love energy, one might think that all human beings would be repulsed by the dark side. But we are not. Or perhaps it is fairer to say that we are repulsed by the dark side but we are also drawn to it. Of course, some of us feel more drawn to it than others.

If you are unsure of your own attraction to the dark side you may want to double check some of the shows you've been watching or even some of the artwork you find yourself drawn toward. Chances are there are some darker elements to what you like than what you first might have thought.

What is it about evil that draws us in? After all, we do not wish to be evil, do we? We do not wish evil on others, right?

The draw to the dark side is not about us being evil or wishing evil on others. The allure comes in the form of a lust for power, a desire to be free of constraints, a crystal clear purpose to life and having fear of nothing!

The clarity of purpose comes from the primary and perhaps only objective of that which is evil: the pursuit of power. To have only one desire and a charter that permits one to pursue that goal with complete abandon is certainly appealing.

The acquisition of power ultimately corrupts the powerful. There is no way around the inevitability that power corrupts and that absolute power corrupts absolutely. While the pursuit of power might not be an evil thing by itself, it becomes evil when the pursuer disregards respect for life in favor of the pursuit of power. Let's take, for example, "an evil demon." When the demon hurts someone else in order to become more powerful or maintain an existing modicum of power, the journey to more power has now become evil.

This brings us to the second and perhaps most seductive aspect of evil: power without guilt. It is the ultimate in authorization! An evil demon is authorized to do whatever it wishes to do. It is completely free. In fact, an evil demon would be expected to do whatever it wanted and there could be no valid admonishment from any external source because the demon would be "just being himself." The evil demon is permitted and expected to do whatever it wants to do. It experiences no guilt from its actions and it has no conscious, warning it that it is acting wrongly.

This lack of a conscious is the third aspect of the allure of evil. The complete lack of constraints to action. Pure freedom to be and act. If you can think it, you are permitted to do it. This is total chaos and complete anarchy. It is akin to being a storm that rages across the land destroying all in its wake. But worse than that because of the intent. A storm is not evil, it is just violent and frightening. Evil is terrifying because it has the same elements of violence and fright but it also has intent. The intent to cause harm (for whatever reason) separates random chaos from actual evil.

Finally, it would seem that evil has no fear. This turns out to be a shortcoming, but nonetheless, a release from all fear is certainly enticing to those of us who have lived in fear or who understand calamity is always just a hair's width away from us at any given time.

It doesn't take much thought to see why evil is bad! But for those of us who are working to make this world a better place, perhaps we can see why there is an allure to that kind of freedom.

December 9 – The Fallacy of Power

Yesterday we considered the allure of evil. Today's meditation is on the mistake of being evil and what it would look like if we were to succumb to the allure and choose to go over to the dark side.

The pursuit of power over others to the exclusion of all else while creating a wake of pain and suffering is evil and yes, there is an allure to that kind of unbridled power and the lack of guilt that accompanies it. To have a crystal clear objective with no doubt or hesitation and the pure freedom to do and act however one desires being unbridled by guilt or conscious may have its appeal.

But the appeal should stop as soon as one thinks about the bigger picture. We do not need a large god standing above us shaking his finger at us and threatening to make us suffer in order to turn us away from a path of evil. If the love of life and respect for others isn't enough, all we need do is consider the rest of the story.

Where does the pursuit of power end? Evil is not just a violent storm with the intent to harm, but it really is the pursuit of power to the exclusion of all else. And as the storm becomes more and more powerful it consumes more and more life. What we begin to see is the definition of Anti-Life. (See also, *Not.*)

It is the antithesis of Life and it has only one end: complete annihilation of everything until the only thing that exists is that which consumes all else. It is a paradox and it cannot exist. Therein is the fallacy and the mistake of the dark side.

DECEMBER 10 – THE VOID

Over the last two days we have been discussing evil. Before we move on, there is another type of evil you may have had the misfortune of encountering in your life. If you have not encountered this particular evil then I hope you never do.

It is an aspect of the evil already described in the meditation titled, *The Allure of Evil*, though in that entry it is not called out by name.

For those of us who have encountered it, a good description of it is simply, "the void." When you encounter this in another being it feels like a complete void of love or feeling. It is an immeasurable vacuum that sucks in anything and everything that you give it and absolutely nothing comes back out. The void is infinite and can never be filled up. (See also, *The Opposite of Love*.)

You might be tempted to consider Not a void, but Not is not evil and the void is. Not has no intention behind it or around it whereas the void does have intention. There is presence around the void.

When you are near someone who has this void quality you can discern the evil nature of the void because of the pervasive intelligence around the void. That is to say, the person. The person is a warm, light, active presence in the world and therefore they are an intelligence with intent. But the void of love energy within them is palpable and you should try to get away from such an entity or at the very least maintain your boundaries such that you are not harmed.

It may be possible that this person will find a path to goodness and light, but until then there is nothing one can do to fill an infinite void.

DECEMBER 11 – ADDICTION

As long as we're still talking about evil, we should cover one more topic: addiction.

One might argue that addiction cannot be evil because addiction by itself has no intent. But it is part of the insidious nature of addiction to make you think that. Perhaps, by itself, it cannot have intent, but addiction is not by itself. It is rooted – it seems – all the way down to the spirit-consciousness. Thus, the self is driving the addiction and provides the intent to allow for the brand of "evil." Alcoholics describe it as a spiritual malady that is cunning, baffling and powerful.

If addiction is a spiritual illness that would certainly explain why science has so much trouble dealing with it.

Have you ever watched yourself with horror as you undertook an action that you are ethically and morally against? This maddening behavior epitomizes addiction. It is truly remarkable and horrifying to watch yourself perform actions which you do not wish to perform.

Those who have never experienced addiction for themselves or in a loved one cannot understand the insanity. "How is it even possible that one can do something that one does not want to be doing?!" This is where the insanity begins and it does not get any better as one continues down the road of addictive behavior. You find yourself asking, "Which one of us in charge? Am I in charge, or is it me?"

If you find yourself having conversations like this, seek help from family, friends or external organizations. You can also reach out to the Church of Not. No matter how far down you fall and despite how unbelievably lost you might feel, there is a path to sanity. There is a path of liberation from the chains of addiction.

December 12 – Sanity and Insanity

Sanity, of course, is the other side of insanity. Addressing one necessarily addresses the other. There are two aspects of insanity we should address. One is the "regular craziness" that we all feel and that we all encounter routinely in everyday life. The other is true mental illness.

The majority of people have felt "regular craziness" at one time or another. This kind of craziness results from the "profoundly sick society" that we all live in and our mandate to adhere to its collective conscious imperative. We walk this tight rope between trying to remain part of this sick and twisted society while at the same time trying to save ourselves from it. And all the while we are attempting to heal the world and ourselves. How could one not feel crazy form this?

The cure for this kind of craziness is the pursuit of balance in spirit, mind, emotion, physicality and society. Investigating the Church of Not and Authorism, seeking a spiritual path and pursuing other philosophies or ideologies is part of the healing process. In other words, the fact that you are reading this means that you are keeping your sanity despite the miasma that surrounds you. You are a rational mind who is aware of the fact that you are facing an irrational world. Through the use of thought and will you can imprint some of your own reason onto the irrational world around you and thereby help heal the world.

But when you encounter true mental illness you will find that you are powerless to help. Those who are truly irrational cannot think like you. They cannot think rationally. Nor can you think like they do. You cannot think irrationally. No amount of will or imprinting of manifestation can help these people. Of course, you can be with them and give them your energy, but always ensure you understand the boundaries and never believe that you and the irrational may coexist on the same wavelength.

DECEMBER 13 – REFLECTION AND MANIFESTATION

Have you ever answered honestly when someone asked you how you were doing? I don't mean a sincere query from a close friend or family member. I mean the person who says, in passing, "How're you doing?"

A small and seemingly insignificant exchange such as this is a surprisingly great opportunity for you to change the world. And to change yourself.

In the future, when you are asked this question by someone in passing, do not answer this question honestly. Instead, no matter how you feel, answer that you feel great! Or that you feel excellent! Or some other adjective that describes happiness and goodness.

Sometimes it won't be a lie, but most likely it usually will be. There are two amazing things that result from this lie.

One thing that happens when you respond immediately with such a lie is that you feel a little bit different after hearing yourself saying it out loud. Saying something out loud has a different effect on your whole body and mind than just thinking something.

When the person asks, "How're you doing?" You might think, *I am not really happy right now*. But if instead you respond, "I am doing great!" Your body hears you saying that you are doing great. Your body and mind here the words and you internalize this statement as if it were true. And remarkably, even though you know you were just making up a fake response, you will immediately feel just a little bit better. (See also, *Act As-If* and *Fake it till You Make It*.)

Another thing that happens is that the person – who was likely expecting a mediocre noncommittal response – will be pleasantly surprised that you are feeling good. Also remarkable is the fact that it does not matter if the person believes you or not. They may think, *She's full of it. She's just saying she feels 'great'*. But it won't matter. Their body and mind will internalize the words they are hearing more so than the thoughts they had. Also interestingly, this person will subconsciously want to hear from you again.

Whether they want to or not, your response this will make them feel a little better about themselves and their day. You will have just made the world a better place.

This has an interesting side effect of reflecting back on you. The happiness they feel that results from your lie is real happiness (not a lie) and it is discernable. Their happiness in turn flows out of them affecting everyone around them, including you. As it washes over you, you will feel better about yourself and your day. It is the beginning of a remarkable virtuous cycle.

DECEMBER 14 – CERTAINTY

Be careful. There really isn't any.

Perhaps you are safe in your home right now where you cannot be harmed. Are you so certain?

Did you know that as it circles the sun the earth is flying through space at approximately 67,000 MPH (108,000 KPH)? Luckily, space is mostly empty because traveling that fast would not seem safe if it weren't through empty space!

Life truly is a swirling chaos that envelopes us. We become entrenched in our routines and we begin to feel that nothing can ever change but that chaos can reach out and touch us at any moment. Or is it that we can brush against that chaos at any given moment?

The touch of chaos can be slight and barely affect our day or it can be colossal and completely alter our lives.

Like everything that requires a compromise (see also, *The Tightrope*) so does our sense of certainty. We should strive for a measure of confidence, but do not allow yourself so much certainty as to feel smug.

December 15 – Growth and Learning

What is the purpose of Life?

Perhaps we cannot answer this question quite yet, but growth and learning is Life's mandate.

Or perhaps it is appropriate to say that growth *is* learning.

At any rate, learning brings us knowledge and knowledge makes our lives better in many ways.

Through increased knowledge we can extend our lives thus honoring life. Through knowledge, we decrease ignorance and therefore we eliminate hate and intolerance. This improves our lives and the lives' of those around us as well.

Through learning and knowledge we advance our entire civilization.

DECEMBER 16 – OPPORTUNITIES

This is an old cliché but the truth of it cannot be overemphasized. Every mistake you make is an opportunity for growth and learning.

Here's another cliché for you: We are our own worst critics.

It is understandable that we should criticize ourselves and constructive criticism is quite beneficial, however there is little value in continuing to berate yourself once you have acknowledged a mistake.

Once you have acknowledged a mistake, try to understand how it happened, how you can avoid it in the future and then, of course, look for the opportunity that may have just appeared as a result of the mistake.

Mistakes (or accidents), in a way, are moments of creation. There was a plan, the plan was being executed, then out of nowhere the mistake was made (or the accident occurred) and now there is something that was not part of the plan.

Can something be done to turn this situation into an advantage? There is likely an opportunity here!

December 17 – Loyalty

Loyalty is both an admirable and a dangerous quality to possess. As tribal creatures there is something primal about our loyalty. We want to be loyal to the pack and to the leader of the pack. Back when we were literally running in packs, the pack leader proved himself by being the most powerful member of the pack.

Today, though, how often is the leader of the pack worthy of our loyalty?

Unfortunately, as with most everything, today we must scrutinize who we give our loyalty to in order to make sure it is not misplaced.

There are two entities in which we can maintain unconditional loyalty. One is humanity itself. The other is the self.

A fortunate side effect of having two awarenesses within us is that one can be loyal to the other. In fact, perhaps like the Ouroboros, the other awareness can be loyal to the first as well.

When giving your loyalty to anyone else, it would be wise to double check once in a while if the precious grant of our loyalty is still deserving of those to whom we grant it.

December 18 – Religion as Good

Are you religious? Do you hate religion? Do you love religion? Are you indifferent?

There are many people who are appalled at the atrocities that have been wrought throughout the centuries by humanity's religions.

But hasn't there been some good too?

But perhaps more importantly, what good does religion bring to the world today?

There are many good things we can find in religion.

Religion gives us a moral standard. Not just a moral standard, but a written moral standard. With religion, we have something in writing which explains exactly what is good, what is bad and how we should act. We can depend on this to be the same from one day to the next and this consistency provides a guide for us as we navigate the tumult that is life.

Religion can also provide meaning for us and give our lives purpose. In a world where purpose might otherwise be difficult to discern, religion can help satisfy that longing.

One of the greatest gifts of religion is that religion can provide definitive answers to the great questions of life that nobody else can answer. (See also, *The Mysteries : Album Mysteria Non*.) With these mysteries solved, one can feel confident about their place in the cosmos and move forward in life without fear or trepidation. While other people flounder with no comprehension or direction in their attempts to comprehend the sheer vastness of it all, the religious can put those questions to rest and focus on enjoying their lives (or if not that, then whatever life-purpose has been defined for them by their religion).

Religion is a salve for the spirit-consciousness. For someone who is on a spiritual quest, religion can provide all of the comfort one has sought for their soul. A religion can be the answer for the longing of the soul.

Religion can solve the crisis of loneliness in this lonely but socially networked world. Through religious services, one can meet likeminded individuals and find others who share similar values.

Religion can provide community. Often times, the members of a church will band together to help each other in times of need.

Many religions give back to the world through food banks, home building, clean water projects and other events meant to help people in need.

Nobody can deny there have been atrocities, but we cannot ignore the good just because there is also evil.

December 19 – Religion as Evil

For thousands of years humans have massacred each other in the names of their gods. Human beings have used religion to elevate themselves above other groups of humans and to dehumanize yet other groups of humans in order to justify exploitation, control, murder and genocide.

The great irony is that the religions themselves teach almost identical ideologies when it comes to the love that we should freely give to each other and an overarching respect for life.

But what is this madness? That two different religions can both preach that you should love your neighbor, respect all life and that you should not kill, yet these two different religions engage in murdering each other in the name of … in the name of what? Certainly not in the name of their religions. Their religions are very clear on this matter – Thou shalt not kill. So what do they kill in the name of?

They kill in the name of God.

Therein lies the problem: Whose God? Which god is true? Which gods are true? Whose god is the true god?

Perhaps it should be pointed out here that religion is not evil but that evil people can use religion to do evil things. It is not that people act evil because their religion told them to. Usually they do evil things because their god told them to. This is an important distinction.

The religion is not the problem, the god is the problem.

DECEMBER 20 – GOD CAN'T FIX THIS

The religion is clear on the matter of killing. In fact, the religion is clear on most every matter. And any matter that is unclear has a multitude of holy people who are devout scholars of their religion and can therefore help find an answer based on scriptures and historical precedent.

So where's the problem?

The problem is god.

God is not clear on the matter.

For answers that are difficult to find in scripture or where there is much argument among the holy ones, one might argue that their holy person can commune directly with their religion's god to find clarity.

But often this is not as helpful as it at first sounds. The reason this doesn't fix the problem is because it is never god that speaks. It is always that person who communed with god that translates god's commands to us mere mortals. And when two different holy people commune with the same god and come back with two different answers, we are back to square one.

Why does god not come forth and correct this broken aspect of religion? Because god only exists in the minds of the theistic religious devout.

Since there is no actual god, no actual god can fix this problem with the theistic religions.

December 21 – Winter Solstice

Today is the first day of winter! Or at least the beginning of the celebration of winter! Traditionally, today is the shortest day of the year and therefore the longest night of the year.

Winter gives us a chance to appreciate the darkness. That which was born in the spring has grown through the summer, has now finished its life and faces the ultimate transformation. This is a reminder for us feel grateful for the warm, light, active presence of Life.

If you can perform the Winter Solstice celebration outside today that would be ideal. Or at least, step outside and feel the cold air.

Today's meditation is on this transition point – the halfway point between the autumn and the spring equinoxes. Today we think about the cold, dark, static emptiness of Not.

December 22 – Religion had to Change

The world's largest theistic religions (by number of adherents) are thousands of years old and they have never been updated to align with modern times. Here in 2021, churches do the best they can to make the old scriptures relevant, but stories about god(s) smiting people out of anger or commandments about how to manage your slaves are just no longer relevant in this age of quantum computing, artificial intelligence and global internet.

These giant world religions are painted into a corner. The reason their scriptures have power is because they are claimed to be the actual words of a deity. There is no way to make two to four thousand year old scriptures relevant for today without rewriting them and once you rewrite them, you can no longer claim they are the inspired words of a deity.

This just adds to the argument we have been discussing over the last two days that the root problem with theistic religions is the existence of the godhead. In short, god is the problem.

When you remove god, you are suddenly free to practice the tenants of your religion without contradiction. You can love others and respect life and there is no deity or scripture telling you to kill people who practice a different religion.

If the Philosophy of Not had introduced a deity, I would have been tempted to remove it from the religion of Authorism. Fortunately, for everyone, Authorism has no deities. As such, we must adhere to the principle that human lives are sacred and we cannot kill people just because they believe something different than we do.

DECEMBER 23 – ACCEPTANCE

Acceptance is the other side of 'control.' In other words, we are often inclined to try to control the people and situations around us when in fact we cannot. (See also, *Control*.)

If we want to control a person or situation and we can't, we become frustrated and uneasy. What are we to do instead?

This is where acceptance comes in. We must accept the fact that we have no control over people, places or things. When we let go of our attempt to control an outcome, surprisingly, other possibilities will appear before us.

When we release our iron grip on the situation, we can relax and this opens us to possibilities that we may have otherwise overlooked.

Acceptance brings us a peace of mind that allows us to act with more decisiveness and confidence.

Acceptance does not mean accepting defeat. The acceptance is not an acceptance of our position as a loser, a victim or having received the short end of the stick. Those things are all a matter of perspective (see also, *Perspective*.)

But rather acceptance refers to a matter of fact perspective on the situation. Here are the facts. Is there something I can do to make things better for myself right now? No? Then I let go and move on. Yes? Then I perform that action immediately and reassess.

DECEMBER 24 – THE NEED FOR PURPOSE

There are two major types of purpose and we really need them both. One is a purpose for our own existence. We each need a purpose for being. We need a purpose for our lives. What am I to do with my life? What is my purpose?

The other one is a purpose for all of existence. What is the purpose behind the motion of the planets and the stars? What is the purpose of the galaxy and the universe? What is the purpose for all of life?

The best religions offer an answer for both of these longings for purpose. Purpose is one of the greatest gifts religion has given to humanity. In fact, how well the religion's explanation of purpose resonates with the seeker will often make the difference between whether or not the seeker becomes a convert.

An individual purpose makes us feel we have value. We are something valuable to the world at large. If we are valuable to the world, then we belong to the world. If we belong to something great, we are important. If we are important, we are valid. With this validation comes authorization for being. We are okay. We are authorized to proceed! So by fulfilling our need for individual purpose others can grant us external authorization. This is valuable to some but dangerous to others. As long as you are receiving your authorization from an external source you are chained to that external source for all of your authorization. In short, you cannot act freely without permission.

As for greater purpose, we see from the past and present theistic religions that through their creation stories they offer humanity a purpose for being and they offer an explanation of the greater purpose for all of existence.

This greater purpose can also help us accept the insanity, misery, suffering and pain that we experience and witness within and throughout the world around us. If there is a greater purpose, we can tolerate those horrors as well as other evil that we experience in the world. This greater purpose does not grant us external authorization for being like the individual purpose does but it does authorize the state of the world.

If there is some larger purpose for all of the pain and suffering we see then we can accept the pain and suffering as part of a bigger story that we might not be able to understand. With this in mind, we can take comfort in knowing that it is not for naught. The pain and suffering of the world serves a greater purpose because it is authorized by a greater authority. It is okay. Not only is it okay, but it is meant to be. There is a purpose for it. With this in mind not only should we not worry about it but really there is no action we need to take to stop it. (It is the will of the gods.)

This underlying need for purpose that lies deep within each and every one of us is a critical aspect of the self. It is a valuable tool for those who might seek to control us and an extremely important aspect of the self that each of us should fully explore.

Intrinsically, Authorism does not seek to provide a purpose for all of existence. The core understanding here is that nobody can really know what the purpose is behind all of this. (See also, *The Mysteries : Album Mysteria Non, Is There Purpose?* and *What It Isn't.*) Nonetheless, in the work titled, *The Postulations*, there are many explanations for greater purpose including postulations put forth by Authorism.

As for individual purpose, if you are still looking your own purpose, we do offer a standby for you while you are seeking.

Each of us has a right and a responsibility to life, fitness, relationships, our own personal code and to our community.

The best thing we can do toward that end is to respect our own life, maintain our own fitness, foster our relationships, continually maintain our personal code and be positive contributors to our local, regional and greater communities.

Above all of this, we should learn as much as we can about ourselves and our world. The more we learn, the more we understand that we are all the same. The more we learn, the more we understand that fear comes from lack of knowledge. Fear of the unknown is the seed for all other fears and more specifically fear of the unknown is the core of the ignorance, hate and intolerance that some people have for other people.

Education and learning is the best weapon against this deep fear that drives such awful human behavior. Love, tolerance and understanding are natural fruits from the work of learning.

December 25 – Seek and Ye Shall Find

There have been many days throughout the year where we have touched on manifestation of reality through thought. We know from living life, the truth in the words, "Seek and ye shall find." When you put forth into the world that which you want from the world, you will find that it happens for you.

However, today's meditation is not about bringing what you want into the world. Today's meditation is about not bringing what you don't want into the world. This is the other side of "seek and ye shall find."

When you look for evil, you will find evil. When you look for scandal, you will find it. When you look for deceit, you will find it. This is one of those simple truths that are so simple it is difficult to comprehend.

I am not recommending you try this, but if you spent all day today, looking for something bad today, you would find it. When you found it, you could then nod to yourself and say, "Yep, I knew there was something bad to find." You could then make tomorrow's goal to find two things bad. You would find them. Then three, then four, and so forth.

As long as you keep looking for negativity in your world, you will find it. Part of living an examined life is to double check with yourself periodically to see if you are seeking the bad or the good. Because either way you will find what you are looking for.

December 26 – Seek and Ye Shall Not Find

Paradox is prevalent in truth. And the truth is that when you seek something out, you will find it. But also true is that when you seek something out you will not find it.

Surely you have seen this in your life. This usually happens with things that are tied to people. In other words, relationships.

The most prevalent examples of this are romantic relationships and jobs. You may encounter many times in your life, a situation where you feel lonely and want to give and feel love. This loneliness drives you to seek a partner. You try and you try and you cannot find anyone. You seek, but you do not find.

Or perhaps you are between jobs and you are looking for a good fit. You try and you try but you cannot find a job.

There is one more example where "seek and ye shall not find" seems to be a truism. It is in the journey to the center of the self. In an effort to find yourself, you seek and you seek and you still cannot find yourself. (See also, *Finding Yourself*.)

All too often in the case of the relationship, when we finally give up seeking either because we find a partner or we no longer want one, suddenly we have two or more prospects appear for potential relationships. Or in the case of the job, once we finally stop seeking because either we have taken a job or for some other reason, we suddenly receive an excellent job offer "out of the blue." And people who have found themselves most often report that the realization of having found themselves came suddenly out of nowhere when they had either stopped looking or were not actively searching for themselves.

How is this possible? If everything we have said about manifesting our own realities is true, how can it be possible that with all of this seeking we are doing we cannot find what we are looking for? Doesn't seeking the thing put into the universe the idea that we want the thing?!

This "not find" aspect of seeking is a fascinating divergence from the other aspect of seeking we talked about yesterday (see also, *Seek and Ye Shall Find*).

What's the difference?

There are a couple of reasons seeking like this can "backfire." One is the vagueness of what we want. If we are unclear as to what exactly we are looking for, our results may vary. In other words, "I want a girlfriend," or "I want a boyfriend," might not be clear enough to get the results we want from the universe.

The other thing that can add to this kind of anti-result (not finding what we want) is the frenetic energy of desperation that can creep into our desire. Another way to look at this is the expression "we are trying too hard." This is not unlike thinking too hard about something your body knows full well how to do. For instance, you may be quite good at swinging a golf club or a tennis racket but when you try too hard, you over think it and your conscious effort interferes with your body's ability to do make the move on its own.

One of the ways to get around this problem is to detach from outcome. In fact, that is why when you end up in a relationship or a job two prospects might pop up suddenly that were not there before. Once you stop seeking, you detach from outcome and allow the universe to provide for you.

December 27 – Don't Wish Your Life Away

We all end up in situations where time seems to slow to a standstill and it becomes difficult to think of anything other than wishing it was later.

On a more shallow level you see this in "wishing it was 5 o'clock," "wishing it was the weekend," or "wishing the first day of your vacation was here."

During these times it may be tempting to wish it was later but we should strive to remember that this is essentially wishing our lives away. If I am not having fun today but I think I might have fun tomorrow, so I wish it was tomorrow, I am basically saying that I wish I did not have to live through all of today.

It is true, a situation can be so utterly devoid of any kind of fascination or sparkle that many of us would gladly trade that time just to make it be over.

Since we cannot, however, a good stopgap is to see if you can find something else to enjoy during this dreadfully slow creeping passage of time. Perhaps you can hyper focus on an item in front of you and try to "count the number of atoms" inside it. Take a trip into the subatomic. Or imagine what your situation looks like from outside. Then from further and further out (see also, *The Linear Spiral.*) Try just being present. Breathe in. Breathe out. Feel the air moving in your body.

Another approach is to fully immerse yourself in the experience of this dreadful malaise. Really feel it. Ask how it came to be and what you might change to make sure it doesn't happen again. Whatever it is you do, try to make it be something other than wishing your life away.

December 28 – How Do I Be?

Balanced.

It is tempting to leave today's meditation as just the word "balanced." Sometimes less is more. But while that might be the most succinct way to convey the point, it might not be very helpful.

First let us give some context to the question. The question, "How do I be," means, "What do I do in the face of such a myriad of advice coming from a hundred different sources?"

On the path to finding one's self, one will encounter a plethora of advice. We've talked about splinters of truth (See also, *Splinters of Truth*) and how when one finds a splinter of truth one recognizes it immediately and this often entices one to dig deeper into the ideology which surrounds that truth. It is awesome to find a truth and to recognize it and to then add it to one's bundle of truths.

The problem arises when you need to decide how to act on a day to day basis. On the surface one might wonder how this could be a problem at all. You just "be," right?

But if you have gathered four different splinters of truth from four different sources, you will likely have four different sets of rules laid out for how to be.

For the sake of argument, let's just take two. Let's say that you have only discovered two splinters of truth (two is a lot, when it comes to actual truths, by the way.)

From the ideology, philosophy or religion where you found one of your truths comes the mandate that you should pray daily and arrange your days in a clearly defined pattern so that you can retain proper spiritual alignment. From the other comes the advice that you should open your heart to the messages coming from your inner child and act as freely as possible, with no set agenda or pattern to limit your actions.

This is a real problem because you feel the truth in both of these opposing ideologies. So how do you act on a day to day basis?

Back to the first answer: balance. You must balance the two ideologies in your mind. Now it won't surprise you when I say that the other four aspects of self must be brought into this scenario as well. You must balance the splinters of truths and the associated mandates of action in spirit, mind, emotion, body and society.

For example, if one of the ideologies mandates you wear a burka but the other mandates that you go about nearly naked (or completely naked where legal), how do you reconcile these two very different *ways of being*?

The answer is you must somehow balance the two. This is by far, the hardest part of choosing your own path instead of following a path someone else has already paved for you. In the example offered, perhaps you wear clothing that is not all the way to burka, but also not all the way to naked. Or perhaps you choose to wear a burka on one or two days out of the week.

It is often difficult to blaze your own trail through the wilderness and there will be many times when you do not know which direction to go. Only your personal code can guide you and there is an inherent paradox involved in "using your personal code" to help guide you in "creating your personal code."

But the balanced approach is the only way to find *your* right path. Only time and self-examination can hone the principles of your own truths that will define your actions. Keep trying different things and keep asking yourself, does this work for me?

DECEMBER 29 – THE OPPOSITE OF LOVE

The opposite of love is not hate. The opposite of love is complete indifference.

Believe it or not, if you were isolated from humanity for an extended period and came back into contact with people, hate would be a much more welcome feeling than indifference.

Speaking generally, love and hate are very close together on the spectrum of passion. Both are extremely powerful emotions and when a person allows themselves to be swept away by the strength of an emotion like love or hate, a person can literally become confused as to which one they are experiencing.

But neither hate nor love can be confused with indifference. The feeling of indifference from one being to another is akin to evil. (See also, *The Void*.)

December 30 – Religion Without God

The reason religion maintains a foothold in the soul of humanity is because we need it. We *need* the things that religion has promised to give us. It does not matter that religion continuously breaks its promise and fails to deliver. The need remains and we continue to seek acceptance, validation and authorization from some higher power. Humans will keep seeking this acceptance externally until the "divine" truly does spring forth from the fountain of life that is our spirit-consciousness.

There are good things that come from religion and we should hold on to those things. We should embrace those things and feed them so they become stronger. We should love that part of our religion. But what of the things of religion that we should not love?

What of hate, sexism, bigotry, intolerance and ignorance? We should allow those things to perish with complete indifference.

Of the inappropriate and offensive things that religion has brought forth we should not feed them with love or hate. By feeding them nothing but complete indifference, they will go away. They lose their power when they are not fed with energy.

You should be religious in your conviction to find authorization for yourself from within yourself. You should be religious in your conviction to seek the truth and always question what one presents to you as being "true."

There is a higher power than ourselves and it is all around us but only because it wells up from within us. This power accepts us, validates us and because it also permeates us, it naturally grants us the authorization we seek. The power is warm, light, active presence. You are warm, light, active presence.

December 31 – Do Not Wait For the Afterlife

The purpose of life is in *the journey*, not the destination. Should we suffer now and get our rewards after death? Or should we revel in the gift of life and deal with the afterlife after life?

Most religions teach that the purpose of life is merely to prepare oneself for what will come after death. What an ironic mistake this is. The irony is that life is the gift one should revel in, not an unknown life hereafter.

Teaching people to suffer now and expect a great reward once they have died has been an effective method of controlling the masses and building wealth for the churches. Your reward is not waiting for you after death, your reward is the life you have right now. Do not squander this gift. There may be a lot more going on after death than we can possibly imagine, but one thing is certain: the journey through life here and now is what matters to life *here and now*.

Do not make the mistake of disregarding your life or your health because you think that the only thing that matters is what comes next.

Take control of your life here and now and save after death activity for after death. There will be plenty of time to do things in the afterlife once you arrive there.

Your Birthday! (and Yearning)

If you hear the calling, answer!

It is not uncommon for us to feel a yearning but to not be able to identify what it is a yearning for. We do not have a good word for this in English, but the German's call it "sehnsucht."

Until you can pinpoint exactly what it is you are yearning for, the best course is to move forward with your other pursuits. In other words, take a step forward in your master plan for your life. (See also, *You Have to Have a Plan* and *Achievement*.)

If you are fortunate enough to hear the calling – if you can actually articulate your yearning, go and satisfy the yearning if you can.

Afterward

I spent my teen years and my entire adult life looking for a religion I could call my own. A religion I could belong to. Something I could believe in completely. I was desperate to give my love and undying loyalty to something or someone. I wanted *belonging*. I wanted *community*. I wanted belief, and I wanted to *believe*. I wanted to be part of the congregation. And Life knows, I've tried!

But I do not believe in their gods. Not like they do. I do not believe that their prophets, priests, pontiffs, ministers, vicars, saints, popes, teachers or preachers have any more of a clue than anyone else. History seems to bear this out.

In fact, the true seeker, I am sure is more connected to a higher power (a higher truth) than most of those who claim they know. For "those who know" stop seeking. And when you stop seeking, you stop learning. There is risk of stagnation in discontinuing the journey. As long as you continue to seek, you continue to learn and therefore you remain open to knowledge. As soon as you think you know, you have stopped seeking and you have lost the gift of the pursuit of truth.

I do not claim to have the answers to the great questions, but I can tell you that after nearly four decades of searching, all the while being told by most everyone I encountered that my quest was futile, I have found many answers to questions I feared would never be answered in my lifetime.

As I write this now, I see that the creation of the Church of Not and Authorism was inevitable. I had wanted this so passionately for so long and I finally came to understand that what I had sought all those years did not exist.

When I was a teenager desperately seeking answers, I felt a void. I saw the miraculous wonder that was existence and I was stunned that nobody else seemed to care. I was even more confounded when I discovered that of the few people who would discuss it, nobody seemed to have the answers to *The Mysteries*.

And being told there were no answers just drove me to seek harder. But it felt like an effort in futility and I felt completely lost in a world that did not care.

That boy grew to be a man and he finally discovered many of the answers he sought. There are other questions which do not yet have solid answers but they are now framed in such a way that I no longer feel lost without their answers. In fact, though I continue to seek answers, I feel completely "found."

When I think about Authorism, the Church of Not and Authorian Philosophy, I think about the desperation I felt when seeking some kind of path and my hope is that through the vehicle of this religion and ideology, I can help some other person who may be seeking answers.

Acknowledgements

Thanks to my wife, April, for her embodying the examined life, for always looking for the way forward and focusing on the positive. Thanks for being a sounding board, the CFO, the COO and the general manager. Thanks for your perpetual support, for carrying our children (especially in Memphis (and especially in August in Memphis)), for mothering our children and for taking on the full time job of taking care of our family. Your dedication and sacrifice to our family has immeasurable worth. Thank you for being the earth for our sky.

Thanks to my mom, Chris Frederick, for her unconditional love and acceptance, her depth of spirit, her spiritual thinking and being and for never letting go. My mother showed me the value of perseverance, culture, diligence and love.

Thanks to David Kurtz for following me to any depth and for teaching me to widen my scope, to think bigger, to see the breadth and depth of words, to look beneath the surface and to flicker through multiple perspectives before making a decision.

Thanks to Aaron Merriman for showing me by example that we are the captains of our own vessels and that societal constraints and expectations have absolutely no sanction to direct our course. Aaron taught me that we can get what we want once we know we want it even if the rest of the world would tell us it is not within our reach.

Thanks to Derek Gloden, for showing me that we are never too old to have zest for life and for showing me that tolerance for others is not a burden but a joy. I don't believe that Derek has ever met anyone he did not genuinely love as another human being.

Thanks to John DeFacio for your friendship and your dedication to Atheism despite all of the evidence against it.

Thanks to my sister, Dani, for being a friend and for getting me through childhood. Thank you for letting me hang out with you and the cool kids. That acceptance validated me and helped prop me up while I learned to stand on my own. My sister introduced me to music and reading and showed me what it meant to "be cool."

Thanks to the random student at Columbia College night school who told me "Don't wish your life away."

Thanks to everyone who puts forth poetry, writing, artwork, music, movies, etc. into the world.

Thanks to all of the world's students and academics for studying and expanding the boundaries of human knowledge. You are the people who advance human civilization thereby expanding our tolerance for each other and making more room for love.

Thanks to the soldiers who risk their lives in an effort to save ours. Thank you, also, to everyone who works in service of our country. Your efforts to support something larger than ourselves contributes to human civilization and makes a difference.

Thanks to my sons, Tavin and Bleys, for teaching me about human nature and confirming for me that the simple things in life are the most important things in life. Thank you for your blazing spirits and for your genuine gratitude for life.

Thanks to Colorado for being one mile closer to the amazing sun, for having perpetual blue skies, clean dry air, abundant sunshine, mountains, forests, high desserts and great plains.

APPENDIX A – ALPHABETIZED LIST OF ENTRIES

In this appendix is the entire list of 366 entries sorted by title in alphabetical order with their associated day assignment. When reading through the text and you come across something like, "(See also, *Trust*)," you can use this list to find Trust, then look to the right to see that the meditation titled "Trust" can be found on October 26th.

A Day is a Life – November 12 – 450
A Full Solar Eclipse – August 14 – 320
A Measure of Health : Balance – July 25 – 292
A Visual Aid for Manifestation – May 30 – 196
Absolute Authority – September 28 – 392
Acceptance – December 23 – 503
Achievement – November 2 – 436
Aciem Exacuitur – June 19 – 228
Act 'As-If' – July 29 – 302
Activity – April 18 – 133
Addiction – December 11 – 488
Alchemy 2.0 – August 21 – 333
Alien Life – January 16 – 27
Aliens – August 11 – 317
All Life – January 15 – 26
All Religions are False – May 18 – 175
All Religions are True – May 14 – 168
Animal Life – January 12 – 22
Anniversary Ecclesia Condita – February 5 – 49
Anti-Not – April 27 – 145
Ardentis Animae – November 29 – 474
Are Humans Animals? – August 7 – 312
Are there such things as Accidents? – September 14 – 376
Articulating Your Code – February 27 – 71
Aspects of the Self – June 2 – 202

Authorization – May 3 – 152
Authorization for Crime – May 10 – 162
Authorization for Magic – June 1 – 200
Authorization Loopback – May 5 – 154
Autumnal Equinox – September 22 – 385
Awareness of your Awareness – June 13 – 218

B

Be Ready for Anything – January 20 – 32
Becoming Religious – May 19 – 176
Being Heard – November 22 – 463
Being Mean – November 11 – 449
Being Part of the Pack – October 6 – 403
Belief – October 14 – 413
Belief in Fate – September 13 – 375
Belonging – October 7 – 404
Blind Faith – September 24 – 387
Born Pagan – July 20 – 284
Bullies and The Martial Arts – October 29 – 432
But Anti-Not Cannot Be – April 29 – 148

C

Can Life Stop? – August 12 – 318
Can Not Exist? – August 13 – 319
Center Yourself – February 28 – 72
Certainty – December 14 – 493
Chaos and Order – July 26 – 294
Choosing a Religion – May 13 – 166
Cinereo Ascensus – June 17 – 225
Cinereo Modo – June 16 – 223
Civitas – June 28 – 246

Code Seeking – March 4 – 77
Codice Personalum – June 24 – 237
Coldness – April 3 – 113
Communication is the Key – October 25 – 428
Communities within Communities – March 10 – 84
Community – March 9 – 83
Comparing Yourself to Others – May 12 – 164
Computer Life – January 13 – 24
Control – November 13 – 452
Conviction of Belief – September 9 – 366
Creating Relationships – February 22 – 66
Creation and Destruction – August 20 – 330
Creation Hasn't Stopped – September 8 – 365
Cultivating Relationships – February 20 – 64

D

Darkness – April 4 – 115
Day and Night – August 15 – 321
Death is Life – April 23 – 139
Deeper than Good and Evil – March 26 – 103
Depths of Thought – October 12 – 410
Detach from Outcome – September 25 – 389
Dichotomy – October 21 – 422
Dictate to the World – September 4 – 358
Divinity – December 3 – 478
Do Not Wait For the Afterlife – December 31 – 515
Don't Be Afraid – September 11 – 371
Don't Be Evil – March 31 – 110
Don't Wish Your Life Away – December 27 – 510
Doubt and Self-Doubt – August 16 – 323

E

Effective Bailout Value – January 5 – 14
Emotional Exercise – February 2 – 46
Emotional Fitness – February 1 – 45
Emotional Nutrition – February 3 – 47
Emotional Rest – February 4 – 48
Emptiness – April 6 – 119
Enveloped in Energy – November 28 – 472
Everyone is Orange – December 2 – 477
Everything Happens for a Reason – September 15 – 377
Everything is Connected – June 12 – 216
Evil – March 29 – 107
Existing Structures of Belief – June 25 – 239
External Authorization – May 4 – 153

F

Faith – September 23 – 386
Fake it till You Make it – September 6 – 362
Fear – November 6 – 443
Feel the Awe – October 23 – 425
Financial Independence – March 16 – 91
Finding Evidence – November 21 – 461
Finding Yourself – August 19 – 327
Fine Lines – November 8 – 445
Fitness – January 22 – 35
Free Will – September 16 – 378
Futility – November 9 – 446
Future Humans – May 28 – 192

G

Get Involved – June 29 – 248
Give Peace a Chance? – August 9 – 315
Giving Time – February 19 – 63
Go to the Woods – October 18 – 418
Go with the Flow – March 24 – 101
God can't Fix This – December 20 – 500
Good God! – May 20 – 178
Good Mandates Evil – March 28 – 106
Good Religion + Good Science = Not – August 27 – 343
Good Religion, Good Science – August 26 – 341
Growth and Learning – December 15 – 494

H

Halloween – October 31 – 434
Hate – November 24 – 466
Healthy Skepticism – March 1 – 74
Heaven or Hell? – December 7 – 483
Honoring Life – January 9 – 19
How can Death be Life? – September 20 – 383
How Can I be Good? – September 17 – 379
How Deep Should I go? – December 1 – 476
How do I "do" Fitness? – January 23 – 36
How Do I Be? – December 28 – 511
How does Magic Work? – May 31 – 197
How should I act? – February 29 – 73
Humanity's Destiny – August 29 – 348

I

I am God? – May 11 – 163
I Think Therefore I Am – June 15 – 220
If You Are Lucky, You'll Hit the Bottom – October 8 – 405
Immortality – February 24 – 68
Inconcussa Fundamenta – July 17 – 279
Indomitable Spirit – October 9 – 407
Infinity – November 20 – 460
Intellect – October 28 – 431
Introduction to Not – April 2 – 112
Is Religion Good or Evil? – March 25 – 102
Is there Purpose? – August 2 – 307
It is a Violent World – September 3 – 356
It's Not a Simulation – July 4 – 255

J

Jobs and Career – July 1 – 251
Just do Something – July 30 – 303

K

Knowing Right from Wrong – September 19 – 381

L

Liberation – November 19 – 459

Life (big "L") – April 20 – 135
life (little "L") – April 21 – 136
Life After Death – September 27 – 391
Life Destroys Life – January 17 – 28
Life is Death – April 26 – 144
Life is not Death – April 24 – 141
Life, Not and Life (Not and Space) – April 25 – 142
Life, Rocks – April 22 – 137
Life, the Disease – July 13 – 271
Light – April 17 – 132
Living with Intention – September 5 – 360
Love – September 26 – 390
Love Others – June 23 – 235
Love your Past – September 21 – 384
Love Yourself – June 22 – 233
Loyalty – December 17 – 496

M

Magic – May 29 – 193
Maintaining Life – January 8 – 18
Make the World a Better Place – March 15 – 90
Manifestation of Chaos – July 11 – 267
Mental Exercise – January 29 – 42
Mental Fitness – January 28 – 41
Mental Nutrition – January 30 – 43
Mental Rest – January 31 – 44
Mine, Yours – January 10 – 20
Modern Humans – May 27 – 191
Money doesn't Exist – March 17 – 92

N

Necessitudo – June 20 – 230
Neighborliness – March 11 – 85
Never in the Same Place Twice – June 3 – 204
New Year's Day (Yesterday) – January 2 – 9
Nobody Can Ruin Your Day – October 1 – 397
Nobody Has a Clue – July 27 – 295
Non-Love Relationships – February 23 – 67
Not – April 7 – 121
Not in your Mind – April 15 – 130
Not isn't Everywhere – April 12 – 127
Not must not Exist – April 10 – 124
Not to be Seen – April 9 – 123
Not, God? – April 1 – 111
Not, Perfect? – April 8 – 122
Nothing isn't Not – April 11 – 125
Nothing Matters – September 2 – 354
Nothing Touches Anything – March 19 – 95

O

Only Life Exists and it is Eternal – May 1 – 150
Opportunities – December 16 – 495
Original Innocence – July 22 – 286
Origins and Destinations – August 3 – 308
Our Most Valued Commodity – December 4 – 479
Ours, Theirs – January 11 – 21

P

Pain and Suffering – May 2 – 151
Paradigms of Truth – July 14 – 273
Paradox is Prevalent in Truth – April 14 – 129
Passion/Dispassion – November 25 – 467
Perfection – October 15 – 414
Personal Fulfillment – March 5 – 78
Perspective – November 7 – 444
Philosophy – October 5 – 402
Physical Exercise – February 7 – 51
Physical Fitness – February 6 – 50
Physical Nutrition – February 8 – 52
Physical Rest – February 9 – 53
Pick-up Sticks – March 13 – 87
Plant Life – January 14 – 25
Points of Present – November 27 – 469
Pray to What? – September 7 – 364
Preferred Ignorance – June 26 – 242
Presence – April 19 – 134
Presence for Past and Future – July 24 – 290
Preserving Life – January 4 – 12
Pressure and Stress – October 30 – 433
Proof of Manifestation – July 18 – 281
Pruning Relationships – February 21 – 65
Pursuing the Truths – July 15 – 275
Putting Good Into the World – July 2 – 252

R

Reconciliation – November 14 – 454
Reflection and Manifestation – December 13 – 491
Reigning in the Chaos – July 12 – 269

Rejection – May 8 – 159
Relationships – February 15 – 59
Religion – June 30 – 250
Religion as Evil – December 19 – 499
Religion as Good – December 18 – 497
Religion had to Change – December 22 – 502
Religion Without God – December 30 – 514
Religious Delusions? – September 12 – 373
Right and Wrong – November 26 – 468
Righteous Indignation – December 6 – 482

S

Sanctify Life – January 19 – 31
Sanctuary – November 1 – 435
Sanity and Insanity – December 12 – 490
Scarcity & Abundance – June 9 – 212
Science – October 4 – 400
Science & Religion – August 25 – 340
Seek and Ye Shall Find – December 25 – 507
Seek and Ye Shall Not Find – December 26 – 508
Self Actualization – March 7 – 80
Self and Life – February 16 – 60
Self-Authorization – May 6 – 156
Self-Worth – May 7 – 157
Shake Your Foundations – March 2 – 75
Should I Worship Something? – August 31 – 351
Size and Scope – May 24 – 184
Sleep or Die – August 30 – 349
Social Exercise – February 12 – 56
Social Fitness – February 11 – 55
Social Media – February 10 – 54
Social Nutrition – February 13 – 57
Social Rest – February 14 – 58
Spiritual Exercise – January 25 – 38

Spiritual Fitness – January 24 – 37
Spiritual Hunger – August 17 – 324
Spiritual Meals – August 18 – 325
Spiritual Nutrition – January 26 – 39
Spiritual Rest – January 27 – 40
Splinters of Truth – May 17 – 172
Stasis – April 5 – 117
Summer Solstice – June 21 – 232
Superstructures – March 3 – 76
Survival of the Fittest – January 21 – 34

T

Take a Step – March 6 – 79
Take Care! – March 12 – 86
Taking Life – January 18 – 29
The 21-Day Deity – August 22 – 336
The All-Truth – May 15 – 170
The Allure of Evil – December 8 – 484
The Breath of Air – October 24 – 427
The Church of Not – August 24 – 339
The Collective Conscious Imperative – December 5 – 480
The Comfort of Familiarity – October 17 – 417
The Detriment of Here and Now – July 23 – 288
The Emotional Self – June 6 – 207
The Empath – October 19 – 419
The Fallacy of Power – December 9 – 486
The Framework (of Thought) – November 4 – 438
The Future – November 18 – 458
The Garden – November 23 – 464
The Glimmer – July 8 – 263
The Gradient Yin-Yang – March 27 – 104
The Great Tapestry of Life – July 5 – 257
The Highest of Authorities – October 27 – 430
The Interconnect – January 7 – 17

The Linear Spiral – July 6 – 258
The Love-Spark – February 17 – 61
The Mainstream – March 22 – 99
The Mental Self – June 5 – 206
The Mind/Body Connection – October 11 – 409
The Mistake of Atheism – July 19 – 283
The Most Important Thing In The World – January 1 – 7
The Mysteries : Album Mysteria Non – July 28 – 298
The Need for Purpose – December 24 – 504
The Need to Believe – September 29 – 394
The Nucleus – November 5 – 441
The Occult – May 26 – 189
The One True God – July 21 – 285
The Opposite of Love – December 29 – 513
The Past – November 16 – 456
The Pebble in the Pool – June 10 – 213
The Physical Self – June 7 – 209
The Power of Prayer – May 23 – 183
The Present – November 17 – 457
The Principles of Not – January 3 – 10
The Self, Connected – June 11 – 214
The Social Self – June 8 – 211
The Soul – May 9 – 161
The Spark – July 7 – 262
The Spiritual Self – June 4 – 205
The Suffering of Death is Only for the Living – October 3 – 399
The Tesseract – March 18 – 93
The Third Pole – October 22 – 423
The Tightrope – October 20 – 420
The Tree of Not – June 14 – 219
The Truth – May 16 – 171
The Ultimate Expression of Life – April 28 – 147
The Unexamined Life – March 8 – 82
The Universal You – November 10 – 447
The Universe – August 10 – 316
The Universe is Unfolding as it Should – November 15 – 455
The Value of Church – October 2 – 398

The Vernal Equinox – March 21 – 98
The Void – December 10 – 487
The World is Getting Better – September 30 – 395
Time Cannot Pass – March 20 – 96
Tolerance is Easy – October 16 – 415
Toxicity in the Mainstream – August 23 – 338
Tranquillitas Animae – November 30 – 475
Trust – October 26 – 429

U

Unifying the Paradigms – July 16 – 277

V

Veer Away! – March 23 – 100
Victim Mentality – October 13 – 412
Violence and Destruction – August 8 – 314
Vita – June 18 – 227
Vitacentricism – January 6 – 16

W

Walpurgisnacht – April 30 – 149
Warmth – April 16 – 131
We are All Connected – July 10 – 266
We Are not the Center of it All – May 25 – 187
We Need Both – March 30 – 109
What are Dreams? – August 6 – 311
What Does it Look Like? – June 27 – 244

What if You Are Wrong? – September 1 – 352
What is All of This? – July 31 – 304
What is Consciousness? – August 4 – 309
What is Death? – August 5 – 310
What is Greater than Humanity? – May 22 – 182
What is Moral? – February 25 – 69
What isn't Not? – April 13 – 128
What it Isn't – August 28 – 344
Why Are we Here? – August 1 – 306
Winter Solstice – December 21 – 501

Y

You are an Energy Being – July 9 – 265
You Are Deeper than Belief – September 10 – 369
You Have Reached the Top! – July 3 – 254
You Have to Have a Plan – October 10 – 408
Your Avatar – March 14 – 88
Your Birthday! (and Yearning) – 516
Your Family is Whatever You Say It Is – February 18 – 62
Your Higher Power – May 21 – 180
Your Personal Code – February 26 – 70
Your Salvation – November 3 – 437
Your Spirit can do no Wrong – September 18 – 380

End of Appendix A

APPENDIX B – CINEREO MODO

The following pages step you through six flowcharts which assist with the decision making necessary to walk the gray path for any given action. Choosing a "black or white" yes or no answer may be extremely difficult and only the seeker can honestly answer the questions.

It is not expected that utilizing Cinereo Modo in this fashion is realistic for every single situation. Instead, consider these six steps as a general guide to your approach on walking the gray path. Deviation from the steps is expected and it may be good for you to think about the other parameters of a given situation and create your own flowcharts to help guide you.

Ultimately, you may step through Cinereo Modo and decide in the end that despite the guidance your intuition tells you to do the opposite. You intuition may be right!

Following the flowcharts are the steps one must take to go through the flow of Cinereo Modo.

Flowchart for Step 1: (Vita)

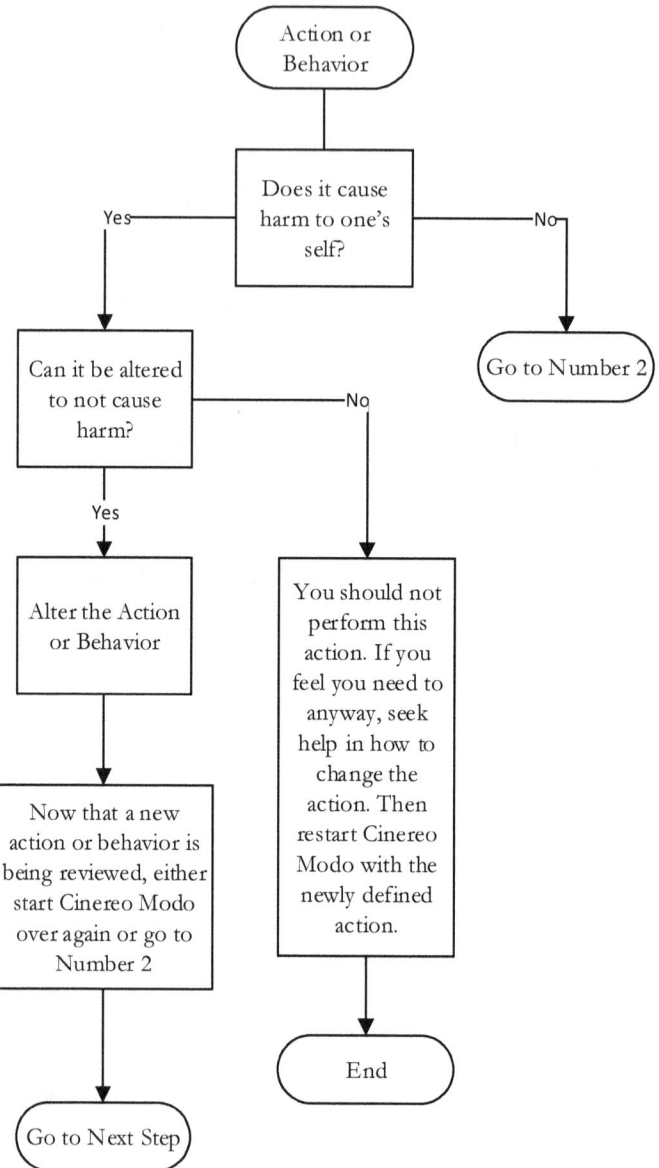

Flowchart for Step 2: (Vita)

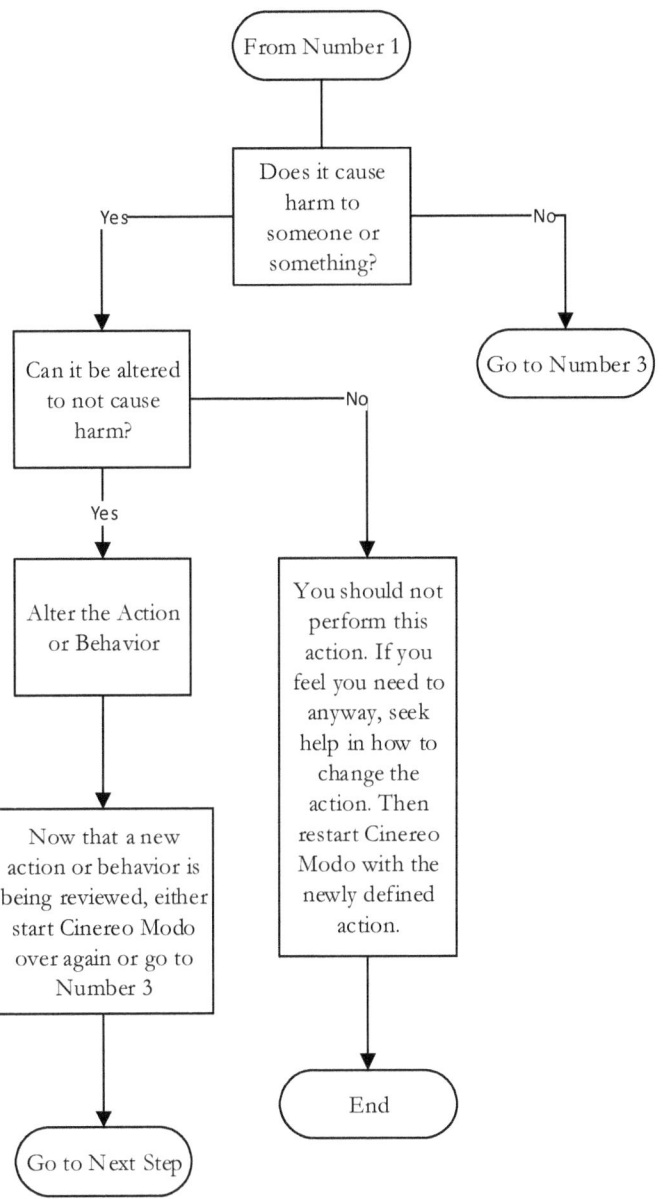

Flowchart for Step 3: (Aciem Exacuitur)

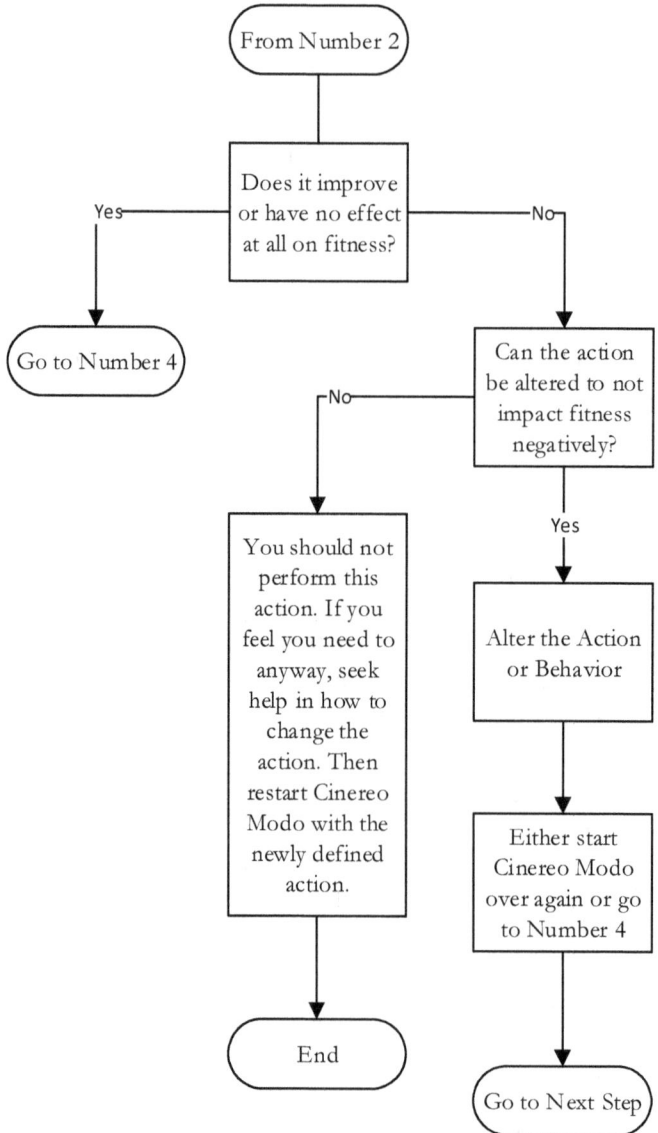

NOT, DAILY MEDITATIONS

Flowchart for Step 4: (Necessitudo)

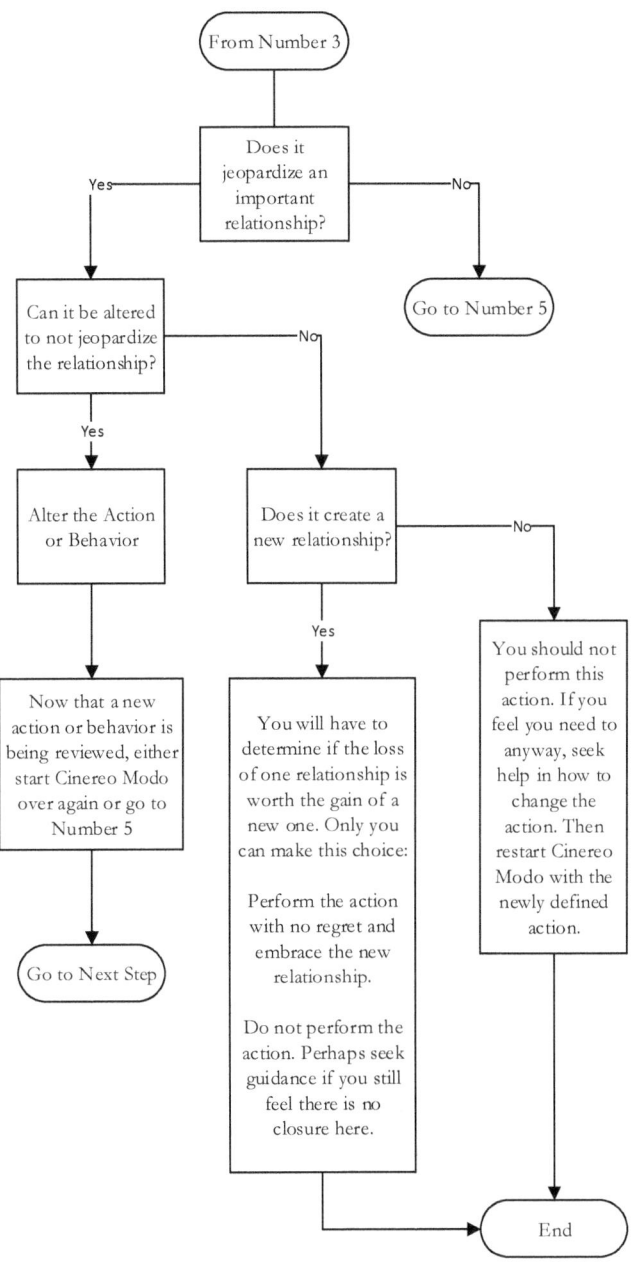

Flowchart for Step 5: (Codice Personalum)

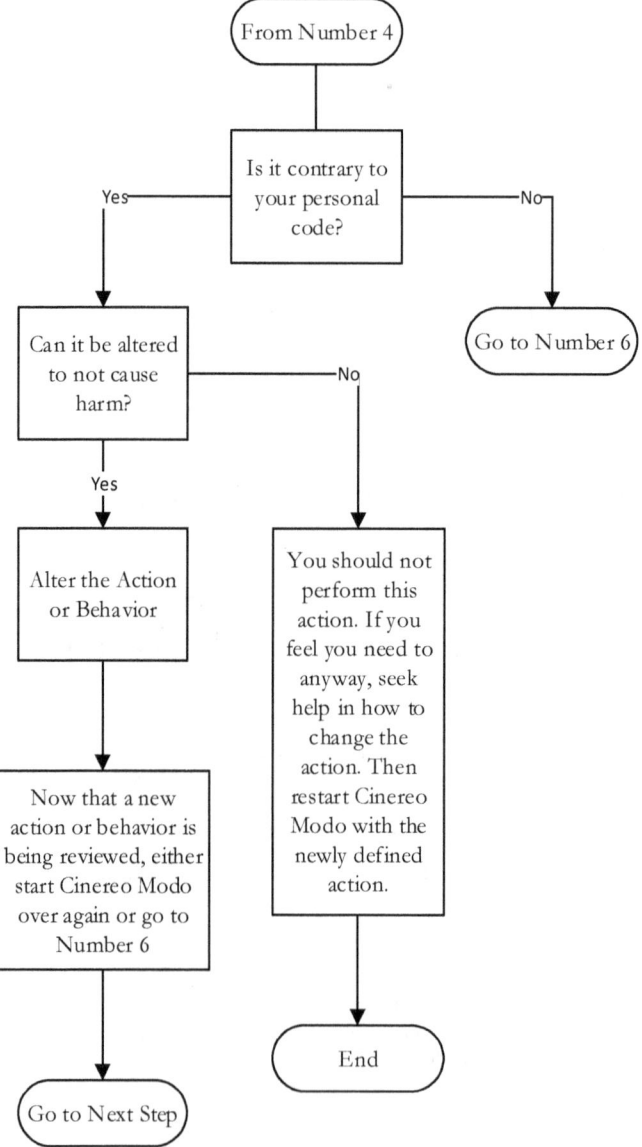

NOT, DAILY MEDITATIONS

Flowchart for Step 6: (Civitas)

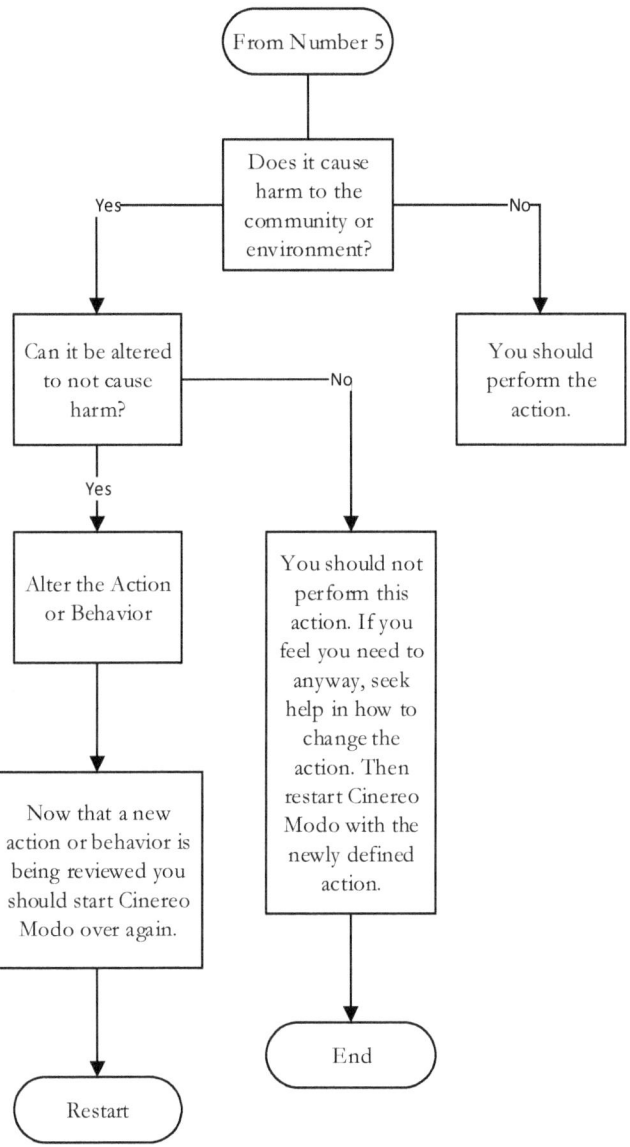

The following steps guide the reader through the gray path.

Consider the action (or behavior) in question.

1. Does it cause harm to one's self? (If yes, find a way to desist from this behavior – seek help if necessary) If not, go to Number 2.

2. Does it cause harm to someone or something else? (If yes, find a way to do it without causing harm. If it cannot be done without harming someone or something else, desist from this behavior – seek help if necessary) If this behavior does not cause harm to other life, go to Number 3.

3. Does the behavior/activity in question increase the overall fitness of the one doing it? If it does improve overall fitness or if it has no effect whatsoever on overall fitness, go to Number 4. If this activity decreases overall fitness one should find a way to alter the behavior to either not affect fitness or to improve overall fitness. If no way can be found and fitness will always be affected negatively as a result of the behavior, the behavior should be stopped. The individual may need to seek help in finding a way to stop the behavior.

4. Does the behavior jeopardize an important relationship? If it does, can the behavior be changed so as to not jeopardize a relationship? If so, it should be changed and one can proceed to Number 5. If the damage of a relationship is inevitable as a result of the behavior one should consider desisting in the damaging behavior. Alternatively, the action/behavior may create a relationship. If so, is this relationship going to improve

life or fitness for life or might it reduce quality of life and fitness for life?

5. Is this behavior contrary to the personal code of the person acting out the behavior? If so, should the person's personal code change or should the person stop the behavior? Can the behavior be changed so as to not be contrary to the person's personal code? If so, go to Number 6. If not, the behavior should likely be stopped. Seek help if necessary in order to stop or change the behavior.

6. Finally, does this behavior or action cause harm to the community or environment around the person in question? If it does, can the behavior be changed so as to stop harming the community or environment? If not, the behavior should be stopped. If it can be altered to not harm the community or environment then it should be changed.

You can use Cinereo Modo to guide your own actions and you can apply this application to other people when they come to you with a question about proper behavior or a question as to which way they should go in any given situation.

We call this Cinereo Modo (the "gray way" or "the gray path") because we do not believe there is a perfectly black or perfectly white path in life. There are only shades of gray. We call this the gray way (or path) to remind us of the inherent innocence of all life and the choice that we have at every moment between good and evil.

End of Appendix B

www.ingramcontent.com/pod-product-compliance
Lightning Source LLC
Chambersburg PA
CBHW060219230426
43664CB00011B/1480